The Handbook of Social, Emotional and Behavioural Difficulties

Related titles:

Roy Howarth and Pam Fisher: *Emotional and Behavioural Difficulties*
Sue Cowley: *Getting the Buggers to Behave 2*
Gererd Dixie: *Managing Your Classroom*
Maden Mall and Berni Stringer: *Understanding Behaviour*
Louisa Leaman: *Managing Very Challenging Behaviour*

THE HANDBOOK OF SOCIAL, EMOTIONAL AND BEHAVIOURAL DIFFICULTIES

Edited by
Morag Hunter-Carsch, Yonca Tiknaz,
Paul Cooper and Rosemary Sage

continuum
LONDON • NEW YORK

KH

Continuum International Publishing Group
The Tower Building   80 Maiden Lane
11 York Road   Suite 704
London   New York
SE1 7NX   NY 10038

© Morag Hunter-Carsch, Yonca Tiknaz, Paul Cooper and Rosemary Sage 2006

British Library Cataloguing-in-Publication Data
A catalogue record for this book is available from the British Library.

ISBN (HB) 0-8264-8893-5
ISBN (PB) 0-8264-8894-3

Library of Congress Cataloging-in-Publication Data
A catalog record of this book is available from the Library of Congress.

Typeset by Fakenham Photosetting Ltd, Fakenham, Norfolk
Printed and bound in Great Britain by MPG Books Ltd, Bodmin, Cornwall

Contents

Acknowledgements

In naming the following people, the editors wish to acknowledge and thank all of the contributing writers, who share their insights and who inspire us to try to find ways of understanding and supporting young people with social, emotional and behavioural difficulties (SEBD) and we wish also to thank their families who provided emotional and practical support for them to make the time to communicate their ideas with others:

- Alexandra Webster, Continuum Books, for making possible the dissemination of the collective experience, knowledge and 'good practice' of the writers;
- Sue Mailley, for substantial editorial support.
- Barbara Hall, Centre for Innovation in Raising Educational Achievement (CIREA), University of Leicester for preparation of the manuscript;
- Ted Hartshorn, Aubrey Nicholls and Margaret Hughes, the 'Sharing Good Practice' conferences team;
- Professor Ken Fogelman and the University of Leicester School of Education continuing professional development (CPD) team and Jonathan Wimberley and Raki Patel; the University of Leicester conference staff, caterers, and to Jonathan Westgate and the university audio-visual services;
- teachers, administrators and teacher educators and advanced degree students who make contributions beyond the call of duty to share their vision, long-term investment and practical contributions to collaborative, research-based, innovative continuing professional education, for teachers' best efforts to be sustained;
- all the voluntary workers, students from Mellor Primary and Community School, Judgemeadow Community College and teachers who contributed to the international conference on communication, emotion and behaviour;
- Joan Pritchard, Ted Cole and the Association for Workers with Children with Emotional and Behavioural Difficulties (AWCEBD)/Social, Emotional and Behavioural Difficulties Association (SEBDA);
- Peter Sharp and Adrian Faupel, and to Peter Hook for their contributions to 'emotional intelligence' and 'anger

management' in Leicester's Sharing Good Practice conference series and for keeping up the momentum of remembered laughter and good humour;

- The late Dr Henry Carsch for his inspirational photographs of the misty Matterhorn and the 'cloudburst of light'.
- Rixa Albrecht for translation and discussion of Joseph Beuys' art that inspired some 'language, art and life' connections reflected through the strands of this book; and
- Claire Baker, who reminded us of Goethe's words:

Until one is committed, there is hesitancy, the chance to draw back, always ineffectiveness. Concerning all acts of initiative (and creation), there is one elemental truth, the ignorance of which kills countless ideas and splendid plans, that the moment one definitely commits oneself, then Providence moves all. All sorts of things occur that would never otherwise have occurred. A whole stream of events issue from the decision, raising in one's favour all manner of unforeseen incidents and meetings and material assistance which no man could have dreamed would have come his way. Whatever you can do, or dream you can do, begin it. Boldness has genius, power and magic in it. Begin it now.

List of contributors

(In order of their contribution to the handbook)

Paul Cooper PhD: Professor and Director of CIREA, University of Leicester; England*

'John': young man who understands SEBD 'from the inside'; England

Sylvia McNamara: Acting Head of Birmingham Support Services, writer; England*

Egide Royer PhD: Professor of Special Education, Laval University, Quebec; Canada*

Morag Hunter-Carsch: Hon. Senior Research Fellow, CIREA, University of Leicester; England*

E. J. Bond: Professor Emeritus, Queen's University, Kingston, Ontario; Canada*. E. J. Bond is the author of *Reason and Value* (Cambridge University Press, 1983) and *Ethics and Human Well-being* (Blackwell, 1996). He has also contributed four articles to the *Encyclopedia of Ethics*, 2nd edn, edited by Becker & Becker (Routledge, 2001), and has contributed many articles to professional journals.

Rosemary Sage PhD: Deputy Director of CIREA, University of Leicester; England*

Alice Sluckin: Chair of the Selective Mutism Information and Research Association (SMIRA), secretary of Leicester Association of Child and Clinical Psychologists (ACCP), social worker; England*

Balbir Kaur Sohal: Local education authority (LEA) adviser, Leader, Advisory Teacher Citizenship, PSHE and Equalities, Coventry Education Authority, international educator; England*

Daniela Sommefeldt: Lecturer, University of Leicester, former headteacher; England

Jennifer Rogers PhD: Lecturer, University of Leicester, researcher, CIREA; England*

Jill Allison: Art, Personal and Social Education (PSE), gifted/talented teacher, Judgemeadow Community College, an inner city college, Leicester; England*

Peter Haase: special education/literacy specialist consultant, Melsungen; Germany*

Gerda Hanko: international adviser, writer on special education, London; England*

Stephen Weiss: Professor, Steinhardt School of Education, New York; USA*

Adrian Faupel: Southampton LEA educational psychologist, trainer, writer; England*

Dominique Wilson-Smith Anderson: Head of Art (in three schools), writer, London; England*

Judith Mullen: British Council, London, former college principal, Leicester; England*

Rosemary Duxbury: Composer, international performer/broadcaster, Leicester; England*

Shiroma de Silva: music therapist with adults and children, Leicester; England

Albie Ollivierre: dance teacher, choreographer, London and Cumbria; England

Neil Kitson: LEA adviser, drama specialist, writer, Northampton; England*

Ian Jones: Police/police training, consultant in mind skills, West Sussex; England*

Chris Comber PhD: Senior Lecturer, School of Education, University of Leicester; England*

Ted Cole PhD: Executive Director SEBDA, Hon. Senior Research Fellow, University of Birmingham; England*

Bill Rogers PhD: Consultant, adjunct-professor, Griffith University; Australia*

Scilla Elworthy: Scientist, peace worker, nominee for the Nobel Prize, Oxford; England*

Yonca Tiknaz EdD: engineer/teacher, Turkey, CIREA researcher, Leicester; England*

* indicates international speaker/writer

List of abbreviations

AD	anxiety disorder
AD/HD	attention deficit/hyperactivity disorder
APA	American Psychiatric Association
BPS	British Psychological Society
CD	conduct disorder
CIREA	Centre for Innovation in Raising Educational Achievement (University of Leicester)
COGS	Communication Opportunity Group Scheme
CPD	continuing professional development
DD	depression
DfEE	Department for Education and Employment (UK)
DfES	Department for Education and Skills (UK)
DSM	Diagnostic and Statistical Manual (USA)
EBD	emotional and behavioural difficulties
EEG	electroencephalography
EI	emotional intelligence
EM	elective mutism
ESBD	emotional, social and behavioural difficulties
FE	further education
HD	hyperkinetic disorders
LAs	local authorities
LSAs	learning support assistants
NGs	nurture groups
NGN	NG Network
NNS	National Numeracy Strategy (UK)
NVC	Non-violent Communication
ODD	oppositional defiant disorder
PRUs	Pupil Referral Units
QCA	Qualifications and Curriculum Authority (UK)
SARs	schools with additional resources
SATs	Standard Attainment Tasks (UK)
SEBD	social, emotional and behavioural difficulties
SEN	Special Educational Needs
SENCOs	Special Educational Needs coordinators
SM	selective mutism
SMIRA	Selective Mutism Information and Research Association
SpLD	specific learning difficulties
UfA	University of the First Age (UK)

CHAPTER 1

Setting the scene

Paul Cooper

The title and themes

In naming the book *The Handbook of Social, Emotional and Behavioural Difficulties* the authors aim to provide a source for practitioners to dip into as well as offer a cumulative contribution to this complex field. It does not pretend to be comprehensive but sets out to explore the dynamic relationship between three themes – communication, emotion and behaviour – a relationship that requires better understanding if practitioners are to be able to provide appropriate support for young people with SEBD.

This chapter provides an introduction to SEBD, different theoretical perspectives and causal factors, prior to noting the rationale for our selection and organization of the lively and diverse collection of chapters and giving a brief outline of the content of the book as a whole.

What are social, emotional and behavioural difficulties?

SEBD are most obvious when they appear in the form of disruptive behaviour in schools. Such disruption can take the form of behaviours that interfere with the learning and teaching processes and in extreme, rare cases can involve violence against pupils and staff. Emotional difficulties may sometimes manifest themselves in the form of severely withdrawn behaviour. It is estimated that between 10 and 20 per cent of all school-aged children in the UK and USA experience such difficulties to a significant degree at any time. This represents, on average, between 3 and 6 pupils in every class of 30 pupils, although such pupils are not evenly distributed either between schools or between classes in schools. SEBD affect approximately three times as many boys as girls, although girls may be under-represented in such figures because of their tendency to internalize rather than externalize difficulties. A review of research and clinical data spanning the 50 years between 1945 and 1995 (Rutter and Smith, 1995) suggests that the rise in externalizing difficulties among girls has increased at a greater rate than among boys. However, girls are still more likely than boys to experience anxiety, depression, eating disorders and to commit self-harm. There is, however, also an increase among boys presenting with these kinds of difficulties.

The incidence of these problems is more pronounced in mid- to late adolescence and is on the increase, although the rate of increase is greater among children of primary school age. Although there are special facilities for pupils with extreme manifestations of these difficulties, such as special schools, child and adolescent psychiatric units and pupil referral units, such placements only account for between one-tenth and one-twentieth of the SEBD population. The overwhelming majority of pupils with SEBD are, therefore, in mainstream schools – or at least they should be. Pupils with these kinds of problems are highly represented among the 9,880 children who are permanently excluded from English schools (DfES figures for 2003/4), and among the unknown population of pupils who are unofficially excluded or whose frequent absences from school are unauthorized. These problems are reflected in the wider society in terms of mental health difficulties and delinquency among the school-aged population, the incidence of which has been shown to have increased throughout the world since 1945 (ibid.).

The interaction between communication, emotion and behaviour

Central to this book is the argument that while surface behavioural problems are experienced as disruptive, and as a source of major upset in educational environments, such problems are often underpinned or accompanied by emotional difficulties. Whether the emotional dimension follows from behaviour, or precedes the behaviour, it is often emotional difficulties that provide the stimulus for developing defensive and offensive behaviours. In these circumstances a third factor comes into play: the social dimension. Hidden emotions provide the spark for behaviours that produce either positive or negative reactions from others. Positive social reactions reinforce the negative behaviour, and the continued development of social affiliation becomes dependent on continued and escalating deviance. Where the social reaction is negative, however, the basic human need for social acceptance and affiliation is thwarted, leading to further emotional distress. Affiliation needs either remain unmet or are met through association with other behavioural deviants.

The deviant sub-culture that is thus formed serves to promote the further development of deviance. Communication patterns are deeply implicated in the processes described here. Deviant students' difficulties are compounded and promoted by their limited repertoire of communication skills. These problems do not reside solely at the level of specific 'social skills', though this level of communication is often implicated. More fundamental communication skills are also often in deficit here.

Specifically, students with social, emotional and behavioural difficulties often experience problems in formulating and communicating basic verbal messages, and in understanding and articulating their emotions. The skills required to overcome these difficulties encompass linguistic competence and social and emotional literacy that play major roles in helping students to escape the cycle of escalating behavioural problems.

What causes these problems?

Popular opinion (as reflected in the press) often seeks to place the blame for SEBD on such factors as poor parenting; poor teaching and discipline in schools; biological predispositions; the negative influence of some outputs of TV, film media and popular music; and the inherent 'badness' of some young people. While there is evidence that *links* some of these factors with emotional and behavioural problems, years of research has failed to establish any simple causal relationships between any of these factors and SEBD.

Having said this, it is important that we take account of the empirical and theoretical literature. By way of illustration we can identify four powerful approaches to understanding the development of SEBD that lend themselves to therapeutic and remedial intervention. These are the social, the psychological and the biopsychosocial approach. A fourth approach considers the influence of culture and society in defining and constructing SEBD.

Social factors: the family and school

Patterson *et al.* (1992) propose a social learning model to describe the life course of individuals who become what they term 'career anti-social adults'. This model is based on intensive study of incarcerated adult males who are defined as being anti-social. Common features in the life histories of individuals studied by Patterson *et al.* were experience of:

- social disadvantage
- ineffective parental discipline
- lack of parental supervision
- parental use of physical punishment
- parental rejection
- peer rejection
- membership of deviant peer group
- academic failure
- low self-esteem.

What is interesting about the model is how these factors appear to have interacted in the lives of the incarcerated adults. They describe a four-stage process:

Stage 1: basic training
This is the pre-school phase in which the child is 'trained' in coercive behaviour in the home setting. Parents and family members are often unwitting trainers who provide models and reinforcement for coercive behaviour through their daily interactions with the child. Their lives (and those of others) are made difficult by the coercive behaviour of the child, but the parents lack resources, knowledge and/or the skills necessary to change the child's behaviour.

Stage 2: the social environment reacts
Behaviours that were functional for the child in the home setting are challenged when he enters school. The school's attempts to challenge his behaviour through punishment or coercion, or unsuccessful attempts at remediation, cause the child's coercive behaviour to escalate. This leads to the pupil being in further conflict with and being rejected by parents, peers and the school.

Stage 3: deviant peers and polishing anti-social skills
The experience of rejection combined with affiliation needs lead the child to seek out like-minded children and they form a deviant peer group. Here the skills of coercion are further reinforced and developed.

Stage 4: the career anti-social adult
The adult is socially marginalized. His main way of relating to others is through coercion. He experiences disruption in personal relationships, has difficulty securing and sustaining gainful employment.

He is at increasing risk of mental health problems, substance abuse, criminality and imprisonment.

The Patterson *et al.* study shows how family and school factors can interact in negative ways to produce and exacerbate SEBD. There is also a long history of research in schools that points to the vital role that schools play in creating and promoting deviance (e.g. Hargreaves, 1967; Schostak, 1982; Cooper, 1993; Cooper *et al.*, 2000; Shelvin and Rose *et al.*, 2003). A perennial feature of these studies is the perception, shared by many pupils, that school is a demoralizing, demotivating and dehumanizing experience. It is important to add that more recent research, while supporting this view, points to the many positive and constructivist things that schools can and actually do to overcome these problems. That these problems need to be acknowledged and addressed, however, remains a key priority for schools.

Psychological factors
Psychological models of deviance often revolve around the concept of human needs. One of the most well known of these models is Abraham Maslow's (1970) hierarchy of needs. SEBD can sometimes be understood in terms of a failure to have crucial needs met, preventing the individual from accessing higher-level needs.

Maslow's hierarchy of needs consists of:

- self-actualization
- self-esteem
- affiliation
- safety
- physiological.

Individuals who have difficulty in getting their safety needs met may experience profound levels of insecurity that interfere with their ability to relate to other people in prosocial ways. This in turn limits opportunities to form affiliations with them and inhibits possibilities for having certain needs met.

John Bowlby's (1975) Attachment Theory suggests that a major source of such problems can reside in the child's early life experience and difficulties encountered in forming a secure emotional attachment with their primary carer. This gives rise to problems in later life that can be understood in terms of an 'attachment disorder', characterized by severe difficulties in forming satisfactory reciprocal relationships.

In Glasser's (1993) *Control Theory*, the hierarchy of needs is defined in terms of needs to:

- play and have fun
- be free and make choices
- exercise power and influence
- belong and to love others
- survive.

Difficulties, for example in having one's needs for power and influence met, may lead to illegitimate (e.g. 'coercive') behaviours.

A further psychological dimension relates to issues of attitude and belief. For example, an individual's capacity to exert control over their behaviour will be influenced by their attributions as to the causes of their behaviour, and whether those causes are within or outside their control (e.g. Munton *et al.* 1998). This is not to say that the individual's capacity to control his or her behaviour is entirely determined by their attitudes and beliefs. Skill and competence play important roles here too. However, the extent to which an individual is able to make the best use of their current level of skill and competence will be influenced to a considerable degree by attitudes and beliefs.

Biopsychosocial interactions

Uta Frith's (1992) model of the relationship between biological causes and behavioural difficulties (see Figure 1.1), shows how biology and environment can interact. The main point of the model is to show how experience, maturation, motivation and compensation act as mediators between biological characteristics and actual behaviour. This suggests that biologically identical individuals may behave in quite different ways, depending on the quality of their experience.

A key implication of Frith's model is that biological factors do not predict behaviour in a straightforward and lineal way. This means that a clinically defined 'disorder', such as attention deficit/hyperactivity disorder (AD/HD), which evidence suggests has a strong biological component (Levy and Hay, 2001), is not determined by the presence of biological abnormalities alone. The quality of the social environment, interpersonal relationships, educational interventions and individuals' attitudes, beliefs and attributions will all play a significant role in determining whether 'difference' equates with 'disorder'.

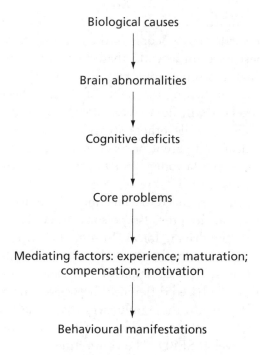

Figure 1.1 *The interaction between biological, cognitive and social influences in developmental disorders (based on Frith, 1992)*

Culture and society

These models go only some way to explaining where SEBD come from. On their own they cannot tell us, for instance, why these problems appear to be more widespread now than they were, say, 50 years ago (Rutter and Smith, 1995). Nor can they tell why the enormous increase in these problems (as shown by, for example, rising crime rates, rising prison populations and the increased demand for mental health services) is common to most advanced industrial and post-industrial countries of the world.

A persuasive argument would appear to be that many SEBD and some of their assumed causes are actually best understood in relation to social and cultural factors. Chief among these social and cultural causes are the related phenomena of the breakdown in community and the increase in individualism that characterizes the evolving state of advanced economies. In a culture in which self-actualization through material consumption and self-seeking behaviour are highly valued, it is not surprising that increasing numbers of young people are disturbed and sometimes enraged by the gap they perceive between what they are told are their entitlement and the reality of their situation in terms of what is available to them.

In these circumstances it is extremely hard for parents and teachers to persuade young people of the importance of selflessness and social conscience. In a world that is obsessed with the rights of the individual it is sometimes difficult to promote awareness of responsibility for protecting the rights of others. Of course, many parents and teachers still do a tremendously good job in the face of these difficulties, while others struggle. It is more difficult to achieve one's ideal as a parent or teacher in the kind of setting in which Damilola Taylor (a young black boy in London) lived and died than it is in a leafy suburb.

When societies are reduced to collections of unrelated individuals the law of the jungle prevails: personal survival and personal advancement are the driving forces. In some instances while adults retreat from the streets children face the choice of a life of solitude or the precarious self-preservation of the gang. Temperamental, and even biologically based differences between children can make some more vulnerable to these influences than others, which helps to explain why not all people experiencing these disadvantaged circumstances develop SEBD. The commitment to delayed gratification required by schools is difficult to sell in places where there are no positive role models to show that it really can pay dividends.

On the other side of this coin schools in such areas feel the negative brunt of punitive government policies, which degrade pupils and communities through the instrument of crude and unfair league tables, while at the same time imposing a curriculum which constrains schools and teachers in ways that inhibit them in their efforts to meet local community and pupil needs.

A simple illustration of this last point can be provided by observing that between 1992 and 1998 the annual number of permanent exclusions from school in England steadily increased, so that by 1998 there were four times as many pupils excluded as there had been in 1992. It is hard to avoid the conclusion that this increase was not in some way related to the radical changes to the education system imposed by government in this period. These changes included the imposition of a National Curriculum and national tests at ages 7 and 14; league tables of school performance; increased parental choice in the selection of schools for their children and the introduction of Ofsted accompanied by a massive increase in the frequency of school inspection. The enormous pressure placed on teachers by these measures is reflected in the increased stress-related illnesses and early retirement due to ill health among teachers during this period. Stress was further transmitted to pupils, the most vulnerable of whom found themselves failing in an inflexible and high-paced curriculum, being dealt with by staff who had diminishing power to respond to children in difficulty in flexible ways. The system became simply less tolerant and this had a negative effect on both teachers and pupils.

The education system is of course simply a reflection of the culture in which it is embedded. Our culture has become increasingly dominated by the Darwinian logic of the market forces perspective. This view states that everyone has an entitlement to choose what is 'best' (e.g. in terms of public services, such as schools), though these choices are not related to responsibilities in relation to promoting improvement and quality. These responsibilities reside with the service providers (e.g. teachers), who, in turn, are motivated by their own survival needs. A flaw with this 'market forces' model of social development is that inequalities in the distribution of economic and cultural capital mean that social groups (defined by cultural and economic capital correlates) are differently placed in terms of their ability to make effective choices. In extreme cases this state of affairs creates, at one end of the spectrum, an 'underclass', which can be defined as:

> A social group or class of people located at the bottom of a class structure who, over time, have become structurally separate and culturally distinct from the regularly employed working-class and society in general through processes of social and economic change (particularly de-industrialisation) and/or through patterns of cultural behaviour, who are now persistently reliant on state benefits and almost permanently confined to living in poorer conditions and neighbourhoods. (MacDonald, 1997, pp. 2–3)

Furthermore, the plight of the underclass is perpetuated and exacerbated by the fact that it becomes a target for avoidance by those best placed to make social choices.

In a Darwinian (market-forces driven) society, as opposed to the 'communitarian' society championed by Amitai Etzioni (1995), inclusive social participation is replaced by competitive individual engagement. The goal of engagement is not social belonging (i.e. a process that links individual fulfilment with social improvement), which communitarians promote, but individual self-actualization (Maslow, 1970). 'Advantage' for one person, in these circumstances, is often dependent on the 'disadvantage' of others.

The destruction of community has further specific consequences for children. On the one hand they are expected to operate as autonomous beings from an early age. They have their own catalogue of individual civil and human rights. They are empowered as a consumer group. On the other hand the breakdown of community means that the full weight of the responsibility for their upbringing falls to parents, who themselves are increasingly isolated from traditional forms of support in the extended family and the wider local community. In these circumstances, parents who themselves may not have been exposed to models of effective parenting, or who have no experience of a cohesive extended family and/or community, are at a loss. Furthermore, in a society that overstates the importance of personal over social responsibility, they are more likely to be blamed for their failures than supported. Meanwhile the pressure to consume, to which children are subjected and that is reinforced by the mass media, acts as a source of conflict between parents and children.

SEBD, competence, volition and opportunity

It should be clear from the preceding argument that the view being proposed by this book is that SEBD are rarely the product of individual choice in any simple sense. Furthermore, it is clearly the case that there are many and varied routes towards the development of SEBD. In so far as SEBD is a matter of individual choice, the choices made are often drawn from a narrow and unreasonable range of options. An example of this would be the individual who engages in anti-social or delinquent behaviours in order to meet his or her needs to be held in high esteem by others. The problem here is often the absence of opportunities to attain the positive regard of others through means that are widely approved. This state of affairs may exist because the opportunities are not available, or because the individual does not possess the competences necessary to take advantage of such opportunities.

Making the necessary opportunities available and promoting the development of appropriate skills are complex matters that are at the heart of this book.

The importance of the individual and individual experience

One of the things that makes the study of SEBD so fascinating is the way in which it forces us to seek answers to fundamental questions about how human beings operate and what influences them to behave in different ways. One of the motives for putting this book together in the first place is a recognition of the human cost of SEBD, coupled with the perception that intervention has to be humane and growth promoting for all individuals concerned. The problem, of course, is that it is all too easy to judge the effectiveness of intervention in terms of the extent to which it relieves the effects of SEBD on the families, classrooms and other settings which are disrupted by the presence of an individual with SEBD. This narrow view of intervention not only ignores the influence of the apparently disrupted environment in creating the SEBD in the first place, it also fails to address the central theme of this book, namely that SEBD are more often than not best viewed as evidence of unmet need at the individual level.

This book is structured around this important insight. At the heart of the book is the voice of an individual whose first-hand experience is highly pertinent to the understandings that we hope readers will gain from this book.

Introducing a different voice

'John' is the fictitious name that we have given to a key contributor to this book. As you will see, John is a young man with a long history of being labelled 'with SEBD'.

John's words are shared, unedited, in six 'episodes' that punctuate the voices of the academics and professionals. John's story begins with the following chapter. Cumulatively John's chapters are devoted to illustrating the personal dimensions of SEBD and the complex ways in which different factors come to interact in the creation of SEBD.

Readers are encouraged to empathize with all of the authors. It is on the sustained engagement of this spirit of empathy that the value of the whole book depends. It is through exploring all of the writers' perspectives that readers can carry out an exploration of ways in which deeper insight can be gained into why young people sometimes develop SEBD and what can be done to overcome these difficulties.

The shape of the book

There are three parts to this book. The first, 'Exploring the Issues', has nine chapters of varying length and style. It starts and finishes with parts of John's story. Other contributing writers present their views on key aspects of how we conceptualize SEBD. While all three themes, communication, emotion and behaviour, are addressed, different writers tend to illuminate the roles of each aspect in different ways. Various professional and theoretical perspectives are explored. Particular issues dealt with here include: the challenges posed to local education authorities by SEBD (McNamara); the training needs of teachers working in such settings (Royer); the role of emotional literacy in relation to SEBD and its links with specific learning difficulties (Hunter-Carsch); a philosophical exploration of the relationships between communication, emotion and behaviour (Bond); a psychological perspective on communicative competence and its role in the facilitation of effective social engagement (Sage); an illuminative exploration of selective mutism (Sluckin); and a multicultural perspective on SEBD (Sohal).

The second part of the book includes a substantial cluster of 24 chapters, again of different styles and lengths. The emphasis is broadly on further approaches to supporting as well as under-standing SEBD. This part, entitled 'Practical Perspectives', includes four more chapters of John's story, interspersed with perspectives on practical responses to SEBD, policy and provision. Specific topics in this section include: evidence on the ways in which LEAs respond to meeting diverse needs among pupils (Sommefeldt); nurture groups (Cooper); the Communication Opportunity Group Scheme (Sage); mathematical communication problems (Rogers); an illumination of the visualizing and verbalizing processes and the visual arts (Allison); a neuro-educational approach to intervention (Haase); the importance of empathetic understanding and respect (Hanko); a range of classic psychoeducational approaches (Weiss); the value and efficacy of emotional literacy programmes (Faupel); the role of art in promoting pupil self-confidence (Wilson-Smith Anderson); and the use of emotional intelligence (EI) in leadership in schools (Mullen). The focus on the arts is further developed by Duxbury in relation to the value of musical activity in promoting communicative abilities and spiritual development and DeSylva shares her perspective on music therapy. The role that dance can play in personal development is rhythmically shared by Ollivierre and the case for drama as a vehicle for promoting the development of empathy and sympathy is promoted by Kitson. Jones explores 'the art of influence' and shows understanding of the importance of developing thinking skills as one way of overcoming SEBD, while Comber illustrates the value of the University of the First Age. Aspects of effective school provision for SEBD are discussed by Cole and a critical review of the literature on AD/HD follows (Cooper). John's words are the penultimate voice and this part of the book ends with Rogers' keen observations and advice about teachers' leadership styles and pupil behaviour.

This acts as a bridge into the third and final, relatively shorter part of the book where attention is given to considering the way forward in teacher education and how best to conceptualize SEBD and intervention practices. Hunter-Carsch and Tiknaz analyse their own and other teachers' professional development experiences after an inspirational conference on 'Wise Minds' at which Elworthy shared her observations about how young people address issues of conflict resolution. Elworthy's views are included prior to the final chapter, which is by the four editors. It draws together the broader implications of our ways of thinking about communication, emotion and behaviour to illuminate the links that should inform future educational policy and practice.

PART I

EXPLORING THE ISSUES

Chapters 2 to 10 provide a range of perspectives. Collectively, they aim to provide a context for deepening readers' own relevant and personal awareness as well as potentially broadening their knowledge base.

CHAPTER 2

John's story: Episode 1

Understanding SEBD from the inside: The importance of listening to young people

'John' and Paul Cooper

Introduction

This story was shared in a tape-recorded informal discussion/ interview situation in which Paul's questions prompted John (a pseudonym) and guided the recall of his experiences and reflections on his school career. As a historical account it reports the events shown in the list below.

Time line

- 1988 – started school in X-shire
- 1992 – diagnosed as dyslexic
- 1993 – moved to school in a Midlands city
- 1994 – diagnosed with AD/HD and transferred to mainstream secondary school
- 1997 – referred to emotional and behavioural difficulties (EBD) Special School
- life after school.

The transcription of the story is first contextualized in the following rationale by Paul. With the agreement of the speakers, no attempt has been made to edit the content or to alter the wording other than the place names. The format is as in a play – and it may prompt associations with the very concept of theatre and its relationship with life (see also the publication by the Royal Academy of Arts, 1998 of the exhibition of Charlotte Salomon's story, 'Life? or Theatre', which includes references to her original writing on *Life? or Theatre: A Play with Music*).

Why should we listen to young people?

- They have a right to be heard.
- They have important things to say.
- What they have to say is useful.
- Teaching and learning are transactional processes – effective teaching depends on the ability of the teacher to listen to his or her pupils.

Some challenges

- We must avoid being patronizing.
- We must be prepared to be surprised.
- We must be prepared to do something on the basis of what we hear.
- 'The problem of speaking for others'.

Things can be complicated

- '... I think things should stricter in this school. There should be more rules ...'
- '... of course, if there were more rules, I'd be the one who would be breaking them ...'

John's story: episode 1: causes for concern?

P: When did you first experience any problem?

J: When I first went to playschool. Just things like when your Mum says you're naughty, when you're about 3 or 4 you start taking that in. And then when you start going to school – I don't really think I had a problem then. But my Mum used to think I did. 'Cos I was loud and hyperactive. I used to fidget a lot. So she used to tell me there was something wrong with me. At playschool everyone's like that! So it was all right.

P: Did things change then, over time?

J: Yes, when I was 5 and I started going to infant school that's when the problems started really a lot more. 'Cos then I was being naughty, just to get attention. 'Cos I never used to get any attention in the lessons, when everyone else did. I used to get bullied all the time as well – called racist names – all through infant school and junior school. That's when I really did start to play up. Because when I wanted attention, maybe

I went off in a huff, or started shouting at the teacher, when I wasn't getting the attention everyone else was. But when I look back on it now, sometimes I think it's to do with the racism. It's not like it is now, 'cos that was still in the '80s – early '90s. So things have changed. Things were bad back then, though. Even in places like that.

P: So this was like when you were 4 or 5. Did you know that it was racism?

J: Yeah. I knew when they called me names it was racism. But I never thought the teachers were racist. I just thought they didn't like me, and that's why they didn't give me attention – I had one teacher – I think it was in my first year of junior school. She was the worst. I used to have temper tantrums, 'cos I used to ask for help for ages and ages. Doing something. And she'd come. And she'd look at me. And she'd look straight at me, and she'd help someone next to me. She'd look at me for ages and then just help the person beside me.

P: When did these temper tantrums start?

J: At junior school. 'Cos in infant school I got the racism, but the school work wasn't really the problem then, 'cos the teachers were a lot nicer. And when I went into junior school it got a lot worse. The racism got a lot worse then. All through the years – through different schools, the change. 'Cos you got older people in junior school who were still at the top, going to secondary, and you start at the bottom. See what I mean? It goes down then, don't it then? To other kids. See that's what used to happen all the time.

P: What about these tantrums?

J: Well, they weren't really tantrums – I never used to pick things up and throw them about. I just used to run at the door. Slam it. And run off somewhere. On to the field or something. My Mum used to called them temper tantrums.

P: So you weren't actually having a go at anybody?

J: Not really. I used to walk out of lessons, that's all. That's about it. Or I just used to shout. I never used to swear, I just used to shout.

P: So how old would you be when this started?

J: About 7.

P: And how long had you been in that class?

J: I can't really remember how far into the year it was. I know it wasn't right at the beginning. It was about halfway through.

P: Why did it take that long?

J: 'Cos it takes time. When you start a new school you're just nervous. And you think everyone gets normal – and gets treated the same anyway, when you first go. But then they start getting favourites, and things like that. Teachers, innit, y'know what I mean. From about halfway through you can start to tell.

P: So was it because you started to notice that you were being treated differently that you behaved as you did?

J: Yes it was.

P: So that's what it was like when you were 7. How did it go on from there?

J: Well, I went for a couple of years. I had one good teacher, I remember. I can't remember her name. But she was good. She used to help me a lot. 'Cos I only used to have problems with reading and spelling. I never had problems with anything else. But anything that involves reading or spelling, it became a problem. Because I couldn't do them. It doesn't mean I couldn't do it at all. I just couldn't do it because of the spelling. So they started thinking I'd got other problems with history, geography – all the things that need writing down, apart from maths. Things like that. I wasn't rubbish at them, I just couldn't do them at the time. And there was one time, when they gave me a pencil grip – 'cos I hold my pen – they say it's wrong, how I hold it.

They started inventing conspiracy theories about how I was trying to hide my work. Consciously, I never used to think that I was trying to hide it. I was doing it like that 'cos that's how I wrote. But they thought I was trying to hide my work from them. But it never used to be like that! Then, I remember, it was just about the last year – just a couple of months into the last year at junior school – and that's when it got bad. 'Cos I remember, I went to the headmistress's office, 'cos I'd done something wrong. 'Cos they kept ringing my Mum all the time, as well – all thro' the years. If there were school trips they wouldn't let me go, because I'd have to earn stars to go on the trip. No one else did, but I had to, 'cos I was bad. That's what they used to tell me. I think it was the last year. And I went into the office: the headmistress, she was having an argument with me. She was telling me how bad I'd been. I said, 'Let me out the office!' I wanted to go; to just run away.

P: How old were you?

J: About 9. I just wanted to run away, 'cos I knew they were just going to ring my Mum up again. She was getting on at me, saying, 'I'm fed up of the school ringing me all the time!' So I wanted to get out the office. She wouldn't let me out, so I just punched her in the belly. And then she moved, but she grabbed me again and just kept me in the office. Then my Mum came and collected me – no, my Dad came and collected me. He took me back to his house. Then when I got home they told me that I was suspended for two days. And my Mum came in crying, and complaining and shouting at me, 'Just tell me: oh, John, what are you doing? What did you get suspended for? There's no need for that!' She was crying; making me feel bad. So was my Dad. I think I went back to school for about a month. Then we moved. Mum went to the university and we came and lived here. Well, I didn't live here. I went to school here until after Christmas. Then we moved. That was Y Primary School. I got suspended twice there. And I used to sit outside the classroom with my own desk and chair. 'Cos I wanted to.

P: You wanted to?

J: I wanted to, yeah. I didn't want to be in the class. I wanted to be different. 'Cos I think, from being in Z [previous home town] made me like that. If I didn't grow up there, I think I might have been different. But I wanted to be different. I wanted to cause a fuss. I wanted the teachers to – 'cos I wanted the attention.

P: Did you know that at the time?

J: Yes, I did. Of course I knew at the time. I don't think I really planned it, but I knew what I was doing. When I was sitting outside I used to get more help! [There were] no other kids putting their hand up. They [the teachers] can't see them kids. So it's helping me out.

P: So was this like a strategy for getting help with your work?

J: Yeah.

P: Did it work?

J: It worked, yeah, yeah. It did work. I remember one time – I used to be a bit of a comedian at school. I remember one time, they told me to come in and sit at the back. 'Cos I had my table and chair outside. And I said, 'If I come in, he's gonna take my chair away again. So I can't come in', 'cos the janitor used to come and take the chair. He put it somewhere – I don't know where he used to put it. So I took about five minutes. I got some string and I tied the chair to my back. Everyone was laughing. I walked in the classroom. Everyone was laughing, and then I got sent to the headmaster's office. And a couple of other kids did as well, for laughing. But I didn't see anything wrong with that. I just got frustrated 'cos the guy kept on taking my chair away. When he told me to come in, he said, 'He won't take it.' I said, 'I don't believe you.' So I took it anyway. I did that to. Maybe it was a bit stupid. I think of it now as a bit silly but . . .

P: What should those teachers have done differently?

J: I'd say they should have come and helped me. But that's me speaking, isn't it? Saying I think they should have come and helped me. There's other students as well. But like I said, in Z it was the main problem, 'cos they never used to come over to me. But I was the only black person, and that's what I think now when I look back. All the time. Only certain staff used to do it, 'cos they did have some good teachers there, and they used to give an equal amount of help to everyone. It wasn't the whole school [who were racist] it was individual teachers.

P: So it wasn't just you wanting more than your fair share of attention?

J: No. I just wanted an equal amount of attention.

P: Well, you got it . . .

J: Yes. But that was about halfway through the year. But that's when you learn the most, in the first year. But I didn't really learn nothing. That's why I couldn't really spell. I could read. I learned to read by myself, and spell by remembering words. That's all I can remember. Just remembering a word. And if I write it down and it looks right, it's right. If it don't look right, it gets scribbled out. So when they used to say to, 'just try!' and it didn't look right, I just used to scribble it out and refuse to work. But to me like, it used to annoy me so much. If it didn't look right. It didn't look like a whole sentence; it looked like baby scribbles. That's what I used to be worried about, that they'd think it was baby scribbles, and they couldn't read that.

P: What did the teachers do to make you feel valued?

J: What, at Y school?

P: At any of the schools.

J: Trips, innit? School trips. And I used to like sports. So I used to do sports day and I remember I won some kind of county sports or something. I did well, and I got treated all right for a while. 'Cos I did that. But it all started again.

P: You say you got treated all right. What do you mean?

J: We was in the relay race, and we was falling behind. And I picked up the race, and the guys were at least a couple of metres ahead of me. And when I got the baton, I just raced, and I went to the front of them. So – and I think we came first in the end. So they were all pleased because I got the race back for them. 'Cos this other guy dropped the baton and I got the race back for them. They were pleased with that. All the kids were all right with me for a while, but it all worn off after a while.

P: So the kids treated you better. And did you get more attention from the staff?

J: Yes, a little bit … but that wore off.

CHAPTER 3

Communication, emotion and behaviour:
The challenge for educators

Sylvia McNamara

The challenge for educators in the twenty-first century in terms of managing the issue of pupils who exhibit difficulties with social, emotional and behavioural aspects of their lives is the tension between the twin issues of incidence and time to deal with the incidence.

In Birmingham the headteachers in both primary and secondary phases are adamant that the incidence of these issues is increasing. Many reasons are put forward for this, including poor parenting, different expectations of parents from children, higher expectations of children themselves, mobility, increase in challenges that children have to deal with, better diagnosis abilities of our healthcare system, insufficient investment in mental health in society as whole. There is evidence of a rise in mental health issues among children; a rise in psychiatric disorder; there is clearly a rise in marital break-up although there is no evidence of a correlation between the two. Poverty and deprivation are often seen as associated with the incidence of SEBD although this is hardly a new factor. The headteachers see the rise in both permanent and fixed-term exclusion as unsurprising in the face of such an increase in poor behaviour and in evidence of pupils with SEBD, and point to the plethora of activities undertaken in their schools to deal with these issues as evidence of the fact that they are 'holding' many pupils who otherwise would inflate the exclusion figures still further.

The headteachers are also clear in their own minds that the human rights legislation, with the increase in litigation by parents, has made the issue of responses to this increase in incidence much more fraught than in previous years. For example, if a school decides to exclude a child the chances of that exclusion going to appeal and solicitors being present at that appeal to represent the parents and child are very high. Headteachers and chairs of governors feel inadequately prepared by their LEAs to deal with this situation and consequently find it very stressful.

Meanwhile the curriculum has become ever more focused on attainment, leaving teachers with little time to attend to the pastoral needs of their pupils. This focus began with the National Curriculum in 1988, which prescribed the subjects and amount of time per subject for each phase of a child's education. There has been continued emphasis on this aspect ever since. The second focus was the testing of pupils aged 7, 11 and 14 in addition to the GCSE and A level testing and the publication of results by school in league tables. The third focus has been the introduction of the strategies: the literacy and numeracy strategies in KS1 and KS2 and the literacy, numeracy, science, IT, Foundation subjects and behaviour strategies in KS3. The last has been particularly interesting because the declared focus for all of these strategies is attainment in the tests in English, mathematics and science, yet there is no science strategy in KS1 and 2 and there are additional foci in KS3. Additionally there has been a focus on the exclusion rates for both schools and LEAs.

This has meant that at the same time as the increase in the incidence of emotional and behavioural issues among children, there has been a move away from that of listening to pupils in class time because of the pressure that teachers and headteachers experience in terms of focusing on the curriculum in order to get the pupils through their examinations with as high a set of marks as possible. What would help here would be the notion of readiness to sit an examination, so that pupils sit when they are ready and not when their age dictates they should do so. This would help those pupils such as asylum seekers and others whose command of the English language is not as fluent as others of the same age. What would also help would be the ability and courage of teachers to respond to the evidence that pupils learn in different ways. The clear research evidence of a link between reading difficulties and pupils who are both excluded, and placed in EBD schools, remand homes and ultimately prison points to a compelling argument to address the way in which reading is taught to many pupils who are later identified as having SEBD. Such an approach is not encouraged by the government's strategies for literacy and numeracy where 'more of the same' is still the essential ethos behind the catch-up materials for those who fail to make progress the first time round. Approaches such as kinaesthetic activities and talk for learning would seem to have a good deal of success but end up being in the paradoxical arena of those activities that many teachers feel are only appropriate for those pupils who are well behaved.

Interestingly the DfES suggestions through the remodelling of the workforce agenda that behaviour should be managed by behaviour specialists has been greeted with dismay not jubilation. This is because many teachers say that they see communicating and relating to the whole child as an important and rewarding part of the work they do. The solution may lie in the administrative side of this work being picked up by an adult other than a teacher but, by and large, teachers are ready to learn how to manage the SEBD child more effectively, their proviso at present being so long as it does not take away from curriculum time.

There is also another tension in terms of managing the SEBD child, which is in the perception of the causal factors: the 'within-child view' versus the 'environment' view. Causation is key when looking at responses of teachers, pastoral workers, headteachers and governors and the systems and structures that these key workers put in place to deal with the problem. Many of the solutions to SEBD are based on a within-child view. These include learning mentors, reward systems, time out rooms, learning support centres, an alternative curriculum, courses on anger management, stress management and bereavement counselling.

In this current climate of league tables, competition between schools, performance management and competition between teachers, teacher shortage and fear of teachers leaving, being poached or giving up, it is also a challenge to get heard, to have the debate to develop understanding in the teaching community of the needs of pupils without alienating or blaming teachers. There is an understandable tendency for headteachers to protect teachers because they cannot see what else to do and, with the pressure on teachers to stay in classrooms, it is indeed hard to see what to do, for developing such an understanding is about communicating with each other, exploring ideas and solutions, exploring causation explanations and testing them out. Such a climate is a research climate, one that would be fostered and nurtured in a research/ teaching school along the lines that Professor Brighouse (former Chief Education Officer of Birmingham) has often described, but such schools do not yet exist and such climates are rare in inner city schools. To create such an environment would require a fundamental shift in attitude from the government in terms of expectations targets and focus. It would need a focus on inclusion targets, an acknowledgement that time spent on relationships is an investment and that human resource management is in fact the key to effective education.

Another tension for the educator is the fact that the policy of parental choice has created a skewed catchment for many schools so that some schools have both more than their fair share of pupils at primary and secondary age who have been identified as having SEBD and they have vacancies/spare places. Thus when a pupil is excluded for poor behaviour from another school, when pupils arrive from other countries with little or no English language (perhaps having experienced trauma in their lives in that country) or they arrive new to the city for similar reasons, the only school with vacancies is one where there is already a huge challenge in terms of the pupils on roll. Thus the pupils who need some support and understanding in their first few months of education in their 'new' school are the ones least likely to get it because the need for the teacher time resource has been established by the pupils already there. We see this pattern repeated many times in schools placed in a category – special measures, serious weaknesses, schools facing challenging circumstances.

One of the problems that pupils with SEBD clearly face, and this is identified many times by schools, is that of communication skills. This is evidenced in the research that exists around pupil experiences of exclusion and EBD schools/Pupil Referral Units (PRUs) where they have been interviewed. Here the pupils clearly identify that they had issues of anger to deal with but that they often felt that no one listened to them or helped them. Interestingly, little research has been carried out on teachers' communication skills although the Raising African Caribbean Attainment (RACA) research in Birmingham at both KS2 and KS3 levels shows that pupil experience is that teachers both do not listen to them *and* attribute motives to them based on an interpretation of non-verbal cues. The 20+ volumes of materials that have been written to support the KS3 behaviour strand show that the authors think there is a great deal which teachers need to know and understand. How much is focused on teaching communication skills to pupils and learning more effective communication skills oneself is yet to be seen, although even if there is an identification of these issues as being important the cascade model is the one least likely to effect change in teacher behaviours and responses according to the work of in-service researchers such as Joyce and Shower (1995). In addition to the already identified need to teach communication skills to both pupils and teachers alike, there is another need that is rarely touched on, and that is the need to teach communication skills, especially re-integration/welcome back skills to the rest of the class.

If we are to take the issue of environment seriously and if we are to pay attention to the comments of both teachers and pupils identified as having SEBD, then peer relations are a key aspect of an approach to prevention of increased difficulties for those pupils with SEBD. One of the most common factors in the equation around pupil behaviour and teacher response when SEBD is the issue is the teachers' own feelings of powerlessness, frustration and rejection. Most teachers who are instrumental in having a pupil excluded have tried hard to relate to and support that child. Yet one of the least tried approaches is to teach the rest of the class how to deal with the behaviour that all find difficult, including those who support and encourage the poor behaviour. Restorative justice is one approach that is exploring this avenue. The books that Gill Moreton and I wrote were attempting to teach teachers how to do this (1993, 1995a, 1995b). The issue for us all is in helping teachers to feel that there is genuinely time to spend on the relationships between pupils and the communication skills of all the pupils, as well as teaching the content of the curriculum and, perversely, in order to teach the content more effectively to many pupils. What I am probably describing here is emotional literacy for all (teachers and pupils alike) as a clear, overt part of the curriculum and teacher training package.

It is the case that many pupils who make little progress in academic terms, including those with SEBD, are kinaesthetic, musical, interpersonal or intrapersonal learners, to use the Howard Gardner multiple intelligence model. It is rare for teachers of these pupils to recognize that this is the case, let alone choose pedagogical approaches to teaching that will enable such pupils to learn. Group work, pair work and talk for learning often bring about astounding results, as many of the other authors in this book testify. However, it is also the case that these are the pedagogical approaches which many teachers are most resistant to trying. The challenge for us as educators therefore is to create the climate where teachers will feel supported to 'have a go' and 'take a risk', and if the lesson does not go particularly well the first time to feel that it is OK to have another go.

One of the approaches we have discussed as officers in Birmingham is the possibility of having community cohesion and community inclusion targets for headteachers. The reasoning is that if we are serious about localization and we genuinely see education as the way forward for economic regrowth and a 'rights' issue, then we need to be supporting headteachers and governors to actually prioritise working with the community. If we see the community as the reservoir from which we can contribute to the teaching pool by helping parents and elder brothers and sisters to become assistant learning mentors, assistant classroom assistants and from there to possibly go on to be teachers, we need to support and encourage that reservoir by specific training opportunities, targeted recruitment and family literacy sessions that lead in to this work; in other words, communication becoming a real target for schools with their communities. In this way there is more chance of dialogue, discussion and debate between those who are currently teachers and those who are currently parents in the joint interests of the child.

The cause for optimism in this picture of the future is the amazing ability of the school to embrace change and particularly to embrace collaboration. The development of the groups of secondary schools as a result of the Leadership Incentive Grant has shown how quickly headteachers want to and actually do put aside previous rivalries – developed and perpetuated by the league table climate – and have got on with collaborative approaches. As behaviour is at the top of the agenda in terms of issues to deal with and overcome there are bound to be yet more creative solutions developed as a result of such collaboration.

And what is at the heart of effective collaboration between schools? Communication.

CHAPTER 4

SEBD students and teachers' training

A knowledge base is in search of practitioners

Egide Royer

Introduction

We all know that it is not easy to teach children who present difficult behaviours, and that teachers have received very little intervention training with SEBD students. Nevertheless, we also know that well-trained teachers can effectively manage disruptive behaviours and can improve children's behaviour by, for example, establishing clear rules and directions, providing positive and corrective feedback for adaptive behaviour, and using reprimands, time out, response cost or tokens to decrease problematic behaviour. This chapter addresses some of the knowledge base that is available on SEBD children and adolescents and makes proposals regarding teachers' training and the education of these students.

Background

Over the last 15 years, I have given numerous in-service training seminars and presentations on school intervention with SEBD students in Belgium, England, France, Canada, Thailand and Brazil. One conclusion is obvious: our field is seriously deficient in terms of pre-service and in-service teacher training in educating SEBD students. To say the least, the relationship between research and practice is also difficult.

What does research tell us regarding the education of SEBD students?

From the knowledge base we have at our disposal, we are relatively sure that the following considerations are important for the education of SEBD students:

1. When teaching an SEBD student the school must address the child as a whole. We know that in order to be effective, educators of SEBD students must consider a global school approach that uses a strong interagency component based on collaboration.

2. Academic achievement is an important intervention goal with SEBD students. It is imperative that these students develop academic skills that will enable them to survive academically, as a definite connection exists between school achievement and behaviour disorders (Ruhl and Berlinghoff, 1992).

3. The first line of intervention in schools should not be repression, but an overall improvement of the environment and disciplinary practices. Skiba and Peterson (2000) recommend, among other things, conflict resolution/social instruction, classroom strategies for disruptive behaviours, parent involvement, school-wide discipline and behavioural planning, functional assessment and individual education plans.

4. Setting limits and having positive expectations are essential when teaching SEBD students. We have long known some basic truths about successful teaching practices with SEBD students. As stated by Visser (2002), the field of educating SEBD students has pointed out some 'eternal truths' or core factors that must be present in any intervention with children with SEBD needs, such as maintaining consistent and coherent communication, setting boundaries and providing challenges, which appear to have been effective with SEBD students for as long as one can remember.

5. Assessment is a direct component of intervention. We know that diagnostic categories, be they educational or psychiatric in nature, are poor predictors of intervention responsiveness (Tremblay and Royer, 1992; Cooper, 1996; Strain, 2001). Recent developments in functional analysis support the importance of tailored interventions for SEBD students. The ability to determine the functions of behaviour and to teach replacement behaviour are essential elements of a successful intervention.

6. A staff value system is a crucial element in successfully educating SEBD students. As stated by Cole et al. (1999), 'Good practice in relation to SEBD pupils will not

happen without the existence of strong and appropriate staff value systems which shape the ethos of a school' (p. 13). Good schools thus appear to be a great place to learn. Their philosophy is to support the positive development of their students and staff (Royer, 1995). They promote positive and high-quality, differentiated teaching by enhancing staff skills and problem-solving abilities. Their behaviour policy is to help students not only learn but also maintain positive social behaviours (Bullock, 1999).

7. Individualized intervention is necessary to make education happen for SEBD students. Following a careful functional analysis, a multimodal, multi-environmental intervention must be planned and tailored to the needs of the SEBD student. Each case must be considered on an individual basis and with a carefully designed intervention. This consumes both time and energy; however, it has, in fact, a direct relationship with the complex behaviours many of these children and youths manifest in school. It does justice to their individuality as well as to the complexity of every human being.

The preceding are examples of knowledge strongly supported and well documented by researchers in the field, yet it is not really part of the professional expertise of teachers working with SEBD students.

The two solitudes
There are admittedly very few scientific endeavours that compare to the use by educators of the knowledge base developed by the researchers in the field of behaviour problems in school (Schiller, 1995). As stated by Greenwood (2001), compared to science, education is not impressively effective. Empirical evidence does not support decision-making. Practice is often based on a popular way of doing things and is not scientifically tested for its contribution to students' learning or achievement. Policies themselves are a mixture of ideology and politics, occasionally supported by research.

The lack of knowledge and skills of our teachers in their interactions with SEBD students is problematic, to say the least. More often than not, teachers have no crisis intervention plan or procedure to rely on, which tends for many reasons to make even special SEBD classes unsafe. In this context, many researchers question the ability of regular teachers to deal with SEBD students in inclusive classrooms (Cheney and Barringer, 1995). What is apparent, however, is that even the most effective behavioural strategies are not well implemented in mainstream education (Skiba *et al.*, 1997; Wehby *et al.*, 1998; Royer, 2003).

Many teachers continue to choose less effective methods because the impact of introducing research-supported interventions is not immediately visible to them. Very often, changing their practice – as proposed by research – is not in itself rewarding. Another significant impediment is time. Teachers are reluctant to implement practices that take too much time, regardless of the promising results (Vaughn *et al.*, 1998). Some issues may be related to a cost:benefit ratio for certain teachers. If the cost of change is high and the benefits low or only positive to one student (the SEBD student), teachers may be unwilling to change how they deal with problem behaviours in their classroom (Malouf and Schiller, 1995).

We must bear in mind that teachers and schools are rarely, if ever, sued for failure to apply the most effective instructional intervention or to change a practice that is not working or is found to be detrimental to a student's learning. The common explanation for a student's failure to learn is based largely on characteristics such as poverty, disability, ethnicity/language and family, and rarely on the use of ineffective or inappropriate practices (Carnine, 1995).

Considering the quality of our knowledge base on the preferred teaching practices with SEBD students and the significant problems these students face during and after their school years, not using the best practices available to help them succeed in school truly represents an ethical problem. The situation also has an impact on the quality of research undertaken in the school setting. When we, the researchers, present a new intervention programme for the purpose of evaluation, we assume that teachers already possess the core of basic skills required to implement and test this programme. As an analogy, when testing with a new drug in pharmacology to assess its potential to cure a specific illness, medical researchers assume that the doctors applying the research protocol are able to successfully give a patient an intravenous injection or check their blood pressure. In short, medical researchers trust that the practitioner participating in a study is able to administer the treatment with integrity by referring to a background of basic medical skills. We cannot be so sure when implementing and evaluating a new education programme to help SEBD students succeed academically. This is another reason why we must bridge the gap between knowledge and practice (Carnine, 1997).

One cannot reflect on the problematic relationship between research and practice without directly considering the teachers' pre-service and in-service training on how to work specifically with SEBD students. As stated by Sugai *et al.* (1997), the initial training given to teachers fails to prepare them adequately to educate these students. In this regard, if we are to deal effectively with the quality of education offered to SEBD students, the fundamental issue of adequate pre- and in-service teacher training must be examined.

What type of teacher training is necessary?

We now acknowledge that schools of education must revise their pre-service curriculum (for specific knowledge and abilities, see Bullock *et al.*, 1994) in order to better train new teachers on how to educate SEBD students and alleviate conflict. It is imperative that we introduce courses and training seminars that are coherent with the latest knowledge of our field and are precisely designed to address practical teaching problems in today's classroom. What are the characteristics of an effective pre-service training programme pertaining to the education of SEBD students?

Pre-service training must support the development and use of proactive rather than reactive intervention in dealing with SEBD students. It must be clear to every teacher that two levels of intervention – universal and specific – must exist within the school. Universal interventions are offered to each student by means of school rules, classroom rules and social skills teaching. Specific interventions are tailored, individualized interventions for SEBD students, consisting of consultations, individual education plans, self-control and aggression management training, etc. As proposed by Walker (2000), this pre-service training should focus on solving problems and developing intervention strategies that will truly work in the school setting.

In-service training must enable teachers to integrate the new knowledge and skills supported by research and the preferred practices (Royer, 2001). This training must become part of the school staff's mission and be an ongoing career project. We know now that isolated training sessions may be inspiring or increase awareness, yet these limited workshops rarely alter classroom practices. In-service training must therefore be encouraged by the school administration and will have a better chance of producing change if some kind of entrapment effect takes place. Should this upgraded training lead to a more productive classroom environment as a whole for SEBD students – and no doubt decrease the stress felt by teachers – then these new approaches will be better welcomed as part of the preferred intervention practices of these teachers. In so doing, direct consultation and supervision of teachers will become one of the best ways to train in-service practitioners in the use of behavioural intervention (Nelson and Rutherford, 1987; Veillet and Royer, 2001).

CHAPTER 5

Masks, manners, motivation and mind

Morag Hunter-Carsch

Introduction

This chapter explores the reasons for the apparent success of two seemingly opposite teaching approaches: 'the structured approach' and 'the creative arts approach' in teaching young people with specific learning difficulties (SpLD), such as dyslexia, and those with SEBD. The connections are revealed through looking at what lies behind: (1) the 'relationship structure' component in the original (Cruickshank *et al.*, 1961; Haring and Phillips, 1962) model of 'the structured approach', and (2) what underlies the current methodological conflicts in literacy teaching.

The connections can be explained in terms that require the widening of the idea of literacy to include not only 'basic literacy' but the 'new literacies': 'emotional and spiritual literacy'. A theoretical model is generated to illuminate the role played by 'emotion' as well as 'mind' in motivating young learners (and teachers) and how 'masks' and 'manners' may facilitate or obscure underlying difficulties related to communication and behaviour. In this sense, the chapter is about so-called 'emotional literacy'.

Background

The views expressed here are based on my experience of teaching mainstream and special classes with pupils diagnosed as having SpLD or SEBD or both. In addition, I have taught and learned from teachers of such pupils over a period of 40 years in different parts of the UK, Canada and Malaysia. My initial Scottish primary teacher training provided a good base on which to integrate special education training in the USA, Canada and the UK. The range of experiences has sharpened my recognition of what may be significant differences in approaches to the teaching of the two sub-groups SEBD and SpLD. The differences concern teachers' understanding of the role played by 'structured teaching' as a form of learning support with each of the groups. In particular, the focus here is on appreciation of the role played by 'relationship structuring' in the success of teaching pupils with SEBD and/or SpLD. An interest in neurological processing and the range of individual differences underpins the idea of seeking to understand 'connections' in responses to teaching methods. (For 'definitions' of SpLD and dyslexia see BPS/DCEP, 1999; Hunter-Carsch 2001 and for SEBD see Cooper, Chapters 1 and 32 of this book and Cooper, 2000.)

The structured approach

The original Cruickshank *et al.* (1961) and Haring and Phillips (1962) structured teaching approach that was developed on the basis of the Strauss, Werner, Lehtinen (1947) research was strongly multidisciplinary. It involved a neuropsychological perspective and approached 'structuring' the environment in order to assist pupils with what is now termed SpLD and/or SEBD to engage and sustain their attention on particular, carefully prepared and specially taught lessons. The content and methods were mediated in prepared class-rooms where the following elements were structured: (1) time, (2) space, (3) materials, (4) methods and (5) relationships. Historically, the developments in 'remedial', 'special' education and 'inclusion' during the 1970s and into the twenty-first century, on both sides of the Atlantic, show that the first four elements were readily assimilated into the specialist training for teaching pupils with SpLD. But it is not clear what has happened to the fifth element, which seems to have been 'forgotten' in the UK approach to multisensory structured teaching of dyslexic pupils – and it is not clear to what extent it remains an integral part of specialist training for teaching students with SEBD in either the UK or North America.

Misunderstandings and limited understanding of the structured approach

When the term 'the structured approach' is used in the public arena there can be confusion about what it actually means. Critics may have incomplete information and some may express the view that 'structured teaching methods' may be perceived as boring by the learners and restrictive of teachers' freedom to engage in 'creative teaching'. An example of this confusion can be drawn from the public responses to media coverage of the findings of the House of Commons Education and Skills Committee's Report *Teaching Children to Read* (2005). Below the surface of the report's resurrection of 'the phonics debate' (in this case about which phonics methods to adopt) lie tensions about 'traditional' and 'new' approaches to basic literacy teaching. The terminology evokes associations with educationally 'conservative' or 'progressive' teaching methods and the arguments become confounded by simultaneous challenges to teachers to raise achievement levels while maintaining an 'inclusive' approach that may sometimes vitiate against meeting the range of individuals' needs in literacy learning.

This confusion is also evident in discussions that polarize the 'therapeutic' and 'structured educational' approaches employed in teaching pupils with SEBD. The larger drama is played out in the competition for places in the structured teaching contexts of classes for pupils with SpLD (disability) in the USA, where provision varies from state to state and parents appear to prefer to have their children taught in SpLD rather than SEBD contexts. This is perhaps because there is a perceived emphasis on 'cognitive' factors in the associations with SpLD, whereas the perception that SEBD requires therapeutic approaches tends to become polarized as 'affective' and consequently emphasizes the 'emotional' dimension that appears to be more questionable, if not 'frightening', to some parents. The fear is of the unknown, and the results of the fear can include remaining in ignorance of the role played by structured teaching and what kinds of structuring takes place in both approaches.

In my experience it is the expressed wish of children with SEBD, not only those with SpLD, to be seen as getting on with 'normal' learning and not to have 'therapies', but it is often the case that children with either difficulty make only limited progress with structured teaching unless the vital element of 'structuring relationships' is taken into account.

How does relationship structuring fit into the structured teaching approach?

Inevitably teaching is about emotions. There is increasing research on the role of emotions in teaching (Hargreaves, 1998; Zembylas, 2004) and of how 'the classroom as a stage' affects the emotional engagement of teachers and learners (Pettersson *et al.*, 2004). However, teachers may not always be aware of how the involvement of emotions in their teaching role can impinge on and affect the learner – positively as well as negatively. For example, we do not know the learner's experience of figures of authority but we do know that, by definition, the teacher is not only an authority on the curricular subject(s) but 'in authority'. By virtue of the context of 'school' and classrooms, the teacher comes to represent 'society'. For the traumatized learner it is a sufficient task to devote their energies to concentrating on the learning task. They may have insufficient energy to negotiate their feelings if the teacher, even unintentionally, imposes 'demands' by requiring pupils to 'read' the teacher's emotions (smiles, encouraging looks, words of support).

It can seem like a very strange and initially difficult or even 'unacceptable' state of affairs for the beginner specialist SpLD or SEBD teacher to take on the seemingly 'neutral' emotional stance that is recommended in the structured approach. And to the uninformed eye this may look like a boring scenario. To the participants in the 'drama', however, it provides calm and the necessary emotional and spiritual 'space' and 'time' for the learner to put their energies into the huge task of 'focusing' on the carefully prepared lesson content. That is presented in bite sizes and via a systematic trialling and monitoring (diagnostic teaching) of the effects of different combinations and sequences of sensory channel use, e.g. visual (V), then auditory (A), followed by kinaesthetic-tactile (or K-T), followed by simultaneously A and V – i.e. not 'a blitz on all senses at once' but tailored methods and materials designed to track consistencies among the responses to learning experiences and to diagnose the preferences of the individual.

The teacher's role, sitting alongside the pupil (avoiding direct eye contact), involves skilled 'mediation' of learning so that the experience of increments in success is felt (and personally celebrated) by the learner. In this way the student is helped to experience their own feelings and the teacher may be able to come closer to discerning the student's awareness and interpretation of the events of the moment. There should be no intrusion of the teacher's excitement at the moment of the student's successful learning.

It is a mistake to think that this is either boring or soulless for the learner or teacher. It is simply as unobtrusively supportive as the idea of water in a 'water birth' of a normal baby to a healthy mother. The water does not distract. It simply 'is' there in a supportive and calmly perceived manner. Learning how to become an effective teacher in relationship structuring involves more than 'informed sitting alongside'. It concerns the refinement of the capacity to read your own feelings as a teacher and to monitor them and employ them in the diagnostic teaching process, along with observing, monitoring and recording the learning behaviour of the pupil. This is a demanding professional challenge that involves a very different kind of creativity – one which does not always seek expression in the usual ways or at the time the experiences occur. It seeks to channel energies into a quality of caring that aims to deepen knowledge about the learner's attention and concentration span and gradually promotes and extends the learner's engagement towards facilitating the learner's taking on of the responsibility for his or her own actions and learning.

Avoiding and limiting choices, then gradually introducing them
Part of this approach involves the initial avoidance of presenting choices to the learner, whose relevant emotional energies are needed to address the task itself. It is vital to match the level of the student's tasks carefully, so that they begin well within the learner's capabilities and there can be no risk of failure. Clearly, the diagnostic teaching process is continuous and record keeping is essential, including personal reflective accounting on the part of the teacher. You will appreciate that in presenting what seems to be a specialist one-to-one scenario I am simply seeking to illustrate the principles behind what can also be effected within a group or class situation.

Understanding the purpose of relationship structuring can be helpful in finding ways to cope with grasping the complex interactions that happen in the classroom. The point here is that there is a need for the teacher to be aware of the role played by his or her expectations and emotions that can intrude and even obscure the need to focus exclusively on trying to understand the needs of the pupil with SEBD. The route to meeting the particular needs may be assisted by tracking the pupil across different curriculum classes and exploring with them as well as observing how they respond to the different learning experiences.

It will quickly become evident that there exist differences between the observed behaviour of both the learner and teacher in classes studying the 'creative arts' which are less 'desk-bound' and in those that employ traditional literacy (listening, reading, spelling and writing tasks). The observed differences may play a part in explaining the curious polarization between the 'creative' arts and populistic impressions of the 'structured teaching approach'. We need to look below the surface in order to appreciate the problems caused by superficial or incomplete appreciation of the dynamics of learning that can take place in both contexts and employing both methodologies. We can begin by considering the adoption of a broader understanding of 'literacy' – one that includes its intended purposes and seeks to go beyond basic literacy to include the notion of 'spiritual' as well as 'emotional literacy', which may appear to become more accessible through the creative arts.

This chapter's very brief re-examination (below) of the original 1960s 'structured approach' prompts the suggestion that if we are to offer our children an education which is both balanced and bold in recognizing all children's rights to learn how to understand their own and others' feelings, we may all need to have a wider view of what constitutes literacy, one that encompasses emotional and spiritual literacy along with so-called 'thinking skills'. This includes the ability to 'read' signs of conflict, 'rays of hope' and 'routes to peace' and, reciprocally, adults taking responsibility to assist children in this process that takes us, together, into the unknown. (See also Chapter 6 in this volume for a discussion on 'skills' and other related issues concerning thinking, emotions, language and communication.) The loss of understanding about the role played by this strand weakens the approach and undermines its integrity since the purpose of relationship structuring is to free the learner from any distraction emanating from the teacher's emotional role.

Before considering what kind of theoretical model we need for maintaining empathy, understanding and effective teaching, let us remind ourselves of the actual challenge that is involved in teaching pupils with SEBD.

Understanding 'misbehaviour'

When students 'misbehave' this is usually an indication of the need for attention regarding some facet of social experience (e.g. misunderstanding, ineffective or inappropriate attention seeking). Broadly, the problems relate to communication and behavioural difficulties and often concern difficulties in making appropriate responses to experiences. There can be many reasons for finding it difficult to make an acceptable response. It can be hard to 'hear oneself think' and to cope with feelings generated by some internal message or intruded upon by some external message. Such matters involve making choices about the use and direction of energy, and the resultant behaviour can reveal the confusion. Such problems constitute emotional difficulties. For teachers as well as pupils, it can be difficult to move on beyond the intrusive incident to try to develop the kind of empathy that can lead to understanding about the impact of experience(s) on behavioural responses. For the teacher, the personal quest involves pursuing the route to maintaining 'objectivity' as well as informed subjectivity in classroom interactions.

The challenge of teaching pupils with SEBD: what do you do, and how should you do it?

For teachers of young people with SEBD in mainstream classes, the immediate and pressing problem is often felt to be 'what to *do*' with such youngsters. The underlying immediate feeling tends to reflect the wish that they would just *behave like other* ('*normal*') youngsters. Advice from 'experts' simply to '*do* nothing, but to *stop and think*' (in the manner that the teacher might say to a pupil, 'think before you speak') can, initially, provoke a reaction of irritation, because the dilemma at such a moment is that feelings (e.g. irritation) can 'take over'. They can obscure the teacher's vision and appreciation of the fact that it is the understanding of the nature and timing of our responses (including silence) which is vital if we are to assist the individual pupil to begin to cope with his or her feelings (which relate to their 'difficult behaviour' of that moment). By this I mean that since both '*what* you do' and '*how* you do it' are so tightly connected, we can only begin to appreciate 'what to do' in the light of appreciating, also, 'how you (actually) do it'. If you think of this in terms of the relationship between the words and the music (rhythm) of the well-known jazz piece 'It *ain't* what you do it's the *way* that you do it', you will be able to make the connection easily by singing it to yourself, and thinking about the emphasis (rhythm) in the following defiant rewording (just for reminding yourself at those difficult moments in the classroom): 'it *is* what you do *and* the way that you do it!' – and the coda 'and what you *don't do* ...' (e.g. don't say anything for a moment – just 'think' and recognize your own feelings first!).

So the first hurdle for the teacher in deciding what to do is managing to 'stop, listen and look'. Once you have 'listened to your own feelings, recognized them and looked as well as listened to the student', you may be able to create a 'space' and 'time' to come to a decision about how to respond. But how well do we know ourselves and what underlies our tendencies to respond in particular ways (i.e. 'know first thyself', etc., with appreciation to Shakespeare)? Also, are we aware of *why* it can be helpful to us to reflect at such moments, on the way our own mental theoretical model informs our actions and how well it serves our understanding of complex human interactions in the classroom? Simply by engaging in trying to think of the answer to 'why do I feel/think this?' can be useful in redirecting our emotions away from making a potentially less than helpful hasty response, whether verbal or non-verbal. In this way we can slow ourselves down and create a 'space' or 'time' to use our minds.

Remember, the time we need for the relevant reflection may not be more than milliseconds, but it is important to use it wisely, because it is the only available 'peace tool' (for staying calm) that we have at such moments. Also remember that it may not be possible to 'reach' pupils who are experiencing SEBD unless they can draw upon the necessary energy to concentrate (i.e. sustain their attention) on the teacher's words or the visual information being presented at a moment when their 'minds' are absorbed by more pressing images (mental words, feelings or pictures). We need to be able to enter into the 'third space' (between the two actors) to support both them and ourselves. This useful concept of 'the third space' is being employed increasingly in the literature on multilingual and cross-cultural communication (see Svalberg, 2005). Holliday (2005) sensitively notes that *within third spaces we and other parties are particularly vulnerable; we can see more, and less as imaginations are heightened'*.

To recap: have you noticed that teachers say things three times? So have I! By addressing the first aspect of the challenge, at any moment of 'crisis' in the classroom the teacher with the informed mind (as well as 'the informed heart', see Bettleheim, 1960) will be able to take the essential time to 'be still and know' in the sense of drawing on their own informed theoretical framework. This helps them to listen and look rather than speak or respond in any way without checking their own and the pupil's feelings and respecting their 'unknown' source.

The relationship structuring strand of the structured approach is the one that addresses the management of emotions and at the same time causes us to become more aware of what we are experiencing. It affects both teacher and student, and when well employed can facilitate sustained engagement with exploring emotions and 'surfacing' levels of awareness that connect with mind, i.e. it helps with 'thinking with your inner heart', which helps 'centring' of the self, gaining the energy to 'accept' as well as to 'become'. The vision (imagination) of what self might become sets the internal trajectory of the will (motivation) and the agenda (priorities).

The creative arts, creative teaching and 'relationship structuring'

To fully discuss the issue of how the creative arts 'fit into' this argument about effective teaching methods with students with SEBD would require a longer chapter than this. Such a chapter would require cross-cultural and historical contextualization of the purpose, content and methods of formal education. This would need to be completed in a manner which would reveal the changing fashions in the relative emphasis given to oracy (APU, 1986) and the arts and, additionally to their perceived relationship with ethics, in and beyond Europe and North America and also from ancient Greece to the present. Sufficient, for the moment, to quote the outstanding musician Ashkenazy's comprehensive comment '*Art is something that communicates the eternal*'. In this way he prompts awareness that intimations of soul, spirit and the life of the 'inner self' are intimately connected with and through the arts. It is in the dynamics of the connecting of the emotions through the arts that we 'tap into' this essential and everlasting dimension.

The following theoretical model attempts to portray the relationship between the role of the arts and the 'new literacies' (emotional and spiritual), as well as the structured approach, in understanding difficulties in communication and behaviour. It is represented in a series of four illustrations.

Figure 5.1 relates the personal and social dimensions with the dynamics of masks, manners, motivation and mind. Figure 5.2 cues linking of factors that impinge on and influence the sense of 'identity' and belonging. Structured teaching/healing can impact positively where there are difficulties for learners in making or changing certain connecting links or routes in their learning and behaviour. Figure 5.3 seeks to envisage diagrammatically, by pulling apart the 'glue of experience' that bonds, what may be falsely separated or polarized as 'affective' and 'cognitive' dimensions of being (see also Chapter 6, Bond's reference to the work of Nussbaum, 2001). Essentially, the

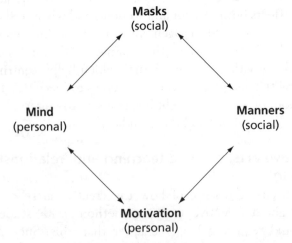

Figure 5.1 *A model for representing the dynamics of communication, emotion and behaviour in relation to personal and social dimensions of experience*

Factors impinging on the development of identity and 'belonging'

ME

Image Mirror

Masks	Experience
sight	representation

Manners	Expectations
hearing	expression

Motivation	Emotion
touch and smell	energy

Mind	Empathy
'dreaming'	humanity

Music
Harmony

Movement, performance arts and the visual arts

Structured teaching
Time, space, materials, methods, relationships

Relationship structuring
Towards metacognition, meta-affectivity and their synthesis into
metacomprehension (see also Figure 5.3)

Figure 5.2 *The role of the arts, the 'new literacies' and the structured approach in understanding and supporting young people with SEBD*

dynamics of learning and reflection in, on and through experiencing at different levels can deepen empathy and 'surface' the potential for the 'seeds of understanding' to germinate into awareness and the will to express, share, reach or become harnessed into the task of 'communicating' (involving listening, speaking, language, literacy and the arts). Figure 5.4 seeks to remind us that, without the facility to read people as if by instant MRI scanning to reveal neurological functioning and the routes adopted by individual humans, we are dependent on 'reading' each other in ways that can be well informed by good teaching and learning through the arts (not only the 'sciences').

Masks, manners, motivation and mind: a theoretical model

We all wear 'masks' much of the time. Often this is a matter of consideration, recognition and respect for others' rights to their own space, time and experience. It would not be appropriate or 'good manners' to subject our colleagues, friends and family to awareness of what may be uppermost in our private experiencing of life at any particular moment. It becomes a social skill to be able to detect the face behind the mask and to acknowledge and respect the placing of the mask by the owner while deciding whether and how to reveal that you think you can 'see through' a particular mask at a particular moment.

The 'navigating' of the masks can form an intricate dance with its own rhythms and music sometimes discernible through voice pace, intonation and stress, silences, glances and facial expression, movements and degrees of engagement or seeming disengagement with dialogue. Essentially it is interpersonal. It holds the potential for relating and it conducts, orchestrates, facilitates or impedes individual, 'solo' expression and harmonizing (see also other chapters in this book regarding music, dance and drama, visualizing and verbalizing, new approaches such the Danis Bois (2003) method of promoting self-awareness through movement and Annie Marie Vaillant's (2003) innovative approach to art therapy through the anthroposophist approach).

Making appropriate responses to the masks requires awareness of 'manners'. According to conventions that can be created between individuals as readily as within groups and across groups, manners can be interpreted as either 'good' or 'bad'. Their connection with

Levels of experiencing	Predominantly	
	Cognitive	Affective
Sensing		*
Becoming aware	*	
Going through		*
Grasping	*	
Comprehending		*
Metacognition	*	
Meta-affectivity		*
Metacomprehension	*	

Figure 5.3 *Connecting cognitive and affective development (based on Hunter-Carsch, 2001, p. 100)*

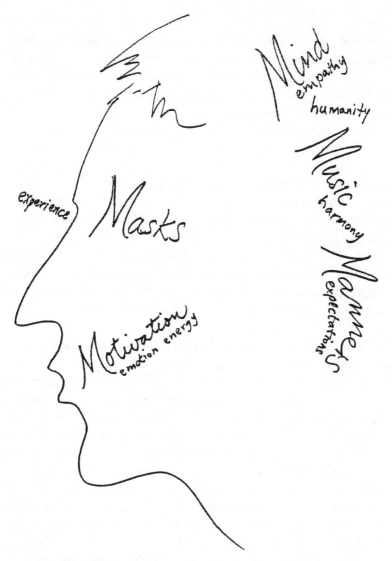

Figure 5.4 *Developing identity and 'reading people': a visual representation of the dynamics of the 'm' and 'e' components of the evolving identity (i.e. the 'me')*

culture (the idea of 'high culture' – cultivated behaviours as well as behavioural customs that help to define borders, barriers and perimeters of groups) is intimate and complex. It defines what it is to belong to a group. In that sense it forms an essential component of identity of the individual and of the group.

It is the motivation to find our identity, our 'self', that drives much of social interaction. This need to 'keep in touch with ourselves' can take many forms and is not necessarily a private experience. To be successful, however, it seems to require both inner and outward expression. It fuels the fires of intention and energizes the individual towards conceptualizing as well as responding through overt actions or resistance to action. It involves the realm of conscious awareness and what may be different levels of dynamics that promote or impede conscious awareness. It is the stuff of 'mind'.

Since school is one of the conventions constructed for the purpose of training young individuals to cope effectively in society – a compulsory experience for all our children, it becomes vital for teachers to consider the breadth and depth of our vision of both school and society. Not one of us can escape the fact that we participate in this ritual and that our masks reveal, in some aspect, our adopted role in every interaction.

Figure 5.4 prompts association of the interpersonal and communicative aspects of behaviour with the physiological and underlying neurological functioning related to perception and cognition, apprehension and comprehension, empathy and sympathy.

The value of the arts: observing, experiencing/participating in dance, drama, music, painting, sculpture

The arts permit transcendence of our routine particular roles and allow each of us to adopt a stance, perspective and potential vision that can not only penetrate the masks but also challenge the manners, penetrate the protective layers of motivation, recognize and respond to mind in a manner which may be rapier fast, leisured as a drifting walk through summer meadows, determined as a journey through deep snow and blizzard conditions to reach a safe home, or warm as a loving glance. The timing, mode of expression and patterns of response are not restricted since they emanate from mental constructions whose control remains private. Such experiences form the basis for developing 'self'. They concern matters of 'the spirit' and may require 'new' forms of literacy in order to be 'read', appreciated, understood at different levels of awareness. For some youngsters, and perhaps particularly for those with SEBD, it can be easier to work with different, perhaps more accessible forms of 'reading' and 'literacy' such as can be offered through arts and crafts. *'What makes the subject [arts and crafts] particularly interesting is that it is not only a matter of using linguistic mediation, but rather, also mediation based on external factors such as the use of specific objects or model learning'* (Pettersson *et al.*, 2004, p. 589).

The links with 'mind' and 'motivation'

In employing my particular theoretical model, the links lead me from considering the impact of masks and manners to how they connect with 'mind' and to recognize the salience of motivation in trying to understand and determine how to support the 'upset' student in the classroom, whatever their behaviour, whether confrontation or retreat, reversal or paralysis. I try to become aware of the dynamics that prompt their behaviour and, using the theoretical plan, to seek to understand the route followed by their connections (see Figures 5.1 and 5.2). I have to ask myself, for example, at any moment in the interaction with them, where was my attention (energy) being directed and where was their energy being directed? I have to consider, was it devoted to engaging with the observed mask or 'under the mask', with the expected/conventional behaviour or a departure in order to make a point (consciously or unconsciously)?

Incidentally, without such deliberations there would be little humour in art, poetry and music and, probably, no 'cartoons' and much less laughter in the world! There would also be fewer heart-rendingly beautiful or sad representations of the tenderest moments of human experience, whether through art, music, dance, drama, poetry and other forms of the written word. The synthesis of some of the art forms through film constitutes perhaps a separate case, but not one that we should neglect in this line of argument. However, with regard to any or several of the arts and creative writers across a range of fields, perhaps it is only through a process of 'apprehension of the spirit', for example of Vygotsky (Vygotsky *et al.*, 1978), Montessori, Kodally or Picasso, that we can 'know' their methods, not the reported actions or even the words, materials, musical phrases or paintings as such. And it is doubtful how accurately we can 'absorb' or 'translate' their methods in the process of letting them become part of our own expression and drawing on their minds in formulating our own responses to the situations we face.

In returning to the use of the theoretical model, the core issue concerns the notion of 'identity', sense of self and the value attached to self (self-esteem) that is intimately connected with other aspects of values and valuing. This is where making the link with the idea of 'mind' (Donaldson, 1992) – one's own and others' minds – becomes essential and the raising of individuals' awareness becomes most challenging. We are dealing with issues that were central to Erich Fromm's (1979) discourse on 'being and having', reliability and falli-bility (e.g. Cardinal Melcher's and Hans Kung's reluctance to concur with the idea of the infallibility of the Pope), beliefs and values (e.g. Walter Kaufmann's [1963] work on 'the faith of a heretic'), matters which explore the bridge between what we regard as the sciences and the arts and that inspired many great thinkers and humanists including, for example, Gallileo, Van Gogh and Ghandi. We are facing the need to explore the nature of 'beliefs' and their impact on our behaviour. We cannot deny that such challenges occur in classrooms with children as well as in the wider contexts of life with people of all ages, languages and cultures, and that they constitute the stuff of potential 'misunderstandings', and require us as teachers to reflect on some of the experiential dimensions of the causal factors involved in human communication and behavioural problems.

In conclusion, I see the value of relationship structuring within the framework of 'the structured approach' as acknowledging the need for teachers to develop familiarity with another level of professional awareness. This they do by consciously 'withdrawing' from the foregrounding of their normally necessary emotional involvement in interaction in the classroom and learning to inhabit a 'backgrounded' and aware emotional state while fostering the calm required for youngsters with SEBD to become gradually more aware of their own potential and actual learning and in so doing to affect, positively, their sense of identity and their self-esteem. Crucially, this can have a positive impact on the youngsters' motivation to learn and to become. The energy necessary to do this will come from our own creativity, awareness and humility. In the words of St Francis of Assisi, from a German book of quotations, *Was der Mensch Gott ist, das ist er, nicht mehr, und nicht weniger* ('What man is in front of God, that is what he is, no more, not any less').

Note

For further information about the pioneering vision of structured teaching see Cruickshank *et al.* (1961); for the historical impact of diagnostic labelling see Hunter-Carsch (2001); and for a review of debates over how to teach literacy see e.g. Soler (2002) and Green and Kostogriz's (2002) use of the descriptor 'new literacies' as employed, differently, by Gee (2000) to refer to *'a growing body of transdiscipline studies in literacy education'*. Also, see Reid (2005) for the impact of environmental factors on learning for pupils, whether described as 'with SEBD' or as 'with SPLD' or 'Dyslexic'.

Acknowledgements

With thanks in memory of my late husband, Dr Henry Carsch, with whom I discussed the synthesis into the 'dynamic' model in Figure 5.3 of an earlier model by the late Professor Beqiraj based on the idea of representing 'levels of experiencing as strata of cognition'; and to Professor Margaret Donaldson for discussions on 'human minds'; Mrs Cornelia Schmidt for the quotation from St Francis of Assisi; Anne Marie Vaillant for an introduction to her inspiring anthroposophical work in art therapy in France and for information about the Danis Bois method; and Marian Adams for sharing a performance with 'masks' as part of an international conference in 2003.

CHAPTER 6

Ways of thinking about relationships: communication, emotion and behaviour

E. J. Bond

I take as my text the following paragraph from Chapter 1 of this volume:

> Specifically, students with social, emotional and behavioural difficulties often experience problems in formulating and communicating basic verbal messages, and in understanding and articulating their emotions. The skills required to overcome these difficulties encompass linguistic competence and social and emotional literacy that play major roles in helping students to escape the cycle of escalating behavioural problems. (p. 3)

The context makes it clear that these skills together are what are called 'communication skills', the lack of them being important causal factors in SEBD.

A skill is something that can be learned or acquired by someone with the necessary talent or ability (an ability that is often though not always minimal), through instruction and practice. Examples of this are driving a car, swimming, skiing, fencing, juggling, riding a bicycle, mountain climbing, sailing, playing a musical instrument, masonry, carpentry, use of a computer. There is much talk of 'communication skills', but does communication belong on this list? (The only example of a communication skill that springs quickly to mind is the skill of being fast and accurate in sending messages in Morse code by wireless telegraphy!)

Ultimately derived from the Latin *communicare*, to make common, 'communicate' originally (sixteenth century) meant (*Shorter Oxford Dictionary*) 'to give to another as a partaker' and thus came to be used as the word for participation in the Christian rite of the Eucharist or Holy Communion – a coming together (or forming a community) as brothers and sisters in Christ. But while interesting and useful, these etymological facts do not reveal the sense of the word as it is used today. The common element of meaning in 'communication' now, not unrelated to its original sense, is transmission or movement from A to B, not only messages but also (less commonly) goods, and not only between persons but between, for instance, towns and cities when they are connected via rail lines (or other means of transportation). Messages may be conveyed by a postal service, various electronic means, telephone, wireless telegraphy or mechanical means of moving paper, thus connecting persons, institutions, or departments within institutions. If the communication is between persons or institutions (or within institutions), then it *consists in* the sending and receiving of (normally verbal) messages. Looking at all this we can see that communication is still a kind of joining or bringing together.

I may communicate with you, by email or postal letter for example, but if two people are simply chatting together, face to face, one does not normally speak of communication. To be communication, properly speaking, there must be a message containing *information* and it must normally be given by a sender to a receiver or receivers from at least a minimal distance. While communication between persons consists in the sending and receiving of messages, such messages *can* be delivered in the presence of the receiver, as, for example, a warning of danger, but such communications are typically read out from a platform or at least a special position in a room or hall. Conversation or discussion, or argument, or pleading, or explaining, or giving advice, or excusing or justifying oneself, or expressing one's feelings, or simply telling how one feels, do not consist in sending or receiving messages and are therefore not, in the basic sense of the word, forms of communication, although *teaching* may be partly just that.

If we look again at the quoted passage that I am taking as my text we will see some serious problems. The claim is that the condition of children with social, emotional and behavioural difficulties is connected with 'problems in formulating and communicating basic verbal messages [note the term], and in understanding and articulating their emotions', two apparently closely related problems that it is supposed can be overcome by the learning of certain skills, namely 'linguistic competence and social and emotional literacy' and that these skills 'play major roles in helping students to escape the cycle of escalating behavioural problems'.

Now a skill – see the examples given above – is something that certain persons (in some cases just about everybody) can learn by training, discipline and practice. Some sense can be given to the notion of acquiring a skill in linguistic competence, including the special skill of composing messages, by these means, but the trainees would have to be eager to learn (as is someone who is seriously interested in excelling at archery and is therefore willing to subject herself to discipline and practice), and I imagine that for the clientele in question this would be most unlikely.

Nor should it be forgotten that talking face to face does not consist in the composing, sending and receiving of messages. But that someone might be *trained* for social and emotional literacy (although it is not entirely clear just exactly what that is) is scarcely imaginable. Never mind the discipline problem, how would one practise? And just exactly what would the trainer, in her role as trainer, do? 'Well, children, we are here today for our one-hour social and emotional literacy training session.' Something that makes sense for reading and writing as well as archery or typing does not seem to make any sense here. Clearly this is not something to be acquired by training, discipline and practice or, in other words, 'skill' is a serious (and hopelessly optimistic) misnomer. Whatever might helpfully be done here must be much more complex than this, for what needs to be induced is understanding and self-knowledge. This is something utterly different from acquiring a skill, and even to attempt to induce such understanding and self-knowledge will require a great deal of calm, patience and understanding (does this equal social and emotional literacy?) on the part of the person in charge.

It is time to turn to emotions. While it is a commonplace to suppose that emotion and cognition are entirely separate, as far back in cultures ancestral to our own as the fifth century BC, Plato believed that the highest form of knowledge, knowledge of the Idea of the Good, was at the same time *love* of the Idea of the Good, while in the seventeenth century Spinoza held that worldly emotions were joy or sorrow accompanied by the idea of an external cause and that the highest form of knowledge, *scientia intuitiva*, was at the same time love of God. And he had this to say: 'No emotion can be restrained by the true knowledge of good and evil in so far as it is true, but only in so far as it is considered as an emotion' (*Ethics*, IV, 14).

It has long been obvious to analytic philosophers that an emotion or feeling cannot be identified as guilt, for instance, unless it involves the idea of having committed a moral transgression, or as fear, unless one believes oneself to be under threat, and in recent times it has been successfully argued (see de Sousa, 1987; Nussbaum, 2001, pp. 3–4) that all emotions, whatever the associated feelings or physiological symptoms, are essentially cognitive. Nussbaum says that her view, essentially that 'emotions are appraisals or value judgments, which ascribe to things or persons outside the person's own control great importance for that person's own flourishing', is derived from the Stoics of the Hellenistic and Roman periods. The important difference is that she, unlike the Stoics, does not see all such beliefs as false, which for them meant that all emotions were to be extirpated.

Some examples, such as guilt and fear, have already been mentioned, and they fit easily into Nussbaum's account. I should mention here that 'flourishing' is a translation of the Greek *eudaimonia*, sometimes translated as 'happiness' and sometimes as 'well-being', but it is not just a matter of feeling or of physical well-being (although it includes both), but a state of the whole person, where we want to say that person is thriving or flourishing or living well. Feeling guilty is, on the Nussbaum account, the judgement that I have done wrong, which I see as adversely affecting my *eudaimonia*, hence a downer, and fear is the judgement that my well-being or even my life is under threat from some source or other, hence the physiological response and its accompanying feeling. To love someone involves a number of beliefs, the most obvious being that the loved one is seen as vital to one's well-being; but less immediately obvious, though no less important, is that the truly loved person's personal well-being becomes a significant part of one's own. An analysis of this kind can be given for any emotion you care to name. But we must not forget the essential element that these are beliefs or judgements concerning things that are beyond our control, such as the grief felt over the loss of a parent, spouse or child, which is a judgement or a recognition that that person really mattered to us. Thus the loss was a grievous blow to our *eudaimonia*.

Now what are we going to say, in this connection, about a lack of 'communication skills', seemingly analysed by the writer quoted as 'problems in formulating and communicating basic verbal messages, and in understanding and articulating their emotions'? The first of these, as I said before, is simply a matter of acquiring a certain linguistic competence, which, given the basic ability and the will to learn, is a genuine skill that, given the right conditions, can be acquired by training, discipline and practice. The second, which is supposedly to be mastered by acquiring 'social and emotional literacy' – and this phrase does not wear its meaning on its face – is a much more difficult notion. But because it is claimed to be the means for understanding and articulating emotions, it obviously needs to be looked at.

It is important that we understand our emotions, and no doubt there is significant failure in this regard with children or adolescents with SEBD. I would imagine that hostility is a factor in every such case, and hostility involves attacking those to whom one is hostile or defending oneself against them. Fear and hatred are obviously involved here – the activities or even the existence of the 'enemy' being seen as inimical to one's well-being. Now I am assuming, and I am assuming also that there will be no disagreement here, that this hostility and the resultant bad behaviour are not the consequence of a badly wired brain, but of something in the history of the disturbed child or adolescent. He or she may have been badly treated by parents, siblings or peers – perhaps hurt and deceived by them. Thus they trust no one. Emotional literacy consists, it is claimed, in understanding and *articulating* one's emotions. Can you imagine that such a person would wish to articulate his or her emotions to just anyone, even if they understood them well enough and had the necessary linguistic skills to do so? To how many people would you or I or anybody be willing to do this? Such children and adolescents are particularly liable to mistrust authority figures, or people they feel are trying to squeeze something out of them, without real sympathy. In the (dubious) sense of articulating their emotions, they do not *wish* to 'communicate'. What is needed first of all is to establish trust and genuine caring. Mere method will not do the job; in fact if simply imposed it will serve only to further alienate, and thus exacerbate the condition.

If emotional literacy and social literacy are not firmly tied together in one bundle, I suspect that 'social literacy' means willing conformity to social norms, which may be exactly what is being resisted in the attempt to attain or regain the personal autonomy and self-esteem that the person sees as necessary for his or her well-being. For these norms are often seen as pointless and inimical to individuality. A person who feels under constant pressure to conform, or to please the authorities, is likely to resist more and more. The remedy for SEBD must consist in something more, indeed something more humane and loving than what is coldly listed in the paragraph I have taken as my text.

CHAPTER 7

Why is communication important in learning?

Rosemary Sage

Introduction

We seldom give thought to our communication. It is taken for granted as breathing is. Yet if we want to improve our performance it is vital to consider communication as the way we conduct our business with each other. This chapter looks at experiencing and using communication as a basis for learning and teaching.

Experiencing communication

Luke woke at the shrill sound of the alarm and put on a CD. The noise of people talking in the kitchen forced him out of bed and into the shower. He could hear Dad whistling merrily in the bedroom. Stumbling downstairs only half awake, Luke picked up the paper and post from the mat, looking at the headline 'Teenager sails around the world', and then at a postcard from Grandma holidaying in France. On the way to the kitchen he glanced up at the picture on the wall – an abstract called 'Life' – that he had bought for his parents as a present. While eating cereal, Luke gazed at the packet for free offers or competitions, grunting in the right place as Mum chatted away. His watch bleeped, reminding him it was time to catch the bus. Downing a cappuccino, and grabbing his school coat, Luke ran down the hall, turning to wave goodbye and swerving to avoid the cat ...

What references to communication are there? The radio, CD, paper, post, talk in the kitchen? We can add whistling, wave of the hand, alarm clock, as well as a glance at the picture, watch, postcard and cereal packet. Details such as school, France, cappuccino, cat, etc., communicate a message about family values and situation.

During a day we speak, and are spoken to, read, write, listen to music and look at pictures and signs, responding constantly to thousands of cues to communicate. We are in touch with many people who give us information and ask us to remember and do things. As we move around, a radar-like system tells us how to dodge things in our way and in all these events we give clues as to our intentions. Even if not fully conscious of our motives and actions we are giving out messages. Today I am dressed in old jeans. The message is that there is no need to make a good impression. As we interpret the actions of people we attribute a meaning to these behaviours. Figuring out why they act as they do has a major effect on our relations with them and the way we might respond to approaches.

Communication is a complex, consuming business. The day starts with a message from an alarm clock or someone calling us. Getting clothed is the result of accumulated habits of previous communication, as we were not born with the urge to wash and dress but have learned through child-rearing practices to do this and live successfully with others. The cereal we eat for breakfast, the clothes we wear and the tea or coffee we drink are the result of environmental conditioning that continually communicates. Communication is everywhere and inevitable, but how do we do it?

Means of communication

Discussion suggests a variety of communication but tells us nothing about how it is used or why it is happening. Two terms describe the process:

1. *Forms of communication* include ways of communicating such as speaking, writing, drawing, dancing, playing music, drama or sport, etc. Forms are distinct as far as they have their own system for putting a message across. Writing uses words arranged according to rules of syntax and grammar.
2. *Medium of communication* combines different forms. Speaking involves words and gestures, facial expressions and tone of voice, so integrating verbal and non-verbal forms in conveying messages. Non-verbal communication reinforces something being said, as when a speaker bangs a hand down and strengthens the voice to add emphasis; or it clarifies an idea, as when a teacher asks a child to fetch a small ball from a basket, indicating the size with a

hand movement. At other times non-verbal signs modify speech. An adult may tell a child off with a smile on their face and a soft tone to the voice, taking the edge off the disapproval. Technology may be used in communication as in a *book*, which produces forms such as pictures, drawings, tables and diagrams. The word *media* refers to mass communication via radio, television, computer, cinema, books, newspapers, magazines and journals, offering words, pictures and music. Media are based on technology that bridges the sender and receiver of the message.

All forms of communication utilize the senses, passing through eyes, ears, touch, feeling and sense of position in space, smell and sometimes taste. We must integrate messages across domains and make meaning from them. Most means of communication are intentional – a church spire presents the function and purpose of the building and a no-waiting sign indicates that we must not park a car near by. Qualities of communication, however, vary. Speech is transient in contrast to writing, pictures, objects or signs, which allow us to return to them. Some qualities of communication are imposed – cartoons are funny but they could be serious. The important thing is whether the sender and receiver of the message connect.

Communication and connections

When we communicate connection occurs between one person and another or between groups. What flows through the connections are the ideas, beliefs, opinions and pieces of information that formulate the content and material of the communication. Speech links us with one another and television links us with the world at large. However, being able to speak to someone does not mean that we can get across what we want to say. We learn to do this through performance techniques and knowledge of audiences.

Particular forms of communication are better at doing some things than others. Pictures are good at representing the physical and material world whereas words are better at dealing with abstracts – ideas, opinions and arguments from the world of the mind. As the tool for describing and discussing feelings, speech is an essential feature of forming relationships. It is quick, immediate and flexible, which ensures that spoken language is the paramount communication in life. Speech links past, present and future enabling us to bring together a series of events and make meaning of them. This narrative ability is crucial to understanding and fundamental to the communicative process of teaching and learning. So what are the types of communication?

Categories of communication

1. *Intrapersonal*: communicating with ourselves. This is when we *think* we are communicating with ourselves, as in solving a problem through a series of steps, completing a task by means of a number of sequenced activities or just reflecting on a past, present or future experience. We do this in words and/or pictures in our heads.
2. *Interpersonal*: communicating face to face or by telephone. Emphasis is on linguistic and non-linguistic forms of communicating but, on the telephone, the voice is the only non-verbal form available.
3. *Group communication*: communicating within and across groups. Large groups will act differently to small ones because they are often brought together for special purposes such as a concert. The messenger has to take into account the range of needs of the people receiving the information. Communication is less personal in groups.
4. *Mass communication*: communicating with large numbers of people. A concert for 1,000 people rather than 100 is considered mass communication. Included in this is large-scale communication as in telephone and postal systems and the mass pop record and DVD industry.

In reality communication fits more than one category. A teacher might take notes at a conference (intrapersonal and group communication) and share them with a colleague (interpersonal communication) before writing the information in a report (mass communication). In addition, the study of one category of communication contributes to understanding another. The way teachers behave in a staffroom is partly explained by how they relate in pairs and communicate between themselves. How we talk depends on our ability to think and see ourselves. Coping with group talk relies on using various conversation moves. The ways we communicate are varied, but how do we define the process?

Defining communication

Two definitions predominate in the literature:

1. *Communication as a process*, whereby a *sender* directs a *message* through a *medium* to a *receiver* with some *effect*. Different components and stages are identified in Lasswell's persuasive verbal model (1960), '*Who says what in which channel to whom and with what effect*'. Others find ideas of *purpose* and *context* of fundamental importance since most communication has an aim and takes place in a social context that influences how messages are formulated and understood. The message must be converted into an appropriate code for the channel used. Thoughts may be encoded in gestures and movements, speech, writing, pictures and sounds depending on the availability of visual, aural or haptic channels. (*Haptic* refers to feeling and touch as well as the sense of position in space – it is ubiquitous over the body, in contrast to localized organs of sight and hearing.)

2. *Communication as a social activity*, where people in a given culture create and exchange meanings in response to what they experience. Focus is on the *text*, which may be a painting, photograph, film or dance sequence as well as speech or writing. An old Esso advertising strapline, 'Put a tiger in your tank', decodes the tiger as exotic, powerful and savage, with an appeal of uninhibited energy alongside the cultural value that speed and power are desirable and good. Communication is thus a study of culture as well as process.

Accounts agree that communication is a basic, non-stop human activity, since even in our sleep our mind rearranges memories in dream images. While we are awake we give out information deliberately and unconsciously. We may say one thing but signify the opposite with an uncontrolled facial expression, such as when an adult praises a child's messy picture with a grimace on their face. Whatever we say, and how we say it, along with our dress, posture and body movements, creates an impression. It is impossible *not* to communicate, even when saying nothing. So how do we describe the process?

The communication process:
The Transactional View
shared experience
COMMUNICATOR (sends & receives) -> MESSAGES ->
COMMUNICATOR (sends & receives) <- responds & decodes
<- decodes and responds
feedback

Communicating is most accurately represented by the transactional view, reflecting that we send and receive messages simultaneously. Consider what might occur as a teacher gives out homework to a class. Several faces grimace, signalling a powerful message while receiving the verbal one. This feedback could lead to defensive behaviour on the part of the teacher. The simultaneous nature of most interaction explains why, in this model, *communicator* replaces *sender* and *receiver*. It is difficult to isolate a discrete act of communication from events that precede and follow it. The way participants act in the exchange will influence all further interactions. Duck (1990) reminds us that 'Relationships are best conceived as unfinished business'. Communication in this view is the result of mutual influence and not something we do to others but what is actively done *with* them. Like dancing, it depends on involvement of both partners, and the skill of one person, alone, will not bring about success. The cooperative, transactional nature focuses on being able to adapt and coordinate activity. The way we communicate will vary with different partners. Research of Dainton and Stafford (1993) shows the quality of interaction between adults and children as a two-way process. Children with behaviour that causes problems evoke more high-control responses from adults. Those with low self-esteem send messages that weaken the self-concepts of children who, in turn, react in ways that make the adult feel worse. This mutually reinforcing cycle suggests how important it is for adults who are involved with child rearing to understand the communicative processes and the principles of interpersonal exchanges:

1. *Communication is both intentional and unintentional.* Unintentional 'sour' expressions, impatient shifting or signs of boredom give out stronger messages than intentional words.
2. *All behaviour communicates.* We are transmitters that cannot be shut off as all behaviour sends a message, which is interpreted accurately or otherwise.
3. *Communication has content and relational dimensions.* We

express information and also how we feel about the other person in the way we speak. Think how you might say 'thanks' to a person you love in contrast to one you hate – the first will convey a bright and the second a grudging tone of voice.

4. *Communication is irreversible.* No amount of explanation can erase a bad impression. Words said and deeds done are irretrievable.

5. *Communication is unrepeatable.* Communication is ongoing so events cannot be repeated. The smile that worked yesterday may not today because situations change.

Popular misconceptions

1. *The more communication the better.* One can talk something to death and produce negative results. We have to judge when to stop talking. Cloven and Roloff (1991) found that thinking and talking about conflicts increases relational problems.

2. *Communication solves all problems.* Sometimes clear communication causes problems. If you are asked about a friend's new dress and say it makes them look fat more harm than good is done. It is important to judge what and how to disclose.

3. *Communication is a natural ability.* People think communication is a natural aptitude. Although most of us function passably without formal communication training, we operate at a level of effectiveness way below our potential. Acquiring techniques to adapt our communication in a variety of private and public contexts gives us the information and skill to assert ourselves, perform successfully in social and learning contexts and control our lives more successfully.

Communication problems

Schumacher (1978) points out that we 'rely on other people's visible signals to convey to us a correct picture of their invisible thoughts'. He describes four steps:

1. The sender must know precisely what thought he wants to convey.

2. The sender must find visible and audible symbols to

externalize internal thoughts in gestures, movements, facial expressions, voice tone, words ('first translation').

3. The receiver must have a faultless reception of visible and audible symbols with ability to hear and understand what is said and observe the non-verbal signs that convey feeling and meaning.

4. The receiver must integrate messages within the context and relationships of the communicators and turn them into thought ('second translation').

Much can go wrong at each stage and this is considered in the following list:

1. *Knowing what to say.* This is easier said than done. Thinking is expressed in language that has two aspects:
   (a) *language structure* – the sound, grammar and syntax forms used to organize words to deliver content;
   (b) *narrative structure* – the use of words in connected events, as in instructions, directions, explanations, recounts or reports of daily activities, and storytelling.
   Language structures are the tools, and narratives are what are accomplished with them. Possessing the tools does not mean you can use them. You need opportunities to learn. We can master language structure and appear competent but experience problems organizing the overall meaning of spoken and written events. This depends on a wide variety of experience, knowledge and use of language to build connections between information, depending on *reference, inference and coherence* skills.
   An example of these necessary skills is seen in the following sentences:

Milly and Mog were wet and *they* sheltered under a tree near *their* house. **After a while**, the sun came out and *it* was dry enough to dash *home*. *Both* were pleased to be inside. Milly took off *her* coat and Mog pulled on *his* **lead** before *it* was removed. **Then** *they both* had **supper**.

The italics are *reference* words, depending on knowledge and understanding of what they refer to and ability to link information by thinking forwards and backwards. *Inference* is involved here but more directly affects whether you understand Mog is a dog (*lead*) and that the couple ate in the evening (**supper**). *Coherence* is understood by recognizing the time markers, **after a while** and **then**, which indicate the passage and event sequence. Critical (sequential and logical) and creative (lateral) thinking skills merge with linguistic knowledge to process and produce narrative discourse. Questions scaffold the thinking required and provide the structure for taking thoughts into action:

Thought – I'd like a party. *Why?* To celebrate my birthday. *When?* On Saturday 28 April. *Where?* A local restaurant. *Who?* Twelve friends. *What?* Budget of £500. *How? Book location, select menu, decide transport, send invites, prepare surprises, check arrangements.*

Tasks and tests tend to focus on assessing specific knowledge and fail to monitor bringing together information as in a summary or explanation. Many students have difficulty with narrative but this is not easily observed if language structure is adequate.

2. *Performing the message.* Since verbal and non-verbal signals are used together, the skill is matching these forms so that they reinforce the message clearly. Actors spend time developing their performance skills but the rest of us seldom devote attention to communication. Opportunities do exist to develop these skills and our lives would benefit from so doing. Sage's book *Class Talk* (2000) provides details of how to do this and become better talkers.

3. *Receiving the message.* Speaking clearly is important, but without *listening* the message might as well not have been sent. If frequency is used as a measure, listening ranks top of the list (Barker *et al.*, 1981).

	Listening	Speaking	Reading	Writing
Learned	first	second	third	fourth
Used	most	next to most	next to least	least
Taught	least	next to least	next to most	most

Comparison of communication activities

The listening process: five elements

- *Hearing* This is the non-selective physiological process of sound waves impinging on ears, ranging from 125 to

8,000 cycles per second (frequency/pitch) and 55 to 85 decibels (loudness). Hearing is affected by auditory fatigue, hearing loss or continuous exposure to the same tone. If background noise is the same frequency as the speech sounds (masking), interference may occur.

- *Attending*   This psychological process filters some messages and focuses on others. Needs, wants, desires and interests determine what is attended to, so that motivations and incentives are more important than skills in taking in messages. Wiio (1991) suggests that we only give full attention for 12 per cent of the time with 8 per cent attention for some of the time. What about the other 80 per cent? Well, 40 per cent is spent daydreaming, 20 per cent reminiscing while 20 per cent is engaged in erotic thought!

- *Understanding*   Paying attention does not guarantee understanding. There are several elements to the process. First, one must know the syntactic and grammatical rules of language. Secondly, one must comprehend the context (a yawning response to your comments will have a different meaning at midnight than at midday). Finally, understanding depends on mental abilities – a developed narrative structure with a top-down and bottom-up thinking style, which puts together an outline of the message and fills in the details. Plax and Rosenfeld (1979) showed that personality traits affect the ability to understand messages. People good at interpreting disorganized messages were personally secure, sensitive to others and willing to understand the speaker. Their thinking was more versatile and insightful. Using questions – *what, where, when, who, why, how* – is fundamental to structuring a set of ideas.

- *Remembering*   Research (Barker *et al.*, 1981) reveals that people remember 50 per cent of what they hear immediately after listening to it. Within eight hours, this drops to 35 per cent and within eight weeks to 25 per cent. Although we forget information, impressions of the speaker are retained. The better our relationship with the speaker the more we pay attention and retain what they say.

- *Responding*   The first four steps are internal processes, but the final one involves responding to the message with feedback to the speaker. Good listeners demonstrate non-verbal behaviours such as keeping eye contact and reacting with appropriate facial expressions. Their verbal behaviour, such as answering questions and exchanging ideas, demonstrates attention and involvement.

4. *Bringing together the message.* This final step merges with the last stage of understanding. You have to *listen* to the message and understand what it means, then *level* the information by bringing together all the different verbal and non-verbal information to make sense of it in terms of the reality of the situation, and finally *legitimize* the ideas and take them on board (even if you cannot agree with them) in order to make a response that develops the communication exchange. This may involve clarifying with the speaker any problems regarding the message and its delivery and reflecting on what it means in terms of your own experience and understanding.

Much can go wrong at each stage, particularly with the two 'translations'. It is dangerous to assume that just because we have been told something we can take it on board, remember and understand the message. Wiio (1987) concludes that typical success rates in communication were only around 5 per cent. A statistician would regard a 5 per cent success rate as not statistically significant and therefore a random event. Wiio's research, however, was concerned with communication through the media – radio, television and newspapers. Face-to-face communication is five times higher if Barker *et al*'s data is accepted. This still means the odds are 3:1 against communication being successful. Most of us speak with much repetition because we sense problems in getting over messages.

Implications
When involved in developing this process we have to be aware of the nature/nurture controversy. There is the assumption that we are born with ability to communicate naturally with no formal teaching. When we look into the complexity of the communicative process, however, we become aware of the difficulties in communicating successfully and the need to develop ways to enhance abilities.

Brigman *et al*. (1999) reviewed literature regarding instruction in communication. They emphasize the importance of formal teaching because of a strong correlation with positive peer relations and academic achievement. Successful strategies for teaching involve individual, small group and whole-class instruction. Although documented internationally over 30 years, the problems of pupils lacking the requisite communication skills for learning persist at all levels of the education system and may be the main reason for inadequate school performances.

Studies such as those by the Carnegie Foundation (1992), which surveyed 7,000 infant teachers in the USA, estimated 98 per cent of the nation's children had insufficient communication skills to engage in successful learning; 51 per cent of the problems were judged serious. Work in Sheffield in the UK supports this situation in the Let's Talk Project (Lees *et al.*, 2001), in which 73 per cent of children tested as language delayed.

The evidence

The reasons for inadequate levels of formal communication are complex. It is suggested by Sage (2000) that a move from verbal to visual ways of gaining information (from television and DVD), along with parents' long working hours, reduces opportunities for children to converse at home so that they lack experience of putting

Table 7.1 *Television hours watched daily by 300 children (aged 13–15) in five schools*

Hours watched	School 1	School 2	School 3	School 4	School 5
0	0	1	0	0	0
1	1	5	2	4	1
2	2	0	1	0	1
3	4	1	1	0	1
4	5	0	3	0	1
5	10	10	11	10	18
6	20	32	28	36	22
7	8	0	0	0	0
8	4	5	10	7	9
9	1	0	0	0	2
10	3	2	4	2	2
11	0	0	0	0	1
12	1	4	0	0	1
13	0	0	0	0	0
14	1	0	0	1	1
Total	360	358	362	360	379
Mean	6.00	5.97	6.03	6.00	6.32

Mean for 5 schools: = 6.06 hr per day
The 'Schools' columns refer to the number of children in the school who were watching for the stated number of hours. E.g., in column 2, 10 children watched for 5 hours each, i.e. 50 hours in total 'watching time'.

Table 7.2 *The frequency of 100 parents reading to their primary age children in 1972 and 2002*

Date	Never read	Once a week	Twice a week	Three times a week
1972	4	15	21	60
2002	25	55	15	5

meaning together from word images alone. When entering classrooms they are unable to handle group communication, which is less tailored to individual needs than informal talk, because they have not learned to thread together ideas in small group conversations. Table 7.1 shows recent daily television habits of 300 children in five secondary schools. The data were collected in September 2002, with students asked to record the number of hours they normally watched television over 24 hours. Of the students surveyed, 60 per cent had television in their bedrooms and some watched cable or satellite programmes throughout the night.

The evidence is supported by the reading habits in 1972 and 2002 of 100 parents of primary age pupils from a Midland town (see Table 7.2). Unpublished study by Sage (2002).

At the very least this suggests a change in social habits regarding reading and talking with children. It is time to think about how we can improve our talk and help pupils develop the formal communication they need to learn. Chapter 13, on the Communication Opportunity Group Scheme, shows us how we can achieve this.

Recently, communication has been included in the curriculum, as the key generic process through which human exchanges are conducted. However, Pring (2004) outlines the danger of *reductionism* (splitting a whole process into its parts), citing the use of the word 'skill' to describe *communication* results in discrete teaching approaches such as vocabulary, sounds, etc. Skills such as maintaining eye contact are involved in communication, as are projecting voice, using hands demonstrably, choosing the correct medium and presenting arguments to different audiences. These techniques are learned and perfected through regular coaching and practice by someone who understands how components of communication slot into the context of the whole operation. Sage (2003) argues, however, that *communication is much more than skills*, being a cognitive *process* requiring understanding of audiences and situations as well as knowing what to say and do appropriately. The pursuit of skills must not be an end in itself. This relationship between thinking and then communicating to audiences is not properly understood in learning and rarely addressed successfully in school practice (Sage, 2004).

In the *social constructivist* approach to education, which underlies inclusion (learning based on participation – see Sage, 2004), narrative thinking connects to communicative competence because social interaction and cultural practices in shaping human development are stressed (Wood, 1998, p. 50). Verbal interactions are 'formative', as talking to and with others exposes us to communicative functions. Listening to and telling narratives monitors communication use, taking account of listener perspectives and planning coherent and comprehensible speech sequences (Wood, 1998, p. 159). Sage (2003) suggests narrative exchanges help children to review and refine thinking, with talking out ideas essential to their mental development. Therefore the sort of communication practices children experience are crucial to narrative thinking, communicative competence and personal and academic success.

Splitting off components such as speaking and listening from the whole process of communication and treating them as merely 'skills' prevents the focus on how we achieve meaning. Understanding depends on what lies behind the words, as when a teacher says to a child: 'There's a chair over there', requiring the pupil to translate a statement into a command: 'Sit on that chair'. Much of our communication resides in the context, and cultures such as Japan (which have a very high-context communication style as opposed to our low-context one) have a great advantage when it comes to learning, as their children are always urged to consider what the meaning is in an interactive exchange. An holistic approach to communication development, as in the Communication Opportunity Group Scheme (as described in Chapter 13), is built on the idea of developing thinking, meaning and communicating, and this contextual approach is found to be more successful than the traditional component one.

CHAPTER 8

Helping selectively mute children at school

Alice Sluckin

Introduction
In 2002 Dr Rosemary Sage, Senior Lecturer at the University of Leicester School of Education with a special interest in improving communication in the classroom, and Mrs Alice Sluckin, a retired senior psychiatric social worker and now Chair of the Selective Mutism Information and Research Association (SMIRA), jointly obtained a grant from the Department for Education and Skills to enable them to make a video showing how children who have difficulty speaking away from home can be helped. The problem they were asked to pay special attention to is a condition known as selective mutism (SM).

What is selective mutism?
The problem is not a new one. Joan Tough, a much respected English educationalist, wrote in 1976:

> Mutism is usually due to a number of reasons, but leaving the child on its own for long periods, hoping that it will in time begin to approach and talk to others, seems likely to make it more difficult; in fact, the child adopts a role and position from which it finds it increasingly difficult to escape.

Selective mutism is a rare childhood disorder in which affected children speak only to intimates in the privacy of their home. They remain silent with strangers. Only two to five per 10,000 children at the age of 6–7 have the condition (Goodman and Scott, 1997). A child with SM may also have difficulty communicating with peers and, as a result, can become totally isolated. They are also often sensitive to noise, touch or crowds, and cannot tolerate eye contact. Onset is from 3 years, and girls are more likely to be affected than boys. Children with a learning disability can be selectively mute, as can very bright children, who appear frightened of making a mistake or being disapproved of. Not speaking to the teacher interferes with their learning, and it is then difficult to assess their learning potential. Teachers find the situation baffling and frustrating, and there is a reference to one such pupil in the *Times Educational Supplement* by a teacher (Matthews, 2004).

The condition was at one time known as elective mutism, a term still occasionally used. Such a child was then thought to be stubborn and contrary. But Klein and Tancer (1992), two eminent US child psychiatrists, recommended that it be reclassified for the *Diagnostic and Statistical Manual (DSM)* of the American Psychiatric Association (1994) to selective mutism (*DSM*, IV, 94, personal correspondence), 'since evidence is lacking to support the implication that children with EM have a deliberate preference not to speak' (Klein and Tancer, 1992, p. 8).

What causes selective mutism?

Recent research findings point to excessive fearfulness as a likely cause. The condition may be related to paralysing social anxiety states in adults, though there may also be other contributory factors (Yeganeh *et al.*, 2003). Often there is a familial predisposition to shyness, a difficult start, a speech problem in early life and unfavourable environmental conditions such as isolated living, frequent moves and past or present family stress. I refer to predisposing factors (probably genetic), precipitating factors located in the environment (such as a move or an illness), and perpetuating factors, which relate to the way in which the problem is being handled in the here and now. Research undertaken into temperamental dispositions of newborn babies has also contributed to a better understanding of SM. Thus Kagan *et al.* (2004) refer to babies, who have difficulty adapting to new people and new situations, as 'behaviourally inhibited'. Their research indicates that such a temperamental disposition can become part of the child's future personality.

These children are noted to have a high, stable heart rate, which accelerates further under stress. It is likely that at least some SM children share the neurophysiological make-up of 'behaviour inhibition'. We know that as a result of anxiety a temporary paralysis of the larynx can occur. It is noteworthy that children and adults, once they recover from SM, cannot tell why they were unable to speak. According to research carried out by neurobiologists (reported by Brown, 2003), the explanation may be that past traumatic events are retained in the emotional memory, which is located in the amygdala, that part of the brain responsible for instant 'fight or flight' responses. Such memory traces tend to resist change, and are separate from our conscious, rational memory located in the prefrontal cortex. However, by using a step-by-step approach it is possible, in time, to override fears located in the emotional memory.

Assessment

According to Graham (1987, 1999), 'the fact that the child shows affectionate social relationships at home and uses gestures to express needs in school, excludes the possibility of autism'. However, there may be borderline cases. Selective mutism is a heterogeneous condition. At home one such child may be placid, another very assertive and troublesome. They may present other, worrying symptoms, hence a check-up by a paediatrician and a child psychiatrist may be indicated, and referral to an educational psychologist and speech and language therapist should be considered.

Current treatment strategies

In the past, treatment of SM was based on psychodynamic concepts and was clinic based. It was often of long duration and had a high failure rate. Later strategies derived from behaviour modification and social learning theory were found to be more successful. An approach known as 'systematic desensitization', used in the treatment of adults with phobias and irrational fears, was also found to be helpful in cases of selective mutism. Such children respond to a step-by-step approach known as 'fading' and 'shaping' used by psychologists in behaviour therapy (Sluckin, 1977; Johnson and Glassberg, 1999; Johnson and Wintgens, 2001). Fading consists of making contact with the child where he or she is speaking, usually with a parent, at home or in an empty classroom. Another person, who may be the teacher or classroom assistant, is then 'faded in', initially staying at a distance, but each day moving a bit closer. Given time, the child will eventually talk to the new person; the parent can then be 'faded out'.

Once the child has responded positively to 'person fading' the next step would be aimed at 'situation fading', i.e. helping the child to tolerate a previously strange environment. Johnson and Wintgens (ibid.) suggest that an SM child should, over a period, be following a structured treatment plan with a key worker at school, as outlined in their *Selective Mutism Resource Manual* (2001). 'Shaping' consists of rewarding any sound that an SM child may be making, in the expectation that this will eventually lead to speech. To quote an example, an imaginative teacher in an infant class in Leicester recently encouraged all her pupils to answer the register by making diverse animal sounds. After a time this led to the SM child speaking in class (reported by Susan Johnson, St John the Baptist School).

Collaboration with school, parents and multidisciplinary specialists

Thus a step-by-step approach enables teachers, with the help of parents, to initiate a 'fading' or 'shaping' programme, provided they are given time and resources and have support from experienced colleagues, as such programmes sometimes need rethinking. It goes without saying that a good relationship between home and school is of paramount importance, and the help of parents is welcomed. There is now general agreement that early intervention, preferably at the toddler stage, when the child's problem has been identified, has a much better prognosis (Imich, 1998; Cline and Baldwin, 2004). Older children are much more resistant to behaviour change, as non-speaking has become part of their self-image, from which they find it difficult to escape. By then, peers have also attached a non-speaking label to them, and one hears comments such as 'what will they say if I talk?' This is why in some cases a change of school may be beneficial. Older children may need more individual attention and may also benefit from a Communication Opportunity Group Scheme, outlined in *Class Talk* (Sage, 2000), and in the video and accompanying book *Silent Children: Approaches to Selective Mutism* (Sage and Sluckin, 2004).

The object of the video – to the making of which parents contributed – is to highlight some successful strategies adopted by resourceful teachers and parents, and to demonstrate how these were implemented.

Bilingual/multilingual children

From reported epidemiological studies (Cline and Baldwin, 2004) we know that bilingual children as well as ethnic minority children are more likely to become selectively mute. To bridge the culture and language gap (i.e. the possible lack of vocabulary in the second language) very close cooperation between school and home is recommended (see also Tabors, 1997).

Links with medical approaches (see e.g. Dr A. Hauck, SMIRA News 2004)

Over the last few years children with SM have also been treated medically with drugs of the Selective Serotonin Reuptake Inhibitor (SSRI) variety. While this approach is popular in the USA, it would appear that UK parents are, on the whole, reluctant to have their children take medication, because they fear possible side effects. Once the child *is* put on medication, a prescribing psychiatrist should work closely with the child, the family, the teachers and others involved in the care of the child.

Finally, a most important chain in the management of SM is the parents' support group SMIRA, a charity formed by parents for mutual support and to make knowledge of the condition more readily available by distributing literature on the subject. Professionals involved with such children are also welcome to join. SMIRA publishes a newsletter twice yearly and organises a get-together for parents once a year. Since SM is a rare condition, meeting others who have a similar problem is very therapeutic. Parents have also started to communicate with one another via the website smiratalk.

Thanks to SMIRA, public awareness of the condition is increasing, as evidenced by a recent article in *Nursery World* (Sluckin, 2005) and a further mention of SM in *The Times* (Kirsch, 2005). Selective mutism is now a less puzzling condition than when it was first described, and treatment outcome appears to be more promising. For information about the video (24 minutes) and accompanying book *Silent Children – approaches to Selective Mutism*, contact SMIRA (smira.leicester@ntlworld.com).

CHAPTER 9

A view of two cultures: the value of dialogue

Balbir Kaur Sohal

The following is a personal perspective of a reflective practitioner in the area of promoting the understanding of cultural diversity and race equality in education. Examples have been drawn from my life and my relationship with education. I have centred the chapter around dialogue because this is at the essence of understanding and breaking down barriers of inequality and prejudice. If there is no dialogue or connection between people then how can we develop and grow?

Even though my father was illiterate he knew the value of education; he would often say, 'even when everything has been taken away from you, remember you still have the power of your mind and nobody can take that from you'. Throughout my life this has been a mantra for me. My own education, my family, community and cultural heritage, my political awareness, the experiences of racism and sexism, of being an immigrant within majority and minority cultures, have no doubt shaped my principles and philosophy on life and work.

Personal life histories demonstrate how our personal experiences shape our outlook on life. This respect that my family had for education was one of the prime reasons why my parents immigrated to the UK in the 1950s. My parents saw for us, their children, opportunities that they had not been able to access. Their plans were to stay a short while and eventually return to the homeland – the migrants' dream. This mantle stayed with us and is still with me to this day. I would agree that:

> the story begins with earlier recollections of childhood and continues through time, each experience building upon the achievements, disappointments, struggles, celebrations, and relationships from past events. What a woman comes to

understand about the world, her sense of self-worth, her skill level, and the quality of life she comes to expect all originate early in life. (Bell and Nkomo, 1992 in Davidson, 1997, p. 20)

Respect for education, strong moral codes and family expectations were the driving force behind what I am today; my philosophy is very much grounded in the principles of equality and justice for all and, belonging to the Sikh faith, there seemed a perfect logic to this.

My wish from an early age to be a teacher was nurtured by my family and especially by my mother, who was educated up to fifth grade and saw in me her hopes and aspirations. I went on to study history because of a teacher, an ardent feminist who made the subject come alive. This was very unusual because not many women in their twenties and with my cultural background were actively encouraged to study, and if we did, it was mainly the science subjects because this was seen as more prestigious. There was resistance from my extended family but my immediate family allowed me the freedom to choose. In fact, I am the only sibling who did study the arts; my brothers and sisters veered towards the sciences.

During my time at university a number of incidents aroused my interest in politics. There was the campaign on sanctions against South Africa; while at home, discussion revolved around the Indian Workers Association, the Grunwick Dispute of 1976 and the lack of involvement of the trade unions with black issues. In 1978 virginity testing was highlighted in the media and I remember going on my first demonstration in London. Asian women mobilizing was nothing new, the Satyagraha Movement in India was testimony to that. My involvement with politics had begun; it just seemed a natural progression of what had followed previously. I think the seeds from resistance to rebellion were sown then (Sivananda, 1982).

Sikhism advocates equal rights for men and women in secular and spiritual matters. The five Gurus emphasized the equality of all human beings and as such gave a woman a status and role in society equal to that of a man. As Guru Nanak said:

We are born of a woman, we are conceived in the womb of a woman, we are engaged and married to woman. We make friendships with woman and the lineage continues because of woman. When one woman dies, we take another one; we are bound with the world through woman. Why should we talk ill of her who gives birth to kings? The woman is born from woman; there is none without her. (Guru Nanak, Va. Asa SGGS, 473)

The Sikh cultural tradition recommends an active life – the life of a householder (*Grihstt*). To live within society, not in isolation, everyone has to make his or her contribution to the development of that society. Every Sikh must work for a living and not be a burden on society, something that my father believed in passionately and in doing so passed down to me.

After qualifying I took up a history and community post in a local secondary school. I was particularly interested in the community dimension because it involved fieldwork and research into the local black community. The school in which I worked was in the process of developing a strategy that was trying to get people to take up the learning opportunities available. My initial small-scale research resulted in establishing English as second language classes, primarily for young women. My formal liaison with adult education had begun.

Working with these young women and discussing a range of issues which were pertinent to them led me to feel that within the Women's Liberation Movement in this country black women were rendered 'invisible' in a sense that very little had been done to relate to black women's issues. The black woman's struggle was largely ignored. In the main:

> Resolution of the conflict between black and white women cannot begin until all women acknowledge that a feminist movement which is both racist and classist is a mere sham, a cover-up for women's continued bondage to materialist patri- archal, and passive acceptance of the status quo. (Bel Hooks, 1981)

Also, most of the theories regarding women's oppression at this time were in the main ethnocentric and eurocentric, as was the West's view on Asian women. Asian women have been subjected to many cross-cultural studies. Most of these seem to perpetuate Asian women's experiences as problematic, i.e. they have an 'identity crisis', they are 'torn between two cultures' (CRE, 1971), and there is the case of 'arranged marriages' and the 'lack of freedom'. The black community was seen as a problem and thinking so patholo- gizes it:

> Some stereotypes do stick and they are invariably linked to colonial and historical interpretations of the Black woman's role. The image of the passive Asian woman subject to oppressive practices within the Asian family – with an emphasis on

wanting to 'help' Asian women liberate themselves from their role. (Amos et. al., 1984)

I did resent the fact that Asian women were being stereotyped as weak, passive and non-assertive. However, the 1980s did see a breaking away from the stereotypical views of Asian women as we saw Asian women rebelling. Parmer (1981) specified women's struggles as being a combination of race, class and gender. Other such authors were Carby and Parmer in The Empire Strikes Back (1982) and Amos et al. in Feminist Review (1984), and collections such as Black British Feminism (1997) went a long way towards redressing these assumptions. Black women were beginning to have their say.

Classic texts that had a major impact on me then, and still do now, were the works of Illich (1972) and Freire (1970). Freire argued that any curriculum which ignored racism, sexism, the exploitation of workers and other forms of oppression at the same time inhibited the expansion of consciousness and blocked creative and liberating social action for change. Although I taught through the medium of English I tried to reflect Freire's philosophy in my teaching. I found his pedagogy for freedom fitted in with my thinking around issues of empowerment. Assisting this group of adults was, I believed, to awaken within them the concept of change that they could act upon. Empowerment was to me the means and the outcome of this pedagogy. I was to be reminded of this many years later when working in the USA with migrant communities.

I can, on reflection, now trace my movement of self through what Freire calls 'critical consciousness'. Becoming conscious is an ongoing process by which a learner moves towards 'critical consciousness'. I feel that I have become aware of oppression and that I am, in part, becoming part of the process of changing the world. I also feel very comfortable with this analysis because critical consciousness has been brought about not through an individual or intellectual effort, but through collective struggle, and this is very much part of my philosophy. Freire's pedagogy of liberation is that students are active participants and not passive consumers. Certainly the future is ours to determine and human beings will be liberated through learning and social change.

I felt that I had found my vocation in life; teaching was an area that I felt so comfortable with. I would describe myself as a 'second generation' teacher (Ghuman, 1995) in that my schooling and further qualifications were obtained in British higher educational institutions, as opposed to the 'first generation', who were teachers that qualified as teachers abroad and migrated to England in the 1960s and 1970s. Even so, during my early teaching career I felt very much that fellow colleagues saw me in the 'first generation' mode. At that time in the LEA there was only one other Asian woman teacher in a secondary school. When I was at university there were only three black (all Asian) students who were training to be teachers. It just so happened that there was one in each year and the thought of quotas did cross my mind!

Identifying myself as black has never been a problem. It is part of my identity and it has been a positive in my career choice. In school if there was any question around the area of black pupils (regardless of their ethnicity) I was asked my 'expert' opinion. It was as though I had given birth to every black child in the school, regardless of their ethnicity. At times this was annoying, but on the whole I welcomed these queries because it was an opportunity to challenge prejudice and racism. During this time I became very interested in the area of what was then multicultural education. I was on the working party at school and remember the impact of the Rampton Report. The publication of this report came at an explosive time – the 1981 uprisings (when black people rebelled in Southall, Brixton and Toxteth). These uprisings came as a shock to most of the indigenous population. Lord Scarman was to lead the investigation as to the reason for these 'riots'. In spite of the shortcomings of both Rampton and Scarman the positive spin-off was that the question of 'race' was on the education agenda.

My work in the area of 'race' as such had started. I worked as a peripatetic language support teacher in the primary and secondary phase in a number of schools. I then moved to join a team that was established as a result of the Swann Report (1985). The main focus was to introduce an anti-racist curriculum into the 'all white' schools. Five years of working in this team gave me grounding in the area of 'race'. Equality and justice were seeds that became embedded in my practice and philosophy. I worked hard to keep these issues alive and on teachers' and educationalists' agendas.

This period was a very politically active one for me as I was involved in a number of areas. During this time I also developed my skills as a trainer and as an advisory teacher of equal opportunities. Incidents in my past personal and professional life were now beginning to make sense and fall into place. It was also during this time that I made a conscious decision to stay as a practitioner, at the chalk face. In initiating and making policy work I had found my niche.

Recent levers of change have firmly put 'race' equality and inclusion on the educational agenda. These drivers of change include the amended Race Relations Act (2000), the Human Rights Act (2000) and recommendations from the MacPherson Report, which emphasizes that strategies are needed in schools 'to prevent and address racism'. The Cantle Report (2001), which was a response to the disturbances in a number of northern towns, draws attention to community cohesion and the role that educators have to play. Communication, dialogue with each other in order to foster an understanding of cultural diversity, is important. By being aware of one's emotions and behaviour we can break down barriers, and education is one such tool that can assist us. My experiences over the past few years, abroad and in the UK, remind me that these areas are so important that they permeate all aspects of life, not just one's personal life but also one's professional capacity.

By being aware we, as practitioners, can more fully meet the needs of the learner. I feel that I have empowered students and adults by enabling them to be 'participants in the decision making process and through an inclusive curriculum' (Osler, 1997). Schon (1986, 1991a, 1991b) raises the point as to the value of being reflective, indicating that it raises awareness 'of tacit knowledge and transforming knowing-in-action into knowledge-in-action'. I feel this is where empowerment comes into play. The 'need to become professional learners' in order to become more 'effective professionals' (Eraut, 1994) is, I believe, true. On reflection I see myself as a 'black woman' and professionally as a 'black educational practitioner'.

In analysing and tracing back my career development I have deployed both a 'holistic' and a 'critical' approach (Tripp, 1994). It has certainly helped me 'in search of self' (Axline, 1975).

> In working on critical incidents from our past, we are not only seeking to recall, document, and explain past events merely for our own interest, we are seeking the presence of the past as a way of illuminating, articulating, understanding, and gaining control over our current professional practice and habits. (Tripp, 1994, p. 69)

By engaging in the process of dialogue the relationship between teacher and learner and teacher to teacher is transformed and 'the purpose of education is to contribute to transformation – the transformation of society, to make it less unequal and less unjust' (Richardson, 1990, p. 45).

CHAPTER 10

John's story: Episode 2

Problems develop

'John' and Paul Cooper

J: When I moved [from town Z to city T, at the age of 10] the bullying problem wasn't so bad no more. That was only in Z. Well, it wasn't but – when I came to T, because there were so many Asians in the school – there still might have been a few black people there, but there was more Asians. So you got integrated more, innit? People just accepted you. 'Cos they were used to seeing people here with colour. I didn't really get treated any differently that way. But because of how I was treated before, my behaviour was different when I went to that [new] school ... [so] I went into [the new school] with the same impression as I had in the one in Z. But it wasn't the same.

P: So are you saying that you went to the new school and immediately started behaving as you had done before in Z?

J: Yes.

P: So in some sense while you could say that the behaviour problems were created in Z?

J: Yeah.

P: When you went to T, you brought them with you.

J: Yeah.

P: How early on did you start?

J: I think I started in November. And then after Christmas – that's when I really started. That's when they suspended me anyway.

P: And how did this affect the relationships you had with other kids?

J: It didn't affect them that much. It's a bit of a posh school, innit? So we had a lot of posh kids from round there. But they were all right. It was just like a normal junior school, like anyone grows up in. I was just bad. So really, everyone used to think I was bad. Y'know, when you're at home with your kids and you think 'Oh, he's bad; he's disruptive.'

P: What, they didn't want their kids to play with you?

J: No. Not like that. But just, everyone knew that I'd be the person to argue if the football went in someone's garden. I'd be the one who'd go and yell at them. Y'know, when you're kids, you remember things like that.

P: So that was your role?

J: Yeah. That's right.

P: But that didn't interfere with you getting on OK with other kids?

J: No. At Y Primary School I fell out with the headmaster really.

P: So this business of you taking your lessons outside the classroom. How did that start?

J: I can't really remember. I think I used to get help outside. Auxiliary help, or something. They used to help me outside, away from the classroom. I used to have this other woman, this half-caste girl. She used to come over, and she used to help me, and she used to come and talk to me about stuff. I can't remember what it was – it wasn't to do with me work. So they used to take me outside. Then I started to take work out there. And it just started to build. I just started to go and sit out there.

P: So what did you used to do?

J: I used to just go and ask the teacher if I could sit outside.

P: And did that work?

J: No. Not at first. But in the end, they just let me sit outside.

P: So how did you persuade them to let you do that?

J: I can't really remember. I just used to go out there when we did projects – y'know how they just let you wander free? I just used to go outside and do it. I used to have a whole desk. I was trying to build a zoo. I had everything. I'd planned it out. I'd made leaflets; a programme, and everything. And that's when I really started sitting outside and doing my work. In the maths lesson he [the teacher] said, 'You can sit out there and do it if you want.' I said, 'Fine, yeah.'

P: So they met you halfway on that one?

J: No. I don't think they did it knowingly. They didn't want me to sit out there all the time. But in the end, they just gave up and said that I could sit out there. So I used to go and sit out there anyway.

P: So I suppose what I'm wondering is: did you ever misbehave to get put outside?

J: Maybe once or twice. But not as a rule.

P: They just let you do that?

J: Yes.

P: How long did this go on for?

J: 'Til the end of the year. 'Til we finished. 'Cos that was the last year. I was only there about nine months.

P: How did these problems at school affect your life outside school?

J: Well, my Mum was in university, so she was struggling for money as well. So she used to get uptight all the time. 'Cos when I used to come home, I didn't used to behave that well. Like any child. But Mum used to think I was worse than any other child, 'cos she never used to see any other parents looking after their kids, without guests. So she assumed that everyone's kids were perfect. 'Cos she'd never seen them when she ain't there. D'you know what I mean – if she went round to visit someone with kids, kids are normally quiet, when she's there, but when she's gone ... And other parents don't normally go around complaining about their kids' problems. They just keep them to themselves. My Mum's never realized that, I don't think. But she's got to tell everyone – 'John, he's the worst kid ever.' And she's like building up a reputation for me. You know, before people have even met me. And they're thinking, 'Oh, yeah, he's going to be a piece of work.' So in the end I used to just live up to expectations. 'Cos she's going on to me, 'Don't misbehave, John, don't misbehave.' And the more she said it, the more I had to do it. Do you know what I mean? Y'know when you're a kid, you just don't want to do what your Mum tells you. 'Cos she used to say it so much, I just used to do it.

It's almost like your Mum thought you couldn't help it. That's why she had to keep reminding you. That's what she thought, yeah.

P: And how did you feel about that?

J: I didn't like that. Always being told I had to be good. Like I was going to be bad every time.

P: So as far as you were concerned, while she was saying to you that she wanted you to be good, what she meant was that she expected you to be bad!

J: Yeah.

P: And you resented that?

J: Yes. I did.

P: So you felt like you were in control of your behaviour?

J: Yeah.

P: You could have behaved differently. But if you'd behaved differently, your life would have been worse.

J: Yeah.

P: So this tantrum behaviour you used to engage in when you were in the junior school, could you give me an example of what it was you used to do?

J: I just used to start shouting. Or saying, 'I don't want to do it.' That's what I used to do when I was in junior school. I'd say, 'I don't want to do it.' Like a kid does: 'I don't want to do it.' And they say, 'You gotta do it! You gotta do it!' And I used to run out of lessons; slam the door. And just walk around the hallway. People could see me through the window. So I was getting attention that way too. Just walking up and down shouting.

P: So what were you thinking and feeling when you were doing this?

J: I can't really remember what I was feeling. But I think I was just getting some attention. People are watching me.

P: So it was positive, then?

J: I don't know. I'm not sure. Maybe it's because – I don't think I wasn't getting enough attention at home. I wanted the extra attention at school.

P: So you wanted more attention than other kids?

J: No. I don't think I wanted more attention. Like I said, I did get treated differently. So the attention I did get I wanted a bit more, like everyone else did.

P: So was it better to get the attention for bad behaviour than to be ignored?

J: Yeah. But I think things could have been better if my Mum had listened to me, when I used to tell her all the time that I used to get called names. She just used to say, 'sticks and stones'. She denies she said this [now] but I remember she said it. You remember those kinds of things when you are a kid. You remember those things. You remember exactly who said it. She used to say, 'Sticks and stones will break my bones, but names will never hurt me!' And because she's white she will never understand what it is like. Never! Even if I told her, she used to say, 'Oh, I used to be called names at school, because of my red hair and my freckles.' And I'd say, 'But that's different. You can dye the colour of your hair. Freckles will disappear. My skin won't change colour.' She didn't understand that. She thought that all name-calling was the same. Of equal, but I don't think she understands what it is like. Dad understands.

P: So you did tell her it was racial, did you?

J: Yes, for a while. Until someone, just before I left Z, and my friend came and told her, as well. And I said, 'That's true.' But she never used to listen, otherwise. She'd just say, 'Sticks and stones may break your bones' – and all that rubbish.

P: So that caused a bit of a problem as well?

J: Yeah.

P: So did you behave like this at home a bit as well?

J: Yeah. A little bit. I was an only child as well. So I used to get a lot of presents; so I used to want more and more and more. I used to get greedy. Not intentionally. I didn't mean it. But maybe if I'd have had brothers and sisters. People get so greedy when they're like that. 'Cos I was the only child, and I was the first grandson of my Mum's Mum. I used to get spoiled. So maybe that was a bad thing. 'Cos my Mum never used to pay that much attention to me. She never really used to listen to what I had to say about school. So maybe all the presents I used to get substituted for that. So instead of getting the love I thought I should have got from my Mum – instead of that – I had presents.

I never really liked sharing either, when I was younger. I don't remember from any age, Mum taking me to see other kids. From when I was little I just used to live with my Mum, who just used to cuss up my Dad every day. She says she doesn't, but she did. She cussed my Dad off. I used to go to school, but after that I'd just go and sit in. She'd put me in front of the TV, and just leave me and eat her dinner, and do some ironing or something. She wouldn't take me out to see no other kids.

P: So did you see much of your Dad?

J: No, not really. I used to see him every two weeks or something. And my Mum used to slag him off because he was a workaholic. So she used to slag him off all the time. 'Your Dad works too hard. He never comes to see you. He never comes and does anything for you.' I've got other problems as well, but she don't really want to hear them! She's talking about how I'm a burden on her. I've got problems at school and she's telling me I'm a burden on her. It doesn't make me feel any better.

P: She told you that you were a burden?

J: Yeah! It's hard to say. I'm not saying she's a bad Mum. Maybe the things she said, she didn't think through, like other parents do. She used to feed me; clothe me. She seems to think that parents ain't expected to do that. She thinks it's a privilege that kids should get that. But it isn't. It's a duty, if you have kids. We don't ask to be brought here. But I don't think she sees it like that. She thinks she's doing me a favour ... that I'm going to repay her when I get older, for all the things she did for me. She seems to think that all the things she buys for you are hers. She's just giving them to you until you decide to leave. I'm not saying – you've met my Mum: she's not horrible! But I think her best intentions weren't the best.

P: It's like you had a lot of things to deal with – the racism, the bullying and these things at home. You must feel like you were really up against it?

J: Yes. I suppose so.

PART II

PRACTICAL RESPONSES

The major theme of this substantial second part of the book (Chapters 11 to 34) is to respond to the issues raised in Part I. Part II sets out to reveal the links in practice between matters of communication, emotion and behaviour and the need for awareness of not only the ideas and ideals but also 'the realities' in the quest to integrate theory, policy and practice.

CHAPTER 11

Perceptions of inclusion:
educational access for all?

Daniela Sommefeldt

Introduction

This chapter looks at how three different schools in the same English LA respond to notions of Special Education Needs (SEN) inclusion, through an exploration of their perceptions, policies and practices.

National context

SEN inclusion needs to be seen within the wider context of social inclusion and the government's agenda for reducing exclusions from schools. DfES circulars (*10/99 and 11/99*), relating to social exclusion and pupil support, place a range of duties on schools aimed at minimizing pupil disaffection and provide guidance to schools on helping those categories of children perceived as being most at risk. Pupils with SEN are included as being in need of support. Resources have been made available through the Standards Fund to promote social inclusion, although these have been mainly directed at secondary schools, where the problem of permanent exclusions from school is more acute. According to the Audit Commission report *Special Educational Needs: A Mainstream Issue* (2002), children with statements in England are three times more likely than other children to be permanently excluded from school. Unsurprisingly, children with emotional and behavioural diffi-culties constitute the largest group within this percentage. Because of the inconsistencies in the way that LAs collect information, there is no national data available on exclusion rates for children with special needs, but without statements. However, the figures available from 22 LAs for 2000/1 for all pupils with SEN (with or without statements) show that this group represents nine out of ten permanent exclusions in primary schools and six out of ten in secondary. One of the pertinent questions posed by the Audit

Commission queries the extent to which exclusions are the result of unmet special needs.

The revised Code of Practice for SEN (DfES, 2001) and the Special Educational Needs and Disability Act (2001) strengthen the right of children with SEN to education in mainstream schools, where parents wish it. However, there is often a gulf between policy and practice and there is no duty to educate in a mainstream school where the education of a child with special educational needs is incompatible with the efficient education of other children. An Audit Commission survey (2002) discovered that children with different categories of special need experienced greater or lesser degrees of difficulty in gaining admission to their school of choice. Those with emotional and behavioural difficulties had the most problems (73 per cent) in finding a school place, closely followed by excluded children (68 per cent) and those with autistic spectrum disorders (68 per cent). The shift of SEN funding from LAs to schools and the removal of the link between statements and extra funding now means that headteachers and governors are more directly responsible for ensuring that a child's needs are met. One of the implications of this is that schools, with competing priorities for funding, need to be fully committed to this principle of meeting (often expensive) special needs. However, commitment on the part of schools is not always a straightforward choice:

> While there are benefits from having a 'critical mass' of children with particular needs attending a school, in terms of planning provision and developing staff expertise, there is also a risk that individual schools may become over-stretched and a polarised pattern of provision develop – restricting parental choice and effectively letting other schools off the hook. (Audit Commission, 2002, p. 14)

Many LAs have been supporting schools to develop more inclusive practice (Whitney, 2002), Newham being a well-known example of what can be achieved when all stakeholders are united in their vision to establish all schools as inclusive.

In the spring of 2000 the DfES provided funding for the *Index for Inclusion* (Booth *et al.*, 2000) to be issued, free of charge, to every maintained school in England, in order to stimulate thinking about inclusion and promote good practice in schools. The Ofsted guidance on evaluating educational inclusion reinforces the ideas in the *Index*, and describes an educationally inclusive school as:

one in which the teaching and learning, achievements, attitudes and well-being of every young person matter. Effective schools are educationally inclusive schools. This shows, not only in their performance, but also in their ethos and their willingness to offer new opportunities to pupils who may have experienced previous difficulties ... The most effective schools do not take educational inclusion for granted. (Ofsted, 2001, p. 7)

Both the *Index for Inclusion* and the Ofsted guidance stress the need to remove barriers to learning for *all* pupils, thus linking inclusive practices clearly to equal opportunities. The Audit Commission report (2002, p. 1) supports this view, when it states unequivocally that not only should pupils with SEN be educated in mainstream schools wherever possible, but that they should join fully in the curriculum and life of the school. This directly challenges the notion of tokenism or locational integration that is still frequently to be seen across some LAs.

Local context

The LA within which the schools in this study are situated became a unitary authority in April 1997, having previously been part of a *shire* authority. The new LA inherited 11 special schools and one specialist nursery covering the full range of special educational needs. In addition, units were attached to mainstream schools for both primary and secondary pupils with visual impairments (two) and hearing impairments (two). A trend was emerging of placing pupils with SEN in mainstream schools, wherever possible, although the success of this strategy diminished at secondary transfer stage. LA support teams existed for behaviour support, learning and autism support, hearing impairment, visual impairment and pre-school.

As part of the review of special education in the new LA, the Education Committee gave approval to a new SEN policy and to a strategy for developing the city's SEN provision. The LA describes the SEN policy as based upon the values and beliefs of social justice and diversity and sees the principal aim as being:

to increase the capability of all schools to meet the diverse needs of pupils, but where special school placement best meets a pupil's needs a broad range of integration opportunities should be offered. (LA, 2001)

With respect to inclusion, the LA's stated aim is to:

• provide opportunities for *all* pupils to learn and achieve

> through meeting individual needs, promoting attainment and progress across their school careers within a continuum of provision;
> - develop an inclusive ethos that will extend the opportunities of pupils with SEN to benefit from teaching and learning of the highest quality.

In January 2003 the LA maintained ten special schools covering the full range of SEN between them and a number of specialist units attached to mainstream schools (see Figure 11.1).

During the autumn term of 2002 the LA put forward its proposals to establish schools with additional resources (SARs), the intention being to enable designated schools to provide specialist on-site support for pupils with SEN to be fully included in the educational mainstream. On the council's website (2005), these are described as follows:

> Schools with additional resources (SARS) are those where a specific number of additional places are given extra funding in order to meet the more complex special educational needs of a wider range of pupils than those normally on roll. The first group of schools is currently being developed ... The focus of the schools in this group is to provide for pupils with significant learning difficulties.

Special schools	Mainstream units	
Emotional or behavioural difficulties: 2 secondary (boys)	Visual impairment: 1 primary; 1 secondary	
Physical difficulties: 2 all-age	Hearing impairment: 1 primary; 1 secondary	
Moderate learning difficulties: 2 primary; 1 secondary		
	Speech & Language: 2 primary	
Severe learning difficulties/Profound or multiple learning difficulties: 2 all-age	Generalized learning difficulties: 1 infant; 3 junior	
Diagnostic: 1 nursery		
Medical: 1 hospital school		

Primary support	Pupil Referral Units
1 student support service 1 assessment reintegration centre	2 secondary

Figure 11.1 *Specialist SEN provision in January 2003*

The LA was, at the time, considering expressions of interest from a number of mainstream schools and has since introduced the first three SARs, which are all in the primary sector: one infants' school, one junior school and one primary school.

The three schools in the study comprised an 11–16, mixed community college with a Hearing-Impaired Unit, an 11–18 mixed special college catering for students with MLD/SLD/ behavioural difficulties and a 3–11 mixed primary school with nursery provision. The criteria used to choose the three schools in the study were:

- covered the statutory age range
- drawn from mainstream (2) and special provision (1)
- recognized inclusive philosophy
- multi-ethnic population
- willing to participate.

All staff in each school were asked to complete the same questionnaire and follow-up interviews were sought with the headteachers and the Special Educational Needs Coordinators (SENCOs).

As might be expected, there were marked similarities in the way the headteachers expressed their commitment to the ideals of inclusion and all were realistic about their own role in promoting good practice. They saw inclusion as a potentially positive practice, recognizing that the term encompasses not only physical access but also philosophical access, requiring a major shift in attitude. Values, ethos and feelings were all cited as aspects of inclusion. While the heads all claimed that their staff regarded inclusion as a positive practice, any supposed staff reservations tended to mirror each head's own stated position:

> They know it works, but only with the right resources. Support and expertise is needed to help mainstream staff (H1).

> Positive, although the unit is not always easy to cope with. Extra training and learning about yourself and others is positive (H2).

> Positive, but very much where it is appropriate. Decisions need to be made by staff and parents at annual reviews (H3).

If these responses are compared with the information from questionnaires, a slightly different picture emerges, with only 60 per cent of the combined staff respondents taking a positive stance, based mainly on consideration of equal opportunities. Of the reasons given by staff for a negative response, disruption to others was identified as a major factor (41 per cent) over funding problems (12 per cent). The range of responses included:

Positive

[Inclusion] provides the student with a different learning environment and further social development (S3).

It helps children achieve their full potential (S1).

It is my philosophy that all pupils should have an equal opportunity to access the mainstream curriculum (S2).

It enables children with difficulties to integrate with a wider spectrum of the population and also provides the children who do not experience difficulties with an opportunity to be understanding, supportive, recognize the importance of accepting (S1).

[Inclusion] allows students to recognize many people have individual needs and requirements in order to learn (S3).

Negative

I think they will be bullied and ridiculed, even with extra support staff (S3).

Inclusion is a negative practice. Pupils with special needs would not benefit from working with large groups (S3).

Negative – especially children with disruptive behaviour. Not fair for other children (S1).

Detrimental to all – both those with needs (lack of specialized/ individual help and attention) and those without (left to cope alone with the curriculum because the teacher's attention ... is focused on [special] needs) (S2).

Mainstream schoolchildren may pick up/copy the behaviour of SEN pupils, regarding their slow learning, abusive mannerisms (S1).

Putting bad apples in good barrels is also disastrous (S2).

Conditional

Children with behavioural problems – good if a personal support programme works and others do not suffer (S2).

Only if there is appropriate funding to allow adequate staffing and resourcing (S3).

Positive – if handled carefully and sensitively and sensibly (S2).

Can be both [positive and negative] – depends on how support is used and how skilled the support staff are in managing included pupils and also on how willing mainstream staff are to be involved (S1).

When asked whether the school had a specific inclusion policy, the three heads reported a mixed picture:

Not stand-alone. Policies reflect inclusion in all our work [but] it needs to be brought together instead of being bits here and there. We need a definition of what we mean by inclusion (H1).

Depends. Not an inclusion policy, but aims and values that promote inclusion. Our aims and objectives are already serving the whole community [therefore] we already have an inclusion policy! (H2).

Yes. [It informs] links with other institutions. One of our college aims [is] to enable students to manage in an inclusive society. Emphasis on social and independence training. A policy should dwell on what ought to be, rather than what can be or is – there are too many constraints operating at the moment (H3).

Interestingly, staff perceptions of the existence (or otherwise) of a school inclusion policy did not always reflect the statements of the headteachers. For example, in school one, where the head admitted there was no stand-alone policy, most staff confidently described both the content and usefulness of an imagined inclusion policy, suggesting that the ideas were firmly embedded, if not yet formally stated. A similar picture emerged for school two, although more staff admitted that they did not know whether a formal inclusion policy existed. In school three, the only one of the three to claim a formal policy, a significant minority of staff respondents were unaware of its existence and a number 'didn't know' how it informed their work.

A further question about the *Index for Inclusion* (Booth *et al.*, 2000) elicited the information that all three heads had seen it, but only one

(H1) had actually used it, to inform the school's understanding of SEN access and parent attitudes, through the questionnaires included. An overwhelming majority of staff from all three schools said they had not seen the *Index*, although in school one it had been used by a handful of staff, including learning support assistants. There was no indication from any of the schools that the LA had either recommended or promoted the *Index for Inclusion* in its schools as part of its desire to move mainstream schools towards greater inclusion.

In response to questions about the types of special need to be found in the school and how these are met, a discrepancy between need and provision emerges across all the schools. This is clearly reported by both the staff and the heads, although the detail differs in some respects between these two groups. The range of needs to be found within the three schools is extensive although, as may be expected, the special school reports a wider range than the mainstream schools. The following lists of needs were identified by reference to the responses of the three heads, supplemented by reference to the SENCO responses (shown in italics):

> *Special school*
> Physical disability (mild)/hearing-impaired/visually impaired/emotional and behavioural difficulties/autistic spectrum disorder/epilepsy/moderate learning difficulties/severe learning difficulties/dyslexia/attention deficit hyperactivity disorder/mental health problems/*speech and language difficulties.*

> *Primary school*
> Hearing-impaired/visually impaired/emotional and behavioural difficulties/epilepsy/generalized learning difficulties/moderate learning difficulties/dyslexia/*physical impairment.*

> *Secondary school*
> All the special needs listed in the questionnaire (Q6) were claimed, but during the interview the following were identified: hearing-impaired/English as a second language/*physical impairment/visual impairment/emotional and behavioural difficulties/autistic spectrum disorder/ epilepsy/generalized learning difficulties/moderate learning difficulties/dyslexia/attention deficit hyperactivity disorder.*

Given that each school has a wide range of needs for which it is expected to cater, it is disconcerting to learn that the actual range that each head feels his or her school is geared up for is much smaller, although one head felt that new expertise and resources were now being built up. Comments about the ad hoc nature of developments were made, as were concerns about what is being expected of schools:

> Access Fund has helped us to get resources, but it's all happening by default – not planned admissions; rather, building up skills to meet existing needs (H1).

> A flexible definition of 'mainstream' could include more creative options … I'm worried about the 14–19 curriculum: kids need a good general education (H2).

> Sometimes the LA makes unreasonable requests for inclusion, such as asking us to take severely disturbed kids who have been assessed as needing a residential, therapeutic environment (H3).

When asked to identify which special needs were most easy or most difficult to cater for, one head felt unable to answer this, but the other two heads both identified moderate learning difficulties (MLD) as the easiest and emotional and behavioural difficulties as the hardest. The choice of emotional and behavioural difficulties reflects the opinions of all staff across the three schools (60 per cent agreement). It is not surprising that the special school staff were most confident about catering for learning difficulties, since the school is designated MLD and staff have built up considerable expertise in this area. The comment of one of the assistant principals from the secondary school sums up the general attitude by claiming that the special needs which are most easy to cater for are 'those we know about and understand'.

Summary

The comments from staff across these three schools suggest that perceptions of inclusion are still varied, according to the experience and knowledge present in each school; in other words, there is little shared understanding, either between staff or between schools, about what inclusion can mean. Policies reflect the values both of the wider society and the school community. The emergence of specific inclusion policies is indicative of a move towards the wider acceptance of the rights of all children to the same educational opportunities. Practices in schools are both informed and influenced by policy statements. The relationship between perceptions and values, values and policy, policy and practice is not, however, a straightforward, linear one; often the different elements will be developing simultaneously or one will trail behind. The role of the LA has, traditionally, been to encourage cross-fertilization of ideas, as well as offering a lead in defining and promoting common ideals. If we see the three schools in this study as representing the wider picture, then it is clear that the impetus for inclusion is still in its early stages of examining values and thinking about policies, while pockets of good practice, as always, work to inform the whole.

CHAPTER 12

Nurture groups 1970–2003

Paul Cooper

Introduction

The guiding theory of nurture groups (NGs) is that many children who exhibit emotional and behavioural difficulties often experience emotions and exhibit behaviours that are developmentally inappropriate. Normal infant behaviour, it is argued, is characterized by extreme egocentrism, and a concomitant disregard for the needs and feelings of others. In order to progress from this state to the level of social competence that is required in the standard infant school classroom, the individual has to go through a nurturing process which equips them with the ability to meet their individual psychological needs through social interaction, through means that are compatible with the needs of others (Maslow, 1970). This process is essential to healthy psychological development in general, since without such progress individuals will be severely impaired in their ability to understand and regulate their behaviour, form relationships and communicate with others. The process is also vital in laying the social and psychological foundations for learning as conceptualized from a socio-cultural perspective (Bruner *et al.*, 1966; Vygotsky, 1987). Thinking about NG practice has been strongly influenced by Bowlby's Attachment Theory (Bennathan and Boxall, 2000). In this way NGs can be located in the tradition of developmentally informed types of provision (ibid.) such as Feuerstein's (1969) 'Instrumental Enrichment' programme and the High/Scope programme (Berrueta-Clement *et al.*, 1984; Sylva, 1986; Sylva and Ilsley, 1992).

Central to a psychological understanding of and justification for NGs is a socio-cultural theory of learning. Vygotsky's (1987) classic work in developing this theory provides us with the key insight that cognitive strategies in learning can be seen in terms of the internalization of functions first experienced in social interaction.

An individual's learning is guided by a more competent helper who provides both support for the individual in the form of direct cues and cognitive 'scaffolding' (Bruner, 1987) that enables the learner to use their existing knowledge as a means of acquiring new knowledge and understanding. The helper also acts as a model for learning behaviours. The helper's adequacy as a facilitator of learning depends on their knowledge and understanding of the learner's existing state of knowledge and understanding in relation to the learning task, and on the extent to which this knowledge and understanding can be stretched towards mastery of new knowledge, that is, their Zone of Proximal Development. Not only has this socio-cultural theory of learning and teaching been shown to have explanatory power in both teachers' and learners commonsense theorizing about effective teaching and learning (Cooper and McIntyre, 1993, 1996), it has also been shown to enhance teachers' teaching performance and teaching effectiveness when it is incorporated into their practical pedagogical theorizing through in-service training (Monro, 1999).

Noddings (1996), drawing attention to the implications of this theory for practical pedagogical applications, highlights the social–emotional components of trust and caring upon which, she argues, such instructional relationships depend. Noddings' construct of 'a caring pedagogy' is both illuminated and extended by the invocation of Attachment Theory (Bowlby, 1975). Bennathan and Boxall (2000) draw on this theory in their account of the psychological characteristics of pupils for whom NGs were initially devised. These characteristics include a range of developmentally inappropriate behaviours that correspond with Bowlby's account of attachment disorders, including severe difficulties in engaging in productive social relationships, which may manifest themselves in either withdrawn and avoidant behaviour, coercive and aggressive behaviour, or erratic and disorganized behaviour. These problems are further compounded by serious difficulties in productive engagement in solitary activities, such as individual play, which often take the form of disorganized and unproductive engagement, inability to sustain attention and difficulties in self-direction and self-regulation. Geddes (2003) has also provided an Attachment Theory-based analysis of learning difficulties among children with SEN, and shown how many common features of learning difficulties that are often signified by the vague and stigmatizing label of 'social, emotional and behavioural difficulties' can be understood and remedied through an application of this perspective.

Following on from Attachment Theory, NGs can be understood as a school-based learning environment specifically designed for pupils whose difficulties in accessing school learning are underpinned by an apparent need for social and individual experiences that can be construed in terms of unmet early learning needs (Bennathan and Boxall, 2000; Boxall, 2002). This is not to say that NGs are synonymous with a view that pathologizes certain parents (ibid.). The key insight here is that for some children the developmental processes associated with early attachment needs are incomplete when they reach the statutory age of school enrolment.

The NG is designed to provide pupils with an educational bridge to permanent and full-time placement in mainstream classrooms. This is achieved by combining features of a caring home environment with formal curricular demands. One of the crucial elements of the thinking underpinning NGs addresses directly the important distinction between the NG and family setting. While NGs contain many of the features of a family setting (e.g. soft furnishings, kitchen and dining facilities) the preferred group size, according to the originator of NGs (ibid.), should have a lower limit of 10 pupils (the upper limit is 12). Educationally, this is designed to give the pupils the experience of involvement in group activities, and to enable the teaching of group participation skills that will be necessary for successful engagement in a mainstream classroom. This measure also helps prevent the development of inappropriate child–adult attachments that might challenge the parent–child relationship. These aims are further supported by the requirement of the classic NG model that NG pupils remain on the roll of a mainstream class, attending for registration in the mornings and participating in mainstream class activities for at least one afternoon per week, and more during the period of phased reintegration that is sometimes deemed appropriate for returning pupils. Rather than attempting to mimic or usurp the parent–child attachment relationship, NGs are intended to produce a form of educational attachment. That is, within the confines of the educational setting, children are encouraged to develop trusting and caring relationships with adults which are carefully focused on enabling pupils to learn and practise prosocial skills and engage in the challenges of formal curricular tasks.

Practical insights from Attachment Theory are exploited in a number of ways. The two adults are always present, and their patterns of interactions with one another are designed to model positive social interaction and cooperation. The daily routine within the group is explicit, uniform and predictable. NG staff engage in intensive interaction (Nind, 1999) with individual pupils, at appropriate times throughout the NG day, and this is balanced with periods of group instruction. The 'classic' (see below) NG day is structured in accordance with the standard school day. Periods of National Curriculum focus, such as literacy and numeracy sessions, are interspersed with various programmed activities, such as free play and structured physical activity. NG pupils also participate in break times with other pupils in the school. A crucial feature of the classic NG routine is 'breakfast'. This commonly occurs at mid-morning, and takes the shape of a formal group meal in which staff and pupils share a simple cooked meal (usually toast and jam) and interact socially. The social and developmental targets for individual pupils are devised on the basis of psychometric assessment of their developmental needs and functioning (the Boxall Profile) (Bennathan and Boxall, 1998) and educational assessments. Individual learning tasks are determined on the basis of staff perceptions of pupils' current needs in relation to this data.

NGs are not a new form of educational provision. NGs were devised by Marjorie Boxall, a local authority educational psychologist, who set up the first groups in Inner London in the early 1970s (Bennathan and Boxall, 2000). They were established in response to what was seen as the alarming prevalence of emotional problems and disruptive behaviour among children entering infant and primary schools. There is evidence to support the observation that NGs, having gone through an initial period of popularity, which lasted for the best part of a decade, dwindled in numbers, with many of the original groups being closed down (ibid.). A national survey (Cooper *et al.*, 1998) found fewer than 50 groups in the UK. Current (unpublished) evidence from the NG Network (NGN) database (NGN, 2003) identifies over 300 groups throughout the UK. This figure reflects only those groups that have registered with the NGN. Over the same period over 800 students have participated in NG training courses, endorsed by the NGN, running in the universities of Cambridge, Leicester and London (Institute of Education) (NGN database, unpublished). These students are, overwhelmingly, active or soon to become NG practitioners. Added to this is the fact that NG training courses are provided by an unknown number of LA providers (e.g. Staffordshire has had a training programme accredited by the University of Leicester in place since 1999, and supports approximately 50 NGs not registered with the NGN; University of Leicester CPD database). The probability is that there are far more than the 300+ groups in the UK. Even at 300, this represents a 600 per cent increase over five years.

There are many possible reasons for this development. A key event in the resurgence of interest in NGs is the publication of the first book on this topic by Marion Bennathan and Marjorie Boxall (2000), the first edition of which appeared in 1996 and was very well received by a number of reviewers. Government responded very positively to this renewed interest in NGs, citing them as a promising form of educational intervention (DfEE, 1997). Other reasons for this renewed interest have to be sought in some of the negative effects of educational practices that followed from the 1988 Education Reform Act in England and Wales. Over the decade of the 1990s the overall rate of permanent pupil exclusions from school increased by approximately 400 per cent, with the highest rates of increase being found in primary schools (Castle and Parsons, 1998). Recent findings suggest that Standard Attainment Tasks (SATs) lead to increased stress levels among KS2 pupils (Connor, 2001, 2003). Other evidence suggests that this period is marked by increasing levels of stress and insecurity in schools which are reflected in perceptions of rising levels of emotional and behavioural difficulties among pupils and work overload among teachers, leading to severe problems in recruiting and retaining teaching staff in schools (Johnson and Hallgarten, 2002). It is reasonable to speculate that such circumstances are likely to exacerbate the difficulties experienced by pupils with attachment-type problems.

Existing research on NGs

There has been limited research into the effectiveness of NGs. Published studies have tended to be retrospective and to chart the progress of pupils in NGs over time, often using the Boxall Profile (Bennathan and Boxall, 1998) as a measure of pupil progress. One often quoted study of this kind was carried out by Iszatt and Wasilewska (1997).

The study found that, of 308 children placed in NGs between 1984 and 1998, 87 per cent were able to return to the mainstream after a placement duration of less than one year. In 1995 this group was revisited, and it was found that 83 per cent of the original cohort were still in mainstream placements with only 4 per cent requiring SEN support beyond the schools' standard range of provision (Stage 3 and above of the 1994 SEN Code of Practice; Action Plus level of provision under the 2002 revised SEN Code of Practice). Of the original cohort 13 per cent were granted Statements of Special

Educational Need, and 11 per cent were referred to special school provision. This finding was contrasted with data on a non-matched group of 20 mainstream pupils who had been designated as requiring NG placement but for whom places had not been found. A much higher level of persistent difficulties was found in this group, 35 per cent of whom were placed in special schools and only 55 per cent of whom were found, by 1995, to be coping in mainstream classrooms without additional support. In the absence of adequate matching measures it is difficult to interpret the significance of differences in outcomes for the two groups. However, the positive performance of the majority of the NG cohort was consistent with studies of staff perceptions of the effects of NG placement assessed in other studies that point to improvements in pupils' self-management behaviours, social skills, self-awareness and confidence, skills for learning and approaches to learning (Doyle, 2001; Boorn, 2002; Cooper and Lovey, 2003). O'Connor and Colwell (2002) assessed the performance of 68 5-year-old children placed in three NGs for a mean period of 3.1 terms. Using Boxall Profile data, they found statistically significant mean improvements in terms of cognitive and emotional development, social engagement and behaviours indicative of secure attachment. Boxall data was also reported on an opportunity sample (n = 12) of the original cohort after two years. Findings suggest that many of the improvements had been maintained, though there was evidence of relapse in some areas of emotional and social functioning.

While these studies do not present evidence of the distinctive effects of NG placement on pupil progress, they do suggest that positive progress in key areas of development targeted by NGs takes place during placement in an NG.

Findings from a national survey

Preliminary to the current project, a survey of NG provision in England and Wales was carried out (Cooper et al., 1998) that identified common perceptions shared by adherents to the NG approach. The first of these was that the practical, day-to-day work of the NG is rooted in an understanding of the developmental needs of children, the interdependence of social, emotional and cognitive factors, and a commitment to the fostering of positive, healthy development. The second finding was that the work of the NG should be fully integrated into mainstream school and LA policies and structures, so as to avoid the danger of NGs becoming an exclusionary form of provision. The third key point was that children's admission to, progress in and eventual departure from the NG should be informed by the use of appropriate diagnostic and evaluative tools, such as the Boxall Profile. A further important finding was that there were four basic variations of the NG theme. These variants can be characterized in the following ways.

Variant 1: the classic 'Boxall' NG

These groups accord in all respects with the model established by Marjorie Boxall (Bennathan and Boxall, 2000; Boxall, 2002). The 'Boxall NG' represents an inclusive form of educational provision, involving the temporary and part-time placement (usually nine out of ten half-day sessions per week) of pupils in a setting designed to meet their specific developmental needs and promote their educational progress. In this model, pupils who attend the NG are exclusively selected from the mainstream roll of school in which the NG is located. In order to maintain the pupil's sense of belonging to the school as a whole, the pupils remain on the roll of a mainstream class throughout their time in the NG. The NG pupils register with their mainstream class every morning, and are collected by NG staff after the registration period. For one afternoon per week pupils from the NG attend lessons with their mainstream class, while the NG staff engage in record-keeping activities and meet with parents. The main purpose of the NG placement is to enable pupils to return to mainstream classes on a full-time basis. This normally takes place after three or four school terms although, where appropriate, this can take place after one or two terms. Initial placement, target setting and the monitoring of pupil progress are facilitated through the use of the Boxall Profile. This is a normative diagnostic instrument designed to measure developmental status as well as social, emotional and behavioural functioning.

As has already been noted, the theoretical underpinnings of the NG approach demand a setting that requires opportunities for intensive interaction between adults and pupils, while enabling pupils to learn how to function as a member of a group. In order to facilitate these needs two adults, a teacher and a teaching assistant, are required to staff groups composed of between 10 and 12 pupils.

The NG provides a holistic curriculum, incorporating the National Curriculum with a curriculum designed to address social, emotional and behavioural factors underpinning academic learning. As has already been noted, acknowledgement of the interconnectedness of social, emotional and cognitive development dictates the creation of a learning environment that combines homely features (such as soft furnishings) with features of the standard mainstream classroom, including play materials. Each school day is organized around a regular and predictable pattern of events that include formal curricular activities, based on the National Curriculum, combined with free play and social activities (such as the daily 'breakfast').

Variant 2: new variant NGs

Variants of this type are based on the principles underpinning the classic model but differ in structure and/or organizational features from the Boxall groups. One way in which the second variant differs is in terms of the amount of time pupils spend in these groups, which, in mainstream schools, can vary from half a day to four days per week. Other versions of this variant may serve a cluster of schools, rather than a single school; be located in a special school; or take the form of an off-site unit. One LA covering a large geographical area has created a 'travelling NG', which moves from school to school. They may also vary in terms of the age range catered for. Classic groups cater for KS1 and KS2 pupils, whereas new variant NGs sometimes cater for KS3 pupils. Regardless of organizational differences, however, these groups retain core structural features, such as small group size, and being staffed by a teacher and teaching assistant, and they adhere to the core principles of the classic approach in terms of developmental emphasis and the holistic curriculum.

Variant 3: groups informed by NG principles

These are groups that sometimes bear the name 'NG', or are claimed to be variants on the NG concept, but which often depart radically from the organizational principles of classic and new variant NGs. They may, for example, take place outside the normal curricular structure of the schools where they are located, taking the form of lunch-time, break-time or after-school groups. Or they may take the form of 'havens' or 'sanctuaries' that can be accessed by pupils at different times. The groups may be run by a single individual or a non-teaching adult (such as a teaching assistant, mentor or counsellor). The activities that go on in these groups will tend to focus on social and developmental issues but will tend not to have the academic emphasis of the classic and new variant groups.

Variant 4: aberrant NGs

These are groups that bear the name 'NG' or are claimed to be variants on the NG concept, but which contravene, undermine or distort the key defining principles of the classic NG. These groups can be found in any of the above configurations but will lack an educational and/or developmental emphasis in favour of control and containment.

The significance of variation

The first two variants might be seen as genuine NGs. The third often provides important social and emotional support for pupils, although it is in danger of being peripheral. The fourth variant is potentially dangerous, through promoting a distorted image of the theorized NG.

The effectiveness of nurture groups: evidence from a national research study

The study reported by Cooper and Whitebread (2003) set out to assess the effectiveness of NGs in promoting positive, social, emotional and educational development. The study focused on variants 1 and 2 (see above) and measured: (1) the effects of NG in promoting pupil improvement in the NG; (2) the extent to which these improvements generalized to mainstream settings; and (3) the impact of NGs on whole schools.

A group of 359 pupils (71.5 per cent males; mean age 6 years 5 months) attending NGs were studied. A further 187 pupils (matched to a random sample of NG pupils) were studied, composing 4 comparison groups: (1) 64 pupils with social, emotional and behavioural difficulties (SEBD) attending NG schools; (2) 65 pupils without SEBD attending NG schools; (3) 31 pupils with SEBD attending schools that do not have NG provision; and (4) 27 pupils who do not have SEBD attending schools that do not have NG provision.

Data-gathering tools were the Goodman Strengths and Difficulties Questionnaire, the Boxall Profile and interviews with staff, pupils and parents. Measures were taken at termly intervals over a two-year period.

Statistically significant improvements were found for NG pupils in terms of social, emotional and behavioural functioning. NGs that had been in place for more than two years were found to be significantly more effective than groups which had been in existence for less than two years. Pupils with SEBD in mainstream classrooms improved in behavioural terms significantly better than pupils with and without SEBD attending schools that did not have NG provision. The greatest social, emotional and behavioural improvements took place over the first two terms, while improvements in behaviours associated with cognitive engagement in learning tasks continued to improve into the third and fourth terms. There were differential effects in relation to the type of problems presented by pupils. Pupils with global SEBD difficulties, anti-social and mainly disruptive behaviours tended to generalize improvements accrued in the NG to mainstream settings. Pupils with primarily social/emotional problems, and pupils whose major presenting problem was hyperactivity, although they improved in the NG, tended not to carry this improvement over to the mainstream. A further important finding is that NGs appear to have the capacity to influence positively the ways in which parents interact with their children. This study sheds new and interesting light on this important area, but requires far deeper scrutiny in future research.

This study suggests that NGs are a highly promising form of provision for young children with a wide range of SEBDs. There is also good evidence to suggest that successful NGs contribute to the development of the 'nurturing school' (Lucas, 1999; Doyle, 2003). The failure of certain sub-groups of pupils to generalize improvement to the mainstream may be taken to highlight the context-dependent nature of certain kinds of pupil difficulty, and suggest the need for attention to be given to promoting the opportunities for nurturing approaches in mainstream classrooms.

Conclusion

Nurture groups have a long history of providing successful intervention for young children with a wide range of SEBDs. They also have the capacity to contribute to the development of 'nurturing schools'. The recent and current demand for NGs in UK schools would suggest that there is an unprecedented, widespread need for this kind of development in mainstream schools. This need most probably arises out of changes to educational practice instituted in the wake of the 1988 Education Act. An important feature of the nurture group is its capacity for development and adaptation. While it is likely that there will always be a need for the 'classic' NG there is clearly a need for innovative applications of the approach that extend nurturing opportunities to ever larger numbers of pupils in a wide range of settings. The current high level of interest among educators in the NG approach suggests that we may look forward to the continued evolution of this approach.

CHAPTER 13

The Communication Opportunity Group Scheme (COGS): Teaching pupils to communicate, think and act appropriately

Rosemary Sage

Introduction

When children enter school they have to shift their informal chat into formal mode to process large quantities of talk or text and produce a coherent response. Although most children grasp **language structure** (*sounds, words, sentences*) to cope with casual conversation, there is strong evidence to suggest many have major problems in **narrative structure** (*explanations, instructions, reports*), requiring them to put together the meaning of a whole series of events (Sage, 2004). Narrative discourse ability is seldom assessed or considered in teaching, depriving children of the means to improve their thinking, communication and performance. Impairments in narrative are commonly seen among students, preventing them from negotiating solutions to both personal and academic problems (Bell, 1991, Sage, 2003). A Communication Opportunity Group Scheme has been successful for a wide range of pupils. It develops formal language and thinking, greatly enhancing the performance of able and less able children. Evidence is presented to illustrate its use in schools.

Background to research

What do you remember about school? Hours of listening to teachers? Being told to shut up and shape up to adult standards? Learning by listening rather than talking is the norm. Unless pupils have opportunities to talk through their thoughts with others, however, they will never learn to frame questions and construct lines of inquiry towards learning goals.

Rehearsing ideas *aloud* results in their review and revision, as facts and opinions are swapped by speakers and related to their own experiences. Thus, through talk, the reasoning processes that underpin learning are revealed and refined. Externalizing thinking builds the topic overview and represents it strongly in memory for later generalization. Teachers instruct for up to 90 per cent of class time, so stifling student talk and thought and strangling discursive dialogue (Sage, 2000a, p. 19). How can children take control of their lives and become decent citizens if they are expected to 'clam up' in class and subvert their needs and motivations? Talk lies at the very centre of the learning experience.

What is the evidence for communication difficulty?

There is strong evidence that children enter school with severe difficulties in talking, thinking and behaving. In the USA, the Carnegie Foundation's study (1992), across all states, found 98 per cent of children had communication problems (ranked top) on school entry and 51 per cent of these were judged serious. This was followed by emotional maturity, again with 98 per cent pupil difficulty and 43 per cent in the serious problem category. In the *Let's Talk* project (Lees *et al.*, 2001, p. 39), 73 per cent of Sheffield pupils tested as delayed in language and behaviour. This evidence is reinforced by Sage (2005), who found that all the children in one city school had a two-year delay in thinking and communication on school entry and this deficit remained on retesting after 18 months in school. No wonder school success, which depends on a facility with words and appropriate actions, is a problem!

Cohen (1996, pp. 105–27) emphasizes the fact that most research on child communication looks at language structure (*sounds, syntax, grammar, vocabulary*) but fails to consider narrative structure competence (*giving directions, explanations, accounts, reports*). She looks at the high prevalence of language difficulties among children with socio-emotional and/or psychiatric disorders and offers a lack of narrative ability, to express thoughts concisely and communicate meaning in emotionally loaded situations, as an explanation for their behaviour problems. In other words, such children are unable to negotiate themselves out of their troubles. This view is reinforced in work by Cross (2005), who asserts that children with social and emotional difficulties are far more likely to have communication problems than their peers.

Studies of adolescents portray a grim picture of children's natural language and thinking abilities. They also suggest that the right kind of educational experience plays a vital role in determining to what extent children are able to gain expertise and use language to explain, instruct and self-regulate. Brown *et al.* (1984) worked with 500 14–17 year olds who were unlikely to leave school with formal academic achievements. Although they appeared confident communicators in informal situations, when asked to talk into a tape recorder or give detailed information or instructions their performance dramatically deteriorated without the support of a live partner. They were unable to organize their thinking and expression. This formal, public speaking ability that demands organized, coherent information is the midpoint between speaking and writing and an essential skill in competent written performances. The Brown research found that when children were taught formal speaking their personal and academic performance leapt forwards and all the 500 students who were predicted to fail their public exams in fact passed them well. This provides the evidence for a scheme that seeks to develop the thinking and communicative abilities of students in order to enhance their school achievements.

A rationale for developing thinking and communication: the COGS

As a child, do you remember being told to 'Keep quiet', 'Control that temper', 'Stop fighting'? Repeated adult commands set up an internal conflict affecting communication with others. The strong, sturdy spirit – '*I need*', '*I want*', '*I demand*' – that we are born with ensures our survival. This self-spirit views the world through one pair of eyes – our own. It encourages us to cry when hurt, scream when frustrated, hit when annoyed and snatch when we want. Adults teach us to deny these strong feelings in order to help us socialize. The direct line from feeling to action is interrupted and rerouted so we lose touch with our emotional needs. Thus we fail to learn how to communicate what we really feel, think and mean. Our true thoughts and emotions are filtered out and we lose touch with our central self. How does this affect communication exchanges in school?

Think for a moment about class talk. It is generally the teacher who does the talking, in a monologue, where he or she controls action and speaks from a personal point of view. To persuade, inform or change the listener, the speaker *and* receiver must be actively involved. True communication is a discursive dialogue – an exchange between teacher and student actively pursuing a shared meaning. If teachers are talking for three-quarters of class time each student will average less than three minutes talk a day! At home, it is normally children who initiate and question while parents listen and respond. Children take the lead and learn what they need in an active, participatory style. The table turns when children start school, and many are not prepared for the move from home to class events. It is like Alice when she fell down the rabbit hole and found the language of Wonderland was quite the reverse of home. She found 'lessons' were so called because they 'lessened from day to day', but this was not Alice's experience. Her confidence cracked and competence crashed.

When children enter school they move from centre to side stage and feel cast from the spotlight. Some submit to the regime but others rebel because of a number of possible interrelated biological and social factors that affect their ability to conform. Curriculum requirements do not help to ameliorate the situation. Teachers feel they must control the discourse, and allow a restricted range of talking opportunities for their students in order to meet National Curriculum deadlines. In turn, the majority of students sense that they cannot stray from the class agenda or they will be thought difficult and deviant. It is not surprising, therefore, that 'by comparison with reading and writing, speaking and listening continue to be neglected in coverage, planning for progression and assessment' (DfEE/QCA, 1997).

Not all educators are able or willing to work for continual, cooperative endeavours with pupils, some preferring to invoke the authority of their superior knowledge or the power of their position to impose their own choice of instruction, whether or not the learners find it helpful. While conforming pupils might accept this imposition, there are others with personalities, attitudes and problems in understanding that prevent acceptance and provoke them to rebel. Limited communication experience will make for student difficulties as well as educators' failure to make themselves clear, whatever the learner's competence. Sage (2000a) and Cross (2005) cite research to suggest that many behaviour problems of children are rooted in their limited communication, which results in their being poor at negotiating meanings.

Studies by Sage (2004) and Sage et al. (2004) suggest that educators, also, may sometimes lack communication experience in relation to children as persons and learners. In these works 50 per cent of teachers and 74 per cent of support staff felt they did not have the knowledge or skill to communicate adequately with the diverse pupils found in today's classrooms. Teaching is not what it was a few years ago, when schools segregated pupils and lessons were delivered to groups with similar cultures and abilities. In today's classes are found children from many different social, educational and cultural backgrounds as well as with differing abilities, interests and motivations, with the result that the language of instruction appears to be one of the major problems that children have with learning (Sage, 2000a).

Teele (2000, p. 49) cites research suggesting that schools which value personal development as well as academic skills score at least 20 per cent above average grades and have few behaviour problems. Gardner (1997, pp. 20–1) suggests that students just go through the motions of education and are unable to apply knowledge and skills to new situations. They need to become active through group dialogue rather than passive listeners in the process of learning.

Literature reviews from the 1970s (Brigman et al., 1999, pp. 323–9) emphasize instruction in communication because it is strongly correlated with personal and academic success. Effective teaching involves individual, small group and whole-class instruction. Although documented internationally over 30 years, the problems of pupils lacking requisite communication for learning persist at all levels and may be the main reason for inadequate school, college and life performances.

The COGS translates what is known about developing personal and academic success skills. It is based on how spoken and written ideas are developed and expressed both cognitively and linguistically over 14 levels. Organization of ideas is considered within four components of communication:

- *clarity* (clear messages)
- *content* (relevant information)
- *convention* (presentational rules)
- *conduct* (appropriate responses).

These elements are bounded by *attitudes, personality, intelligence* and *opportunity*, which influence the way messages are formulated and understood.

The 14 levels of the COGS cover primary, secondary and tertiary education and job training needs. Levels 1–7 develop the full range of narrative structures (see Figure 13.1) and 8–14 extend these in more complex tasks. After ten hours of teaching, participants are assessed on target speaking and writing competences in five activities. The split of tasks is four spoken to one written, reflecting their normal use. Level 1, for example, requires participants to develop a *range of ideas*, choosing items to:

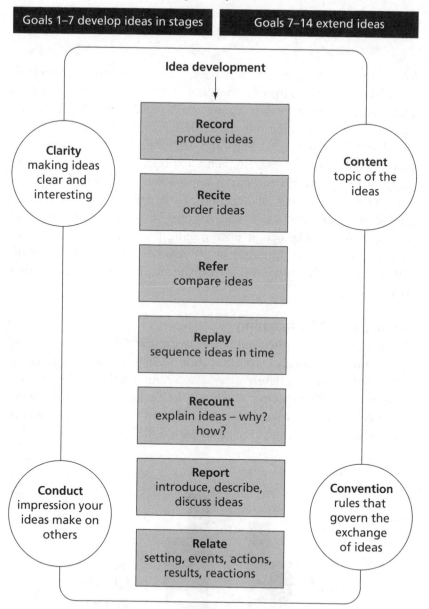

Figure 13.1 COGS *communication model*

- perform a short poem – to examine aspects of CLARITY;
- talk on something that interests them – to consider issues of CONTENT;
- formulate a question to someone – to look at an aspect of CONVENTIONS;

- answer questions from the audience – to understand the role of CONDUCT;
- produce a personal profile as an example of CREATIVE WRITING.

Teaching and assessment activities, reflecting student choices, complement and reinforce ongoing learning. The premise is that students must reason about their *physical* world, involving objects and their relations (paradigmatic thinking), and their *social* world, involving feelings and emotions (narrative thinking), before connecting, organizing and expressing knowledge coherently. A tell, show, do and coach approach is used, which includes systematic sequencing of teaching with review, demonstration, guided practice, corrective and supportive feedback. Group and independent activity occur, encouraging pupils to take control of their learning. In an appraisal of 50 years of research, Wang *et al.* (1994, pp. 74–9) found this to be the most effective instruction mode.

Results of COGS teaching

The question is whether pupils receiving the COGS would show significant increases in communication skills for thinking, learning and behaving appropriately after a ten-hour teaching programme. Results of 2,000 participants (shown in Tables 13.1–13.4) indicate a significant and positive difference between those receiving *weekly* or *intensive* COGS when compared with 2,000 *controls* (75 per cent

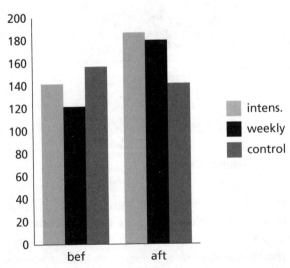

Table 13.1 *Communication tests: primary (2,000 participants)*

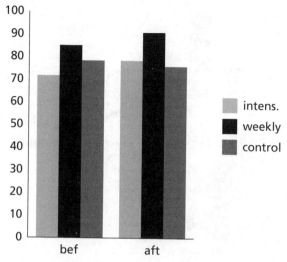

Table 13.2 *Reading tests: primary (2,000 participants)*

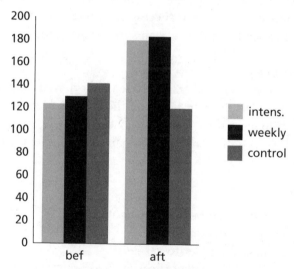

Table 13.3 *Communication tests: secondary (2,000 participants)*

of scores were at the level p = 0.05). The average for *controls* on the pre-test is higher than the teaching groups (by chance rather than design) but is reversed on the post-test. In fact, the *control* group scores significantly lower on the second assessment. Tables 13.1 and 13.3 indicate results from the COGS communication assessments that consider language and narrative structure and Tables 13.2 and 13.4 record National Foundation for Educational Research reading test results.

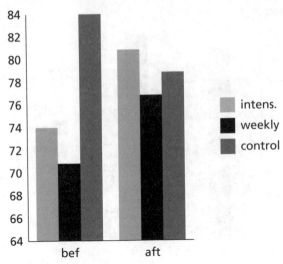

Table 13.4 *Reading tests: secondary (2,000 participants)*

Findings such as these suggest the processes and skills considered most predictive of long-term success can be taught by teachers and produce statistically significant gains in a short time.

Participant views
Students, parents and teachers have been interviewed by independent evaluators to ascertain their views on the COGS. Here is a selection of their opinions taken from interviews in the academic year following the COGS teaching. The parent's comment represents a typical view.

The students

- talking makes you behave better at school
- talking makes ideas real
- talking makes it easier to get help
- help with talking makes it easier to ask questions
- talking helps me to do more work on my own
- clever ones are good at talking.

The parents

I found COGS was really good for my daughter. It pushed her forward and gave her a new outlook. She loved it – it was different from normal lessons. I cannot believe the difference in her. She focuses more and is not frightened of doing new things. I'm really proud of her and her certificate takes pride of place.

The teachers

- much more confident this year both in answering questions in class and in written work;
- works extremely hard and has improved greatly in confidence, communication and behaviour;
- now volunteers answers and has good understanding of the work;
- showing increased confidence and communication in both speaking and writing;
- written work shows improvement in presentation and content and greater understanding of the ideas covered in lessons is demonstrated.

Students receiving the COGS were more confident at school; used an increased range of language and communication; showed improved levels of reading and writing performance and demonstrated improved behaviour.

Discussion

Evidence begs the question: 'Why were these children so inarticulate and disruptive in school?' The fact that pupils were helped in a ten-hour programme proves they could learn, but why had this not happened naturally? Problems of *understanding and using* certain registers (styles) of communication are highlighted. The style of classroom communication is very different from normal. At home, children talk and question while adults listen and answer. In school the pattern reverses and children do not always acquire spontaneously new forms of listening, speaking, thinking and behaving that demand the formal structuring of ideas.

We might argue that the schools concerned had not previously presented students with opportunities to learn new ways of communicating because such skills were not thought to be their major concern. After all, most children can speak and do as they are told when they start school. Speech and language therapists, psychologists and other specialized professionals help children with early difficulties in comprehension and expression by facilitating sound and sentence structures in informal situations and modifying inappropriate behaviour.

When children enter school, however, emphasis is on their ability to *understand, transmit and explain* chunks of information in formalized ways. Children may know how to assert and question but not what to do with answers. Learning demands more than the informal skills of unplanned, mundane conversations and requires an ability to conduct discursive dialogues. These types of discourse combine the sociability of talk with reasoning in order to frame questions and think out answers in an inquiry. Abstract *critical* reasoning, *creative* problem solving and *coherent* linking of events are required, in a structure that describes, discusses and decides appropriately for the purpose. This *narrative talk* is more akin to a formal written style of language.

Evidence suggests that students converse informally but have major problems in speaking and writing formally, when required to process quantities of information and produce coherent, relevant responses in narrative structures. If we are to bridge the talking and thinking demands of home and school, professionals must address this informal/formal talk divide and assist children to shift from oral to more literate styles of discourse. This will help them to think out events and create appropriate responses.

We think, however, not only with our heads but also with our emotions, bodies and spirits – the visions, hopes, values and meanings that are woven into our existence. Everyday language recognizes this when we say things such as, 'He thinks with his head', 'She thinks with her heart', 'He thinks with his guts'.

Thinking, therefore, must be active and available for external criticism to move beyond personal views and feelings. It can be eased into another realm through discursive dialogue with others and this activity lies at the very heart of the COGS. The approach is by no means new, going back to ancient Athens and to Socrates' use of talk to break down his companions' assumptions and stereotypes so that they could expand their thoughts. He believed that talking leads us to find knowledge latent even in the most ignorant and to discover good in every man.

One teenage lad in a COGS group said: 'We are scum, but not just scum'. He spoke of his shattered self-esteem when confronting the boy he had just bullied. Guilt, pain and bewilderment were evident. Given an opportunity to voice his opinions enabled some basic human quality to shine through that was irresistibly likeable to the rest of the group. Bad behaviour is human – an extreme potential of the fragmented, decentred, stunted self. Each of us is a cacophony of sub-selves, relating on occasion as would a dysfunctional family. We have a dominant 'I', but the repressed presence of the others haunts and sometimes overwhelms us in a form of possession. Our consciousness allows us to get in touch with the central self and talk is the way we can communicate with it. The ability to see beyond the moment and place things in a wider framework of meaning depends on our response to life and our contact and communication with others around us.

The COGS is well researched, showing positive effects in many studies (Sage, 1992; Sage and Shaw, 1992; Sage and Whittingham, 1997; Nelson and Burchell, 1998; Sage, 2000c; Orton, 2005; Wilde, 2005). It has a framework that targets formal learning requirements, bridging social and educational discourse styles. It highlights both language and narrative structures and nurtures their use in activities with others, exploring the feelings, views, attitudes and thoughts that influence the way we interpret facts.

There is no suggestion that the COGS is a cure-all for *all* the problems of learning and living together, but it offers an alternative solution for some of the fundamental difficulties that children experience in trying to understand and respond successfully to others. It moves beyond the language structure preoccupation of many teaching programmes and offers a narrative focus, linking with the expressive, informative, social and control functions of talk. The COGS is effective because it does not expect students to write above their levels of talking and thinking, which is a common reason for school failure (Sage, 2000a, p. 139). It considers thinking and communication as a whole, rather than in component parts, and balances academic with personal skill development.

Human Communication International, an educational charity, holds the copyright to COGS and promotes effective communication in schools and workplaces through workshops, conferences and journals. The University of Leicester teaches a postgraduate certificate in Communication, Leadership and Management, preparing people to implement the COGS within a curriculum or work structure. The potential is exciting as the COGS places value on communication, thinking and behaving skills in both schools and workplaces and heralds a new deal for children and adults. It provides an easy tool for personal and professional success. There is no one who would not benefit from such an approach to their self-development as we all need to work at communicating more effectively in order to achieve the responses that we want from others.

Review

The evidence presented here suggests that the COGS could play a significant role in improving the performance of both pupils and their teachers but this will entail a radical shift in educational philosophy and practice that focuses on communication and relationships rather than content. This has happened in Japan with their new moral curriculum in which children are taught the fundamentals of formal talk and participate far more in giving and sharing information than do their British counterparts. Other European countries value teacher and student talk more highly than we do and make oral activities an important part of the public examination system. Italy, for example, has one leaving certificate at age 19, for which students choose their four best subjects to be orally assessed. Speaking and listening performance takes prominence as the dominant activity of daily life, signalling prestige and value for narrative skills. Italian students achieve high academic levels when compared to their British peers, according to teachers on the CamBrit teacher exchange scheme. Discursive dialogue, moreover, is an important part of Italian social life so that students are better prepared to cope with the language of instruction when they enter formal education. A morning pattern of schooling allows more participation in out-of-school events, enabling greater physical and mental stimulation, which helps thinking, communicating and behaving. Targeting formal communication in teaching has greatest impact on disruptive behaviour (Brigman *et al.*, 1999) but we are reluctant as a nation to recognize this fact.

Unless students have adequate language, narrative thinking and structures on which to develop the secondary activities of literacy and numeracy, problems in learning will occur. The Mathematics Report (2005) by academics from leading universities suggests that our poor performance compared with international standards is due to the inability to choose and combine a number of steps to solve mathematics problems. This is a clear example of underdeveloped narrative ability, which also affects reading, as students cannot assemble information to grasp the overall meaning. As power and wealth derive increasingly from 'intellectual property', the UK is in danger of becoming dependent on imported intellect if we continue to ignore this vital issue. It is time to talk and take action as communication matters for achieving appropriate behaviour and effective learning. In particular, we need to target formal communication, which requires the assembly and organization of a large number of ideas to achieve the overall meaning of oracy, literacy and numeracy activities.

CHAPTER 14

Emotional responses to misunderstanding: Early warning signs in mathematical communication

Jennifer Rogers

Following concern about the difficulties that some primary and secondary schoolchildren experience in mathematics, research was carried out with pre-school children in England, Sweden and Japan to uncover the level of their understanding when they start school. The research was designed to investigate their awareness and understanding of numbers with a range of meanings. The findings, which were statistically significant, showed that children of this age have little knowledge of when numerals are used to represent numbers of items (cardinality). In contrast they appear to have a better understanding of when to write numerals to represent the time and the date.

The finding that, as they approach the start of their education, they have little understanding of the numbers they are learning to write in the context of counting is of concern. After all, counting or cardinal number is the basis on which their subsequent study of the number system and arithmetic, or 'number operations', is to be built (Rogers, 1996).

Bearing in mind that these children in pre-school have learned much of what they know in their parents' or carers' family unit, differences in the cardinal and non-cardinal results seem to suggest that innate factors are unlikely to be the only source of young children's limited use of cardinality and that understanding of number is not pure knowledge independent of humans. Young children have to discover what adults mean in order to make the meaning their own. This appears to further endorse the socio-cultural view and support the case for examining the *social* mechanisms of cognitive development and its linguistic-cognitive underpinnings.

Relatively little attention has been paid in research to development of the linguistic-cognitive underpinnings, of when conceptual frameworks are being formed, or of the language and linguistic structures used by adults. There appears then to be an urgent need for children's difficulties, particularly with regard to cardinal number, to be re-examined in relation to their understanding of when symbols are written by others and when children need to use symbols themselves.

This is particularly important in view of long-standing evidence that early difficulties make it hard both to engage children (DES, 1989) and to correct difficulties later. It is also well documented that such difficulties soon become compounded, resulting in further delay (Cockcroft Report, 1982). Equally important, I would suggest, are the negative effects of incomprehension and lack of mastery of a prominent part of the curriculum in which young children are involved on a daily basis. It may even be the case that such incomprehension prompts the early lack of confidence in mathematics that becomes exacerbated by further failure during and beyond the later school years.

Where children 'vote with their feet' they will withdraw from the mathematics lesson. This may be in the form of loss of attention often referred to as 'daydreaming', being 'off task' or 'fiddling/ messing about'. For the teacher this is relatively low level as it may not cause disruption, although it is likely to cause the teacher frustration when the child is subsequently unable to complete the tasks set.

Where the child's lost attention turns to disturbing others there is a higher level of frustration as the teacher becomes concerned about loss of learning among other children as she intervenes to stop the child's interferences. Such loss of attention may in turn be attributed to the learning content being 'too difficult' or uninteresting for the child, particularly if the child has special needs of a generic nature. Although annoying there may not be great alarm when children such as these 'drop out' of the learning, particularly when the wider behaviour and management demands of the class are high or where there is already a broad developmental or learning spectrum to be addressed through differentiation.

The emotional level rises, however, when the lost attention is transformed into greater disruption by calling out, disturbing or sidetracking other pupils into a subversive or confrontational activity. The teacher's authority and class control is threatened and she may find no alternative but to have the child moved away from the lesson, outside the room or to a 'support' unit. In all cases emotions run high for the child, the teacher, the other pupils and eventually parents or carers. Concentration has been broken and learning lost for all concerned – including the child excluded from the lesson.

For some children the thought of personal as well as public failure in mathematics lessons may be too great to risk. This is particularly the case for children who would experience humiliation at their own failure and for children who normally have a confident exterior or 'street cred' among their peers. For them, the bravado of 'cheekiness' and calling out is preferable to exposing their misconceptions and errors in front of their classmates. In fact their persona could actually be enhanced by eliciting laughter – even if a reprimand follows later. Here emotions and stress levels are high for the teacher, the child and for other pupils who may also be reprimanded for laughing, joining in or stopping their work.

Once concentration is lost, confusion and misunderstanding of the lesson content is inevitable and will in turn add to levels of frustration and anxiety for all concerned. For the child who caused the interruptions the negative cycle continues and learning deteriorates further. However, the question may arise: does he now 'deserve' to be helped after being so disruptive?

Much attention has been paid to children's *success and failure* in operations involving written work and symbols, to their performance in class tests, SATs, etc. (Rogers, 1997). In comparison, far too little attention has been paid to the *educational settings* in which the teaching and learning are carried out. The oral component of the mathematics or numeracy lesson can be considerable, with up to 10 minutes of the oral and mental starter, up to 20 minutes for the main teaching activity, with further listening time in the plenary. The effectiveness of the communication during these periods needs to be closely examined for its match to individual learners who are experiencing difficulty. The focus needs to be on the child developing the necessary linguistic-cognitive underpinnings of a new concept. This means the child developing the new idea alongside the language so that the two are interwoven. When teaching involves mainly watching, *listening* and responding to questions this will only happen for children who already have a strong conceptual underpinning of the new topic. Those who have weak prior knowledge are unlikely to 'catch on'.

In order for the child to engage with new ideas sufficiently for the new conceptual framework to be formed, he needs to be involved in a *dialogue* and narrative about the activity. This is more than 'speaking and listening'. It involves the learner in *communicating* for the purpose of *generating understanding within himself.* This is the 'generative' role of spoken language in cognitive development (Rogers, 2004a).

This practice includes all lessons, including those beyond English and literacy (in which understanding and interpretation of symbols are important), such as mathematics, science and geography. Using and applying mathematics is the cornerstone of the National Curriculum for mathematics, as in cross-curricular applications and problem solving. Yet the amount of time devoted to staff training in how to teach mathematical problem solving through the National Numeracy Strategy (NNS) does not appear to equate with the emphasis placed on it in the NNS Framework (Rogers, 2004b). Problem solving takes many different forms, which all teachers need to know about, but each of these is developed through a multifaceted approach that has narrative thinking and generative language at its heart (ibid.). When mathematical processes are used informally and competently to solve problems the grasp of the associated mathematical language is revealed (Hersocovics and Bergeron, 1984) and has the chance to be developed.

A child who displays social, emotional and/or behavioural difficulties because he feels inadequate often responds well when there is no such pressure. This applies to the informal settings in which problem solving is best developed, providing all learners with opportunities to engage with real-life problems. They first need to make sense of the language, not in isolation, but by interpreting the *social situation* that a problem represents.

Despite the extensive work stemming from Vygotsky (1978) and Bruner (1973) on the interrelated nature of language and thought and the generative role of language, relatively little attention has been paid specifically to the role of language in cognition. However, in the case of mathematics, we do know that much appears to depend on the child's understanding of the new symbolic language and on whether it becomes part of *his own* linguistic and conceptual framework. Less attention is being paid to the extent of children's grasp of *oral mathematical communication*, i.e. their use of language broadly. This is far more than their vocabulary as a repertoire of nouns and verbs. Their understanding and misconceptions are best reflected in their ability *spontaneously* to communicate verbally. This is a style of teaching common in Japan, one of the highest-attaining countries for mathematics, where oral, narrative and generative methods reflect an emphasis on understanding and problem solving in lessons *before* undertaking more abstract approaches to calculation for children up to at least age 12 (Cwenar *et al.*, 2005).

The child who 'drops out' of a lesson, whether quietly or disruptively, loses out on the two-way benefits of oral communication and narrative. In terms of assessing knowledge and judging the child's willingness to learn, we need to question the extent to which graphic representation (what the child writes, how much 'work' is undertaken) is a fair reflection of what the child knows and understands. It is useful here to bear in mind that thoughts are described by Vygotsky as 'inner speech'. Given sufficient time, what would the inattentive child express *verbally* in narrative form about his inner representations, in comparison to what he will, can – or *cannot* – write down?

This in an approach to 'assessment for learning' that is both broader and more complex than that often applied in classrooms. Assessment often judges whether or not a lesson's objectives have been met through success in the tasks that were set. However, tasks which require written representation of their outcome, particularly in those involving a correct sequence of expression – or symbols – can present a significant blockage for some learners – children, students and adults (see Rogers, 1997 and 2004).

Assessment for learning can thus be regarded as a two-edged sword. Teaching styles and tasks in numeracy can cause or exacerbate children's fears and failures. Formative assessment that is matched to the individual child's cognitive representation has the power to address and resolve misunderstandings and emotional stress. By being alert to early misunderstandings in maths we have the opportunity to prevent negative emotional responses often associated with maths. We can thereby engender success (not distress) in all children, if assessment as well as teaching is matched to the child's developmental level in maths.

CHAPTER 15

Visualizing and verbalizing

Jill Allison

Making pictures in your head, drawing them and then talking about them was not something I thought about until I enrolled on a course in communication at the University of Leicester.

Questions race through my mind. Do I visualize when I think and remember? Does everyone visualize? Do they ever share this experience? How important is this to comprehension?

Comprehension is the ability to connect and interpret information from the senses – seeing, hearing, tasting and feeling. It is also the ability to recall facts, get the main idea, make an inference and draw a conclusion. It is the ability to reason. It is cognition. Without comprehension learning is impossible, and without information across all sense modalities learning is incomplete.

My experience as an art teacher has concentrated on the visual impression. In today's world the visual image is paramount. Television puts the eye before the ear but is interrupted by advertisements, which break down stories into short episodes. It is a medium in which it is hard to present sustained or nuanced thought. Our students come to school with this fractured experience. They have a superficial knowledge gleaned from foreshortened and fragmented images of the world but no profound reflections on what they really mean.

This is why art lessons must provide opportunities for students to talk about what they have produced as this is vital for developing thinking. Without this chance to put together thoughts, students will leave school with little ability to articulate and explain their ideas. We owe it to them to provide opportunities to converse about their work and share their innermost thoughts. Art is now such a small part of the secondary school timetable that one lesson per week is all they are likely to receive. Value for the creative curriculum has diminished in the drive for improved literacy and numeracy standards. These learning processes emphasize critical, logical thinking approaches, but if students are going to apply this knowledge their creative thinking abilities are paramount.

Recently my role in school has extended to managing the learning of the gifted and talented students. I was fortunate to be able to join a group of educationalists and study the learning opportunities for this particular group of students in Australia. This was an amazing experience. I was struck by the value given in the Australian system to talk in class. There were many more opportunities for students to share their work, not only in school but also in the local community. Communication of ideas and their expression is widely promoted in exhibitions in local community centres and across radio and TV links. Sharing and communicating is at the centre of the learning experience.

In Britain, we have become dominated by the constraints of the National Curriculum and teacher talk has increased because of the need to expose students to ever increasing information. Do they understand this? Does it have value and relevance to their lives?

Somehow we must create space for them to talk about what they have learned and experienced so that they can make meaning of this knowledge. We do not know whether we know something until we have the opportunity to tell it to someone else. This helps us to organize information clearly and present it so that others can understand. The confidence this brings produces commitment and interest in further learning.

Art is a wonderful way to visualize ideas and feelings and stimulate the imagination and thought processes that help us to learn. If we are able to verbalize our visions we can take the thinking process forward, organize the experiences we have undergone and clarify our understandings.

Without visualizing and then verbalizing we may have problems in grasping the whole – known as 'the gestalt'. The gestalt is the entity from which the interpretative skills of identifying the main idea, inferring, concluding, predicting, extending and evaluating can be processed. It enables us to bring meaning to what we see, hear and feel. It is an integral part of cognition. If so critical, how does one create the gestalt? The answer is imagery – stimulated through artistic forms. Imaging is the sensory link to thought and language. It connects up prior knowledge, experiences and existing vocabulary, helping us to create stores in memory.

In 348 BC Aristotle wrote in 'On memory and recollection': 'It is impossible even to think without a mental picture'. The Greeks and Romans taught people imagery to improve their memories. (The number two [2] was visualized as a swan, the shape of which is the form of the figure.)

Helping our students to make pictures in their heads, reproduce them in artistic forms and then talk about them is easy to say but not easy to do at a time when we are pressured to produce. It may appear a waste of precious time. Let us be imaginative, however, in putting creative ideas into practice.

Although the curriculum constrains activity, visualizing and verbalizing is so important to the achievement of meaning that we cannot neglect it in teaching and learning.

Note
'Gifted' refers to students with high achievement, or potential for high achievement, in academic subjects (top 5–10%).
'Talented' refers to students with high achievement, or potential for high achievement, in art, drama, dance or sports (top 5–10%).

Acknowledgement
With thanks to Dr Rosemary Sage for assistance with condensing a longer presentation of this short chapter.

CHAPTER 16

A neuro-educational approach to SEBD

Peter Haase

Introduction

This chapter describes a successful intervention for teaching children with social, emotional and behavioural difficulties and specific learning difficulties and tells the story of Tom to illustrate its use. The approach involves using a computer-based, self-pacing basic literacy programme in the context of a holistic, thematic approach to learning. The multimodal approach includes the use of 'phonomimics' (which is reminiscent of the semaphore alphabet) and draws upon Hebb's rule (1949) to incorporate neuropsychological research findings into teaching practices. The approach also includes the use of colour coding of German orthography in learning handwriting (see Alliger and Haase, 2000) and the use of colour to indicate syllables in the presentation of texts for learning to read.

Historical background of the phonomimics aspect of the approach

Phonomimics was first developed by August Grosselin, a French teacher of deaf students. It was adapted for primary school education by Sczukras, who published her method in 1903. From 1925 onwards, the use of phonomimics formed part of the Hungarian primary school curriculum. Following the First World War, Franz Josef Koch, a primary school teacher working in the Ruhr district with students of multi-ethnic origin, introduced phonomimics into German primary school education. In the early 1990s the North Rhine–Westphalia authority recommended the use of phonomimics in the remedial teaching of dyslexics.

In 1993 the phonomimics approach was questioned by Renate Valtin because in her view it required children to learn a third coding system. Whether or not this is the case, it appears that children find phonomimics helpful in the process of learning to read, write and spell. This has been spontaneously endorsed by the children themselves.

The use of phonomimics in the Haase approach

This section is reported in the first person as a historical account. My employment of phonomimics includes the use of 35 illustrations, each showing the face and lips forming the typical shape required to produce the sound belonging to the letter/letter group (grapheme or digraph). The hand forms the sign for the phonomimic and touches that area of the face in order to feel the vibration of the sound on the skin. Left-handers have to form the phonomimics with their right hand, while right-handers use their left.

In the first phase, I model the phonomimics for the learners, making hand movements to accompany the reading of a chart/ pictures of the basic sounds (vowels and consonants). The idea is that the learners can associate the movements with the sounds (kinaesthetic and auditory) while simultaneously making and looking at the letter shapes (visual). The movement is dynamic (not static) and the activation of movement along with the use of sight and 'sounding out loud' maximizes the 'learning potential' by involving, simultaneously, as many modalities as possible. The hand movement starts at the lips, mouth, teeth – those zones of the body where students can feel with their fingertips the typical vibration of a specific sound production. For long spoken (closed) vowels, the hand is moved slowly horizontally. For short spoken (open) vowels the hand is moved quickly downwards. For consonants the hand is left resting on the body. The intensity of breath of plosive sounds b/p, d/t, g/k is shown on a chart by the use of a picture of a candle flame blown sideways. The learners are thus also using an interpretative mode (cognitive-associative). The role of song and dance is illustrated in the case history of Tom (see below).

The text for reading is presented on a card. On the reverse there is a blank crossword. To the students, it looks like a crossword puzzle. They can solve it only when they read the text on the front of the card. In addition, I developed 'picture dictations', used from the fifth week onwards. There were 14 pictures representing nouns with a coding line that showed the number of spoken syllables, the number of letters and the phoneme/grapheme correspondences. The learning of each sound/letter correspondence and its phonomimic sign is accompanied by a children's song, which has a key word that starts with the same letter as the new letter or letter group being taught.

Hunter-Carsch has commented, in correspondence with the writer, on the observed value of the singing and the movements that the children learned and practised while standing in a circle. It was evident that they engaged with the thinking (associating), the melody and the production of the sounds within the words. The song allowed the sounds to be felt by the children and heard as the melodies were sung by the group that was led by me as the teacher. It was observed that the children recalled the songs and informally sang during their computer-based work in the classroom – sometimes assisting each other by joining in with the melodies as well as movements and 'reading' the computer-programmed individualized work.

The computer – as a tactful friend

The second phase involves the use of five BETAJ versions of computer programs that I have designed and which are then introduced gradually. Three of these programs help in developing technical reading skills. They include learning and blending sounds in reading and using a 'gliding line of text' from right to left. It can be adjusted to the reading speed of the slowest reader in the group. Experience has shown that the students prefer to see syllables cued by changes in colour while reading the text. I present the texts in a saccadic trainer, so that the eyes can follow the text, word by word, from left to right, with colour changes for each syllable.

For phase three I use a 'fixation trainer', which has a window of a defined size that shows the text word by word, at an adjustable speed. I have also devised a computer program that includes a 'picture dictation' system where a picture speaks its name. The student is required to use the computer mouse to build up the name on the screen from the keyboard or from a selection of correct and incorrectly written syllables. When the student clicks on the text the computer speaks what the student has written at a speed of speech that matches the auditory perception speed of the student. The student is addressed by name and verbally praised by the computer for correct work, while being given hints for finding the correct answer in the event of typing errors. This program can be used by one or two students at a time, enabling them to problem solve through discussion at a metacognitive level.

I also designed a speaking-typewriter program that the students can use to write any text (using the mouse) while having auditory control over their work.

Tom: a case history – 'how success breeds success' diagnosis – family situation

In early spring 1995, when I was working as a special education teacher, I was called into a kindergarten for a consultation. There I met Tom, a tiny but tough 6-year-old boy of low measured general intelligence (Hamburg-Wechsler scale, Vienna Standardization by Schubert and Berlach, General Intelligence Quotient below 65 verbal IQ, similar levels on Raven's Matrices CPM). All his aunts and uncles had attended special schools. He lived in an extended family dominated by his grandmother and appeared to be almost a 'spare part'. He was almost unable to express himself verbally, exhibited all the signs of hyperactivity and had a very short concentration span.

There was no indication at that time of brain damage, so I had to recommend he attend a special school for slow learners – with little hope that he would succeed there. However, his mother argued against this special school so he was put into a pre-school group in a primary school for one year. After this he was reassessed. The test scores were even lower than before.

Start of school: motivation

In September 1999 Tom started with my group of slow learning beginners in a special class within a mainstream school. From the first day he showed the severest physical aggression towards his classmates, over and over. (He must have appeared to them as King Kong – he was so threatening.) My question was: did his behavioural problems and his deficits in speech development (both active and passive vocabulary) originate from his social position within the family clan? I wondered if he could be stabilized emotionally by success in learning.

Towards the end of the first week at school he began to show signs of having non-verbal intelligence that was much higher than all the tests had shown. From Vygotsky (1971, 1991) we learn that any intellectual process can only work in a functional system. For Tom, the backwardness in speech development seemed to be the worst factor, showing an extreme deficit in those functional systems. Was there any chance of a successful start to literacy under such disturbing circumstances?

I decided to run a competition for winning a 'Reader's Passport' to give him the chance of being the winner. (The passport is a licence to take any book home from the class library to study, then to read to the rest of the class.) At the oldest house in the medieval centre of our town I showed the students a bronze plaque and promised to give the Reader's Passport to the first pupil to read it and explain its text.

In the classroom and outside on walks into the town we learned the sound names for the letters A and M, together with the phono-mimics, songs and dances belonging to the corresponding A and M (phonemes/graphemes). Through song and play we discovered that the songs consisted of words and that words consisted of syllables. We learned about printing and reading the word 'Mama' and we learned how to find these two letters in house names, street names, shop names and shop displays in the town. Also through play we developed the concept of order in space and time (see Eggert, Bertrand *et al.*, 2002).

Non-verbal intelligent actions

Despite absences from school Tom progressed steadily in his level of achievement and his aggression decreased at an even greater rate. Excursions into town included reading shop names, street names and house names and, through them, discovering new letter/sound relationships. These excursions were real highlights for Tom. In the first two weeks he had learned five letter/sound relationships.

During the next four weeks I had intended to teach another seven sound/letter correspondences, using the methods described above. However, ten days after the start of the programme I had to go into hospital for treatment for three weeks, followed by another three weeks' recuperation. I was strongly advised to retire, but I hoped to be able to stabilize Tom during my final year of teaching, so I returned to work. For the six weeks of my absence my colleagues had worked in my classroom using my programme. Despite sometimes having three different teachers a day working with my group, the children had nonetheless developed those skills I had intended to teach them. This demonstrated that my method could be used successfully by other members of staff.

Colleagues were able to see that, while Tom had shown the severest level of aggression towards his classmates in conventional literacy lessons in the mainstream classroom situations, in the special group during the field trips he was the 'premier discoverer'. He found new shop window signs and decoded them, making use of phonomimics and remembering those words he had discovered two or more days before. The admiration of his skills by his classmates pleased him greatly.

Sitting in front of the computer, writing a word or a sequence using the picture dictation, Tom could forget the world around him and worked with the utmost concentration. When he made mistakes he accepted correction from the speaking computer even though, from classmates or adults, any criticism was met with aggression. Working at the computer, he even cooperated with a partner without behavioural problems.

Success breeds success

I had made a deal with the group: if there had been no quarrels or fighting for a week, we would cook a meal or bake something in the classroom, then eat what we had cooked. In order to prepare for this the students had to study offers to be found in supermarkets, write recipes and calculate the costs. This demonstrated to the students that reading, writing and arithmetic are necessary life skills.

Step by step, Tom's reading skill improved. He was the first to read small booklets printed in upper case, again engendering admiration from his classmates. On one trip, for example, he discovered a new shop name: 'Drachenstudio'. He decoded it very quickly through the use of phonomimics, and explained that the new shop sold kites.

Finally, I gave him the prospect of going back to the primary school in his home town, on condition that he progressed further, gained the Reader's Passport and stopped being aggressive. Tom began to think about this prospect. His aggression subsequently reduced in intensity, while his motivation increased by small degrees, and in the fourth week of April 1998 he managed to read a bronze plaque stating: 'Kemenate, oldest building in town, part of the court of the Barons of Rohrenfurth. There has been a "Kapelle" in this building since 1356'. 'Kapelle' has two meanings – 'chapel' or 'band'. To Tom it could only have been the recording studio of a band, so that is what he explained, grinning, through gestures. He got his reward. He subsequently underwent the headmaster's reading test and gained his Reader's Passport, which read: 'Tom has proved that he can read texts printed in upper case and in mixed upper and lower case. He explained what he read. He has a licence to borrow and read books'. The research group from Leicester University visited my classroom one week later and Tom showed himself at his best (see Hunter-Carsch *et al.*, 1998).

He steadily improved in reading, writing and arithmetic and in August 1998 we transferred him to the primary school in his home town. Because of his family circumstances we suggested he might learn best among first graders, hoping that, in this setting, he would be in the top group. It worked.

Further development

Tom became the top reader in primary school. He read every book I took to school to his classmates and was admired for doing that. His behavioural problems decreased. He subsequently succeeded in completing his secondary schooling.

A retrospective

When Tom first came to school his behavioural problems and test performances offered no hope of success. The start of his success, however, came through the use of the initial multimodal phono-mimic approach to literacy, making use of the semantic, the iconic and the motor memory in learning letter/sound and sound/letter relationships. Having his classmates regard him as a successful learner helped to reduce his 'King Kong' behaviour. Last, but not least, the BETA SIGN version of the computer program 'Speaking Picture Dictation' (in a monolingual version nothing more than an orthography trainer of about 2,000 words) was a teacher whose criticism he could accept. In this way he could improve his skills and grow steadily.

Success bred success. There is now hope that Tom will escape his early background and continue to succeed in earning his own living without recourse to any public support.

A personal remark

Such a story of success depends on diagnostic skill, observation, patient waiting for the right moment in the education process, subsequent action at fertile moments and last, but not least, an inner attitude, that helps you as a teacher, to look at each student not only as a professional but from the perspective of a father. 'What could I do to help him overcome his difficulties through his own efforts, if he were my son?' was my daily question at any critical moment.

Acknowledgements

With thanks to Sue Mailley and to Morag Hunter-Carsch for assistance with editing an earlier version of this chapter and to the Leicestershire Dyslexia Association for grant aid towards the cost of the research visit of the Leicester University team to observe my work with pupils in Melsungen.

CHAPTER 17

John's story: Episode 3

Problems increase

'John' and Paul Cooper

P: So we've talked about things up to the end of the time you were at junior school. So what about when you left there and went straight on to secondary school A?

J: Well, Mum had to fight to get me into School A. I don't really remember much about that – she used to complain about that as well. 'Cos we weren't in the same catchment area [as the school]. We lived in a different area and they wanted me to go to the local school, B. But my Mum wanted me – I wanted to go to School B because everyone I knew from my junior school was going there. So in the end I got to go. And at first, when I first went there, it was all right. Teachers were nice. It was different; definitely different from the junior school. So different. 'Cos you had to buy your dinner and different things.

I don't know how it really started. I started changing a little bit. Making new friends. I made new friends. I was changing. My behaviour wasn't temper tantrums as much any more. It was more – it was a bit more aggressive. I did used to swear a bit more. I used to get up and cuss the teachers. Not swearing all the time, but I just used to call them names or something ... I can remember one time – it wasn't me who was in trouble – some other kid was in trouble and we used to have this French teacher, and every time there was a problem in the class, she used to go and send for the Head of Year. Every time! And once she did this and I said, 'What are you? Are you a wimp? Can't you just deal with it yourself?' I got suspended for five days! For that! That was in Year 7. I think. I was about 11 years old, and I got suspended for calling a teacher a wimp. And what did she do, as soon as I called her? She called the Head of Year! [laughs]. He says, 'You shouldn't call teachers wimps!' I say, 'Yes, but she is! She calls you every time and she should deal with it herself. She's a teacher.' Do you know what I mean? She wouldn't deal with anything, and I got suspended for that.

P: So that was Year 7. When in Year 7?

J: I can't remember. 'Cos when you're younger a year goes slower. So a month feels longer than it does now. So I'd say it might have been just before – it could have been November, something like that.

P: Oh, so quite early on, then?

J: Yes it is now, but I was younger, then. So a lot had happened.

P: So what was that all about, then? Was this a different version of the tantrum behaviour you had before? Was it still about getting attention?

J: Yes, because I never used to get the help there either – not the help I needed. All I ever wanted with work was someone to help me spell. Reading I could cope with. I couldn't read as fast as everyone else, but I could still read. That's why I could understand questions, but I could not spell. And they couldn't seem to understand that. They seemed to think that there was a problem with everything you do. If you say you've got a problem, they think you've got a problem with everything. They think you've got a problem with thinking about stuff. That's what they think. They just forget what you're saying. You see, I only wanted help with my spelling. But again, as I say, there's teachers like in every school – there's teachers you don't like and don't get on with. And there's teachers you do [get on with]. And I remember, I never used to do any homework at School A. I always used to say I'd lost it. My Mum spilled coffee on it or something.

   ... like sports – I never got into the football team. I remember that, 'cos I grazed my leg first. And I never got my goalkeeper gloves. The first time of trials. The second time, I dived to make a wicked save, and I scratched all my leg up 'cos I was wearing shorts. So I didn't play ... so I never got picked. I got in the B team once. I played one game. That was about it really.

P: What about the teachers you did get on with?

J: There was about three teachers I liked the most. There was Mr D, Miss E and Mr F, the geography teacher. There was another one, a history teacher. He was all right. He was all right with me, so. Most of the other teachers didn't like me, though.

P: What was different about the ones you got on with?

J: They projected that they liked me. And they was helping me out in lessons. And I felt like I was actually getting help. And they really wanted to help me. You felt like they actually wanted to help you; to make a difference. Other teachers didn't – you don't feel like that. The thing was, like I was saying, I never used to do homework – we used to have diaries they'd give us. Y'know, you'd write – I'd never write anything in them. Y'know, not one thing. Never.

P: Didn't they check them?

J: No, they never checked them at all. If you don't bring it in, they don't check them. 'I ain't got it.' [I'd say] or 'I forgot it.' I thought it would be so hard to get away from homework, but it was so easy. I just didn't do it, and they didn't say nothing. After a while they didn't say nothing.

P: So what did you think about that, at the time?

J: I used to think it was all right, 'cos when it came to a test, when we were supposed to do revising, I still used to get a high percentage in marks on the tests, even though I never revised. I never revised for any tests. Just like when I did the one GCSE I did, I didn't revise anything. I got an 'F', because I didn't put the working out. I put the answers, but I didn't put the working out. I didn't know you got marks for writing down your working out. So I just wrote the answer down. I just worked it out. And I put the answer down. So I was still good at tests. I was good at taking things. If they were oral – if they came out of someone's mouth – I could understand. I took it in, even though they thought I wasn't listening. They were shocked when my test came through, or when I did work they didn't think I was listening to. They were pleased.

P: Did you ever tell them that you learned better by listening?

J: All the time. All the time. But then they started to try and give me Dictaphones, so I gotta listen to lessons. But I just never got the time to listen to it. It used to bore me. I used to be in the lesson one time and then they'd expect me to listen to it again. I'd always have to listen to the same thing all the time. Like taking down anything off the whiteboard – I could write it down, but I'd have to look up a couple of times, maybe just for one word which was this long – to see what the letters were, because I couldn't spell. Writing down – copying down, was easy. But I didn't learn anything from it, because I didn't used to read it. I just used to write it down – whatever it used to say. And people normally read it when they write it down, don't they? I didn't. I just wrote it down. Put it away! That's my work done! So I never learned anything from that. But everyone else does. So when they used to tell you about it – maybe I would look like I was sleeping, but I was listening.

CHAPTER 18

Supporting young people through empathy and respect: What teachers can offer each other as fellow professionals within and across schools and school services and what young people gain from the offer

Gerda Hanko

Introduction

A new children's agenda charges us with 'making every child matter' by bringing all those who work with them closer together. What can empathy and respect do to promote children's and their teachers' ability to relate across current barriers? How can both qualities be stimulated in the day-to-day work situation?

Empathy and respect as qualities of a 'positive approach to influence negative beliefs and appraisals'

> I loved English lessons because my teacher gave me the impression I could do something she couldn't. (Brookmyre, 2005)

> I could elicit no response from [an unresponsive pupil] if my motive was to 'help' him. But, if I sincerely wanted him to enlighten me about something of great importance about which he possessed knowledge unavailable to me, this put us on an equal footing and allowed this completely unrelating child to relate to me. (Bettelheim, 1990)

> An important positive approach [to influencing negative beliefs and appraisals] is that envisaged by Spinoza in his saying that it takes an emotion to control an emotion. (Peters, 1974)

> [In the struggle to find compensatory strategies ... it is ...] EMPATHY with which we take full cognisance of our natural

emotive sympathy with the other; in the right circumstances it opens the door to sorrow. (Damasio, 2003)

People need to feel that they matter to others ... [which is above all] a question of knowing how to create and how to convey RESPECT. (Sennett, 2003)

Viewing the landscape: knowing the stumbling blocks

To promote children's and their teachers' abilities to relate across often stony and divisive paths will require us to deal with a number of stumbling blocks. How might we, for instance:

- minimize the stultifying effects of the current excessively 'results'-centred teaching climate, for teachers to develop what Elton, almost two decades ago, referred to as an 'affective curriculum', to use children's emotional and social realities as a fertile source of new learning experiences (Hanko, 2003);
- rekindle in all staff, often made to feel inadequate by demands which deskill them, an awareness of possibilities open to them to respond both to the needs of all their pupils and to those of colleagues, to ensure 'that no teacher or support staff feel isolated and alone in their teaching task' (Corbett, 2001);
- stimulate multi-agency collaboration while interagency 'territorialism' seemingly remains embedded within education, healthcare and social work?

It is said that 12,000 letters annually reach the teacher stress helpline for advice relating to both conflict with colleagues and lack of support in problems with pupils who are thus experienced as impeding their professional effectiveness. But, as Mittler (2000) emphasizes, to be able to respond to the needs of all pupils, to be 'prepared' to do so, is a twofold obligation: an individual professional commitment, and a task for each school to help its staff to meet such commitment. As he suggests, 'this may not be as difficult to achieve as it may seem because most teachers already have much of the knowledge and skills they need. What they lack is confidence in their own competence'.

Liberating teachers' understanding and expertise: tapping untapped resources

Views about 'difficult children' can highlight distorted perceptions about a teacher's professional task ('if they don't want to learn they shouldn't be in this school'; 'we are trained to be teachers, not social workers or therapists'). Those who hold such views may not be aware how these may be adding to children's disaffection and failure to learn. Because of insufficient understanding of how children express what they feel or think, they may be missing a child's emotional message, such as the sorrow of masked despair behind a façade of worsening behaviour and even incipient violence. Thus teachers may fail to convey to disaffected pupils that, in spite of a reprimand, they may not necessarily have been 'written off' by an otherwise caring teacher.

Coping alone, teachers may 'cope' by falling back on defensive control just to 'keep going'; feel anger about their competence under attack, and their best efforts frustrated by seemingly unresponsive pupils who make them feel useless. They may not realize that these pupils, while experiencing similar feelings, may nevertheless remember them later as caring teachers who did make them feel worth caring about (cf. Quinton, 1987; Rutter, 1991). But at the time, for both child and teacher, underlying sorrow may remain a lonely experience in a negatively interactive relationship.

Much has, however, been learned from educational pioneers such as Erikson (1964), Winnicott (1965), Bowlby (1969), Vygotsky (1978) about the importance of children's early emotional and social experiences for their learning potential. Practice-applied findings from Attachment Theory (Geddes, 2003) can now inform teachers on how children's responses to new learning are influenced by early secure or insecure attachment experiences as they transfer these to school settings, and how teachers who understand such connections can help to supersede earlier insecurities. Therapeutic intervention projects such as the inspired revival of nurture groups (Bennathan and Boxall, 1996) or 'a quiet place' (Spalding, 2000) have begun to promote therapeutic understanding in other colleagues, raising awareness of their own 'therapeutic' resources for insightful commitment to each child. Such learning-related awareness has enabled many a despairing and disheartened teacher to find a child's 'teachable self' behind a help-refusing appearance.

Developing empathy and respect in the collaborative support group: becoming resources to each other

Staff development approaches geared to solving problems jointly (Hanko, 1999) show how teachers, when learning to 'share the load' (Gamman, 2003), can be helped to:

- contribute to each others' and their own understanding in a process of 'becoming resources to each other' (Sennett, 2003);
- resolve satisfactorily those unhappy situations when well-intentioned but disagreeing professionals from separate services clash over what each may consider the 'best' solution for a particular child (Hanko, 2004).

Such support amounts to developing ways of thinking that can 'liberate' (teachers') expertise, help them to function more effectively and with less distress (Mosse, 1994), experiencing that one can benefit from a learning environment which 'accepts anxiety and uncertainty and promotes thinking and understanding' (Woodhouse and Pengelly, 1991). Years of support work have shown how this can even include those who, after years of relentlessly negative classroom experiences, no longer think that any staff support can make a difference to them or the children they 'have to' teach (Hanko, 2002a).

Steinberg (1989) summarizes the fundamentals of collaboratively supportive consultation as a joint exercise in problem clarification ... which enhances the professional competence of consultees as well as helping them to learn how to consult to others ... (in a) co-equal relationship, where each respects the others' expertise, ... where (non-judgemental) questions can be asked (about a difficulty in a consultee's work setting) which allows the situation to be looked at anew (Taylor, in Steinberg). Applied to a school's twofold individual and institutional task in professional development, these fundamentals can be understood as: (1) a means of opening psychodynamic insights as an integral part of a teacher's empathetic and respectful commitment to each child, and at the same time (as the late Professor Ben Morris suggested when first president of what is now known as the Caspari Foundation), (2) seek 'to change the system as well, however little' (Morris, 1991).

However, introducing groups to these fundamentals as psychodynamically based, it helps to point out that they enable teachers to work flexibly with 'multiple concepts' (Norwich, 1996), offered by other approaches which can also help to understand the complexity of interactive influences on children's learning and behaviour (Hanko, 2002b).

Whatever length of a course has been agreed upon with a group, ranging from one-day sessions to weekly or fortnightly twilight sessions over a term (for variations in detail see Hanko, 1995, 1999), questions that teachers find useful to pursue for developing their understanding of problem behaviour point to them wanting to 'know' about the following:

- causes (what makes children behave as they do?)
- interventions (what more can we do as teachers to help them learn?)
- support (how can we support each other?).

To start such a course, a brief introduction to the basics of joint problem solving (i.e. the skills of asking non-judgemental, enabling questions through which to genuinely explore rather than telling others how 'to do things differently') can be combined with a brief awareness-raising talk about social and emotional factors in learning and failure to learn. To start tuning a group towards exploring such factors collaboratively, I find it useful to mention Bettelheim and Rosenfeld's reference to applied empathic understanding as the 'art of the obvious' (1993), the obvious being to consider as fundamental that:

- children with problem behaviour experience feelings they find difficult to bear; and
- sensitive responses by empathetic others can help them to manage these feelings.

Based on Attachment Theory, Waddell (1998) analyses 'therapeutic' understanding as including awareness that:

- a pupil's current reactions and patterns of relationships may in part relate to important past experiences when her feelings were not well received (e.g. perceiving a teacher's even deserved reprimand as an unbearable threat, since damaging relations in the *past* now colour the *present* situation);

but that

- past damaging experiences can be superseded by new reparative ones (e.g. if a pupil is helped to perceive himself differently in relation to others now important to him, such as teachers and other children).

Thus we can understand how, in the examples referred to, a child's behaviour is influenced by our response to it: whether we convey, for instance, empathetic understanding or, in contrast, respond to a child's negative feelings to us with similarly negative ones towards the child, it is we who influence whether our interaction with him becomes a virtuous or a vicious circle.

How may creating an exploratory climate influence the circle's quality?

Empathy and respect in the process of validating 'implicit know-how by joint reflection' (Claxton, 1998) when neither 'love, nor just wanting to help' (Bettelheim, 1990) are enough

After briefing a secondary school's teachers for a CPD day as described above, including a reference to Bettelheim's way of asking difficult-to-reach children to 'enlighten him on something important to them which they understood better than he did', one of the teachers described her discouraging experience with one of her most disruptive 14-year-olds, whose so far unmanageable behaviour puzzlingly 'changed out of the blue' one day, just when she had felt like giving up on him. In her despair she had asked him, since nothing she was trying worked, what *he* would like *her* to do with him to help him learn. Could he tell her? She noticed him looking puzzled, but got no reply. Since then, however, he was 'different', and in one new encounter, after she lightly reprimanded him about something, he blurted out that 'Nobody liked him anyway – so what's the point?' This now sounded to her like a cry for help from a world he experienced as friendless and unfair and in which he felt he did not belong. She now wondered with her colleagues what might have caused this change of allowing her to look into his world, and how should she react to this?

The teacher found the ensuing exploration heartening: her colleagues thought that, rather than adding anger of her own to his (which the boy still had to learn to manage), she appeared to have communicated some of the despair she herself felt and thus some sympathy with his despair. She had been able to ask him for help which, she had conveyed to him, only he could give her. As a significant person in his life who was not 'writing him off', but who saw him as 'worth bothering about', she had offered him an important new experience as somebody worthy of being asked for advice. The teacher, listening thoughtfully, confirmed her sense of feeling 'on his side', without having been fully aware of its significance. Moreover, her colleagues, non-judgemental sharing conveyed their being on her side and thus made her, on her part, feel supported and cared about, and meant having her strengths recognized and respected when she had herself underestimated these.

When asked how the session had worked for the group as a whole, they felt that contributing from their own existing expertise in such supportive, reflective ways, such as noticing their colleague's apparently 'instinctive' professional response when she asked the boy for his view, was bound to deepen their own awareness in similar situations. Altogether, they had felt enabled to 'look at a problem anew' (cf. Steinberg above).

Similarly enabling for the appreciation of complementary expertise across the professions had been the joint reflections reported elsewhere (e.g. Hanko, 1999), such as that between Jeanie's increasingly despondent teacher and her colleagues (Hanko, 1999, pp. 34–6). There, the brewing conflict between two professionals was no help to 10-year-old Jeanie, nor to her worried foster mother, when teacher and social worker doubted each other's judgement about the child's immediate needs. This unhappy situation was resolved by an inspired redeployment of the enabling skills the teachers had found helpful with seemingly 'oppositional' children: the teacher was able to reach out to her professional 'opponent' to achieve a solution to which both sides could amicably agree. It also enabled her to reassure an anxious foster mother about her effectiveness as Jeanie's carer.

Conclusion

Working together across professional barriers, now the theme of a promising new children's agenda, has of course always been the *raison d'être* of SEBDA and its predecessors (cf. the David Wills lecture that the then AWMC had invited this writer to deliver; Hanko, 1991). Readers of this book will have their own experiences of 'what works' in collaboration, as well as of what may subvert it. This chapter has attempted to forestall the (wilful?) misuse of two concepts crucial for 'becoming resources to each other': that of empathy as uncomfortably 'touchy-feely', and that of respect as something that should be 'demanded' from those to whom it is owed in the first instance. As analysed in this chapter, however, it shows how, in all collaborative sharing thus understood, all participants tend to benefit along their 'Zone of Proximal Development', but that the greatest beneficiary clearly is, as intended, the child, who, in a deeply professional sense, is being 'kept in mind' by all concerned.

CHAPTER 19

Classic psychoeducational approaches to teaching and talking with troubled children

Stephen Weiss

Introduction

Psychodynamic theory proposes that as children interact in diverse social contexts, they characteristically face psychological conflicts that arise from the desire to gratify their own wishes while, at the same time, feeling required to fulfil the expectations of others. At least in part, mental health is thought to depend on the effectiveness of the methods children use to integrate their inner needs with external demands (Freud, 1936).

While all children go through the emotional aches and pains of growing up in their homes, schools and communities, some youngsters may become identified as 'troubled' and in need of counselling when the conflicts become pervasive, long lasting and unable to be resolved without great effort. Conflicts may be experienced in school through interactions with peers, teachers and administrators and be enacted in the form of difficulties in learning, lack of interest and inappropriate social behaviour. Children often come to be considered 'troubling' in the classroom when conflicts turn into struggles with other students or if their behaviours become problematic for teachers and other adults.

Linking such educational concerns with mental health issues, Pollock (1989, p. xvii) writes, 'To enter the world of learning a child must be motivated. To embrace the world of learning, to make it his own, a child must make it one of personal meaning. How we make sense of our encounters with the people and things in our environment – what impels or impedes our lifelong urge to learn and transform ourselves – are central questions occupying professionals in all the human sciences and mental health professions'.

Beginning in the 1890s with the seminal discoveries of Sigmund Freud (Jones, 1953), and later embodied in the pioneering work of clinicians and educators such as Aichorn (1925), Adler (1930), Erickson (1950), Bettelheim (1955), Redl (1966) and Freud (1976), the psychoeducational approach to teaching and learning blends elements of psychodynamic and developmental psychology with education theory and practice (Redl and Wattenberg, 1959). The psychoeducational perspective addresses issues of motivation, meaning and management by providing a person-centred context for relating to all children, including those who present social, emotional and behavioural difficulties. Consequently, the focus is on understanding troubled children as individuals rather than thinking of them according to diagnostic labels that typically emphasize their disabilities and say little about their capabilities. The teacher's objectives are to help children identify their patterns of learning, to build on their strengths and to overcome, or at least cope with, any limitations in their functioning. Although the classroom and therapy session are different venues, and the teacher works differently with students than the clinician does with patients, ultimately they share the same goal: to help children maximize and achieve their potential.

The psychoeducational approach builds upon knowledge from the study of human growth and development, mental health, group dynamics, learning theory and assessment and evaluation and applies that knowledge to learning and behavioural issues. A basic premise is that effective teachers need to draw continually upon a depth of professional knowledge and diversity of skills, as well as from their personal beliefs and values, in a reciprocal-interactive manner, when making the countless educational decisions that characterize the school day. The model has a problem-solving orientation that focuses on teachers learning to become analytic, creative, reflective and flexible, as they attempt to understand and respond to children, instead of being trained to use a set of techniques with little or no regard for the situation or the individual.

The psychoeducational framework is based on the concept that there are reasons underlying children's behaviour which can best be understood in the context of their particular environments and the feelings those conditions elicit. As Knoblock (1983) states, 'Our goal is to understand the many complex ways children interact with their environmental forces, including the significant persons inhabiting that world particularly parents and teachers' (p. 107). As with all of us, teachers' identities – their ways of thinking, feeling and being – are actively constructed over their lifetimes through communications with others and their behaviours, in turn, influence the actions of those around them. The students with whom teachers work develop in the same ways. Significant contributions to the psycho-educational field of study, which had begun before the twentieth century, continue to influence educational practice today. In what follows, much has been drawn from more contemporary sources in the professional literature, such as Kounin (1970), Long *et al.* (1980) and Good and Brophy (1994), to name only a few, as well as from student and collegial communications. Several other major contributors are identified in the continuing text. The illustrative examples are taken from my experiences as a teacher, college professor and psychotherapist with children and adults.

Psychoeducational principles

Ainsworth and Bowlby's (1991) classic studies of attachment have repeatedly shown that children who find a trusting, nurturing, consistent, emotional connection to an adult are more likely to feel secure, develop positive relationships with others and be willing to explore the world around them. In his synthesis of recent research to identify specific teacher behaviours which contribute to student achievement, Stronge (2002) finds that effective classroom communication, learning and management strategies often result from positive teacher attitudes and constructive teacher–student relationships. Ginott (1972) described the importance of the teacher's role in this way:

> I have come to a frightening conclusion. I am the decisive element in the classroom. It is my personal approach that creates the climate. It is my daily mood that makes the weather. As a teacher I possess tremendous power to make a child's life miserable or joyous. I can be a tool of torture or an instrument of inspiration. I can humiliate or humour, hurt or heal. In all situations it is my response that decides whether a crisis will be escalated or de-escalated, and a child humanized or dehumanized'. (p. 15)

Many of the children who challenge us in the classroom bring unresolved problems from home. Of course, teachers are not responsible for what happens in the child's home, nor are teachers trained to be therapists. However, a psychoeducational classroom can be quite therapeutic. Children can find the classroom to be a 'corrective emotional experience' (Alexander and French, 1946). This means that the teacher and the present environment do not reproduce past experiences that, in too many cases, have been so destructive but, instead, offer productive opportunities for children's learning and personal development.

Parents and teachers are constantly required to respond to children's social behaviour. The psychoeducational model bases making decisions about strategies on important assumptions. Dreikurs (1968) suggests that among these are that social behaviour is goal directed. Most of us want to feel significant, to belong and to be important to others. Whether or not we are successful, we behave in ways aimed at feeling valuable to others. At the very least, we act defensively to safeguard against losing the sense of importance that we already possess. Therefore, if we help children to achieve these goals, we are likely to prevent much misbehaviour.

The same behaviour can have many different causes, while the same cause can be expressed in various forms of behaviour. For example, stealing may be caused by physical need, revenge, group status or impulsivity, while feelings of rejection may result in withdrawal, aggression or refusal to learn. Therefore, the psycho-educational approach urges teachers to attempt to understand the cause of misbehaviour before deciding on a remedy. While stealing is never acceptable, children who steal because they are hungry need to be treated differently from children who steal to achieve a position in a street gang or to revenge themselves on a sibling preferred by their family.

Children frequently misbehave out of a sense of frustration and discouragement. When children are unsure of their value to others, and insecure in their ability to gain importance in socially acceptable ways, they may resort to negative behaviour to make themselves feel important.

Carl, a 9-year-old boy, uses such a self-protective strategy with his third grade classmates. Abandoned by his parents as a baby and then repeatedly placed in temporary foster care, Carl is described by his teacher as a marginal academic student, impulsive and of low social standing in the classroom. Referred for special education services, psychological projective tests reveal that Carl yearns for caring and stability in his life, yet feels powerless to become the well-thought-of child that others would desire. The boy avoids tasks that are threatening to his fragile feelings of self-esteem and shows limited tolerance of any perceived failure, his own or others'. For example, during a difficult mathematics test that required him to make many corrections, Carl tore up his paper after rubbing a hole in it with his eraser. He has refused to take any tests since that time. Carl has also become very competitive with Robbie, another student, whom he humiliates when that boy makes mistakes. As Robbie begins to cry, Carl seems pleased when the class laughs derisively at 'the loser'. This further stimulates Carl to provoke the boy to lose control. Through misbehaviour, Carl is trying to avoid the feelings of falling to even less significant status. Therefore, behavioural interventions that deal with the underlying frustration and discouragement are more likely to have lasting effects. Those strategies aimed at eliminating surface misbehaviour may be temporarily effective at suppressing that behaviour but may not address the deeper issues.

Children who continually misbehave have often learned to associate adult intervention with adult rejection, rather than with caring and concern. Children need to learn that teachers are there to protect them as much as possible; but that all behaviour has consequences and children must take responsibility for their actions. Preferred consequences are those that arise naturally from our experiences. However, rules are necessary for groups to function together and when teachers set appropriate behavioural limits as children's needs require, it is a form of caring, not rejection. To use an obvious example, adults would not allow a toddler to suffer the natural consequences of crossing a busy street alone until the child has the cognitive capabilities to make that judgement. The downside risk is too great. Instead, in order to help the child to learn, we would act quickly and decisively. In this context, providing a 'time out' to allow an angry child to cool off, or intervening physically to stop children from hurting themselves or others, is considered to be helpful, not punitive.

Psychoeducational practice: communication with children

The psychoeducational approach emphasizes creating an accepting classroom environment that fosters students' abilities to develop their interpersonal and intrapersonal skills as well as their intellectual abilities. Based on Gardner's (1993) theory that children have 'multiple intelligences' for teachers to build upon, Armstrong (2000) describes the interpersonal domain as 'The ability to perceive and make distinctions in the moods, intentions, motivations and feelings of other people'. He defines the intrapersonal realm as 'Self-knowledge and the ability to act adaptively on the basis of that knowledge' (p. 3). While school is a place where academic skills are taught, children's 'emotional literacy' typically is addressed as part of the learning process as well (Bocchino, 1999).

Learning to become aware of self and others is expected to lead to children's ability to express their needs and to make more sensible and sensitive behavioural choices. Rogers (1979) postulates that teachers facilitate children's social and emotional learning by communicating attitudes of realness, acceptance and empathic understanding. Realness means that teachers are aware of their feelings, understand that they are entitled to the feelings, can choose to act on those feelings and can communicate the feelings to others if appropriate. When teachers' behaviour corresponds to their feelings, they would be described as 'authentic'. Rogers believes that this quality of realness makes the teacher a desirable person with whom others can identify and relate to in a positive, trusting manner. Authentic teachers say what they mean and mean what they say.

Acceptance means that teachers see the student as a valuable person, worthy of care and understanding. Students are respected as persons doing the best that they can at the current time and place. Through the attitude of acceptance, the teacher communicates confidence in the ability and potential of the student. A teacher's comment such as 'You worked hard on that project, and I admire your effort' may well engender feelings of self-esteem and basic trust in the student. Teachers who prize students are likely to be valued and trusted in return.

Empathic understanding is the teachers' ability to see life from the student's point of view. Sympathy means to feel sorry for another; empathy is defined as sensitive, non-judgemental awareness of another's feelings. When empathic expressions occur in the classroom, students sense that the teacher actually understands what they are thinking and feeling. Consequently, the attitudinal quality of the relationship between teachers and students creates conditions for significant learning to take place.

The importance of the teacher's ability to effectively communicate with children is illustrated in the following example and commentary. At her request, I was consulting with Mrs Smith, a new teacher, who was a New York University graduate student in my course, where we were studying children with special social and emotional needs. She wanted my help to learn how to work more skilfully with Chris, an aggressive student in frequent conflict with other children in her fourth grade class. As an undergraduate preparing to become a teacher, Mrs Smith had been trained primarily in Skinner's (1972) behaviourist techniques for changing students' conduct primarily through reinforcement and punishment. These interventions corrected some behaviours by focusing on their immediate consequences but had limited effect upon problems that seemed more rooted in the child's personality. Thus far, Chris had frustrated her efforts. The teacher wanted to learn to use more preventive, proactive social strategies.

Each consultation session began with my observing Mrs Smith in action with her class. Afterwards, we met to reflect on her decision-making skills with Chris and to discuss her effectiveness in implementing the psychoeducational theories we were discussing during my seminars.

The last of my weekly planned observations took place towards the end of 'choice time', when students opt to work independently on activities at learning centres situated around the classroom. Chris can be heard arguing with Jose, another student, about taking turns at the newest of the three computers in the computer centre. Apparently Jose has been occupied at that computer and is unwilling to give up his seat. As Chris becomes more agitated, he begins to pull at Jose's chair. Other students are being distracted by the growing tension between the boys. Mrs Smith, who is with a group in the library area, looks up and says: 'Chris, I see that you are getting angry at Jose.' 'No I'm not,' Chris replies defensively and in a challenging way. 'How do you know?' 'Because you're starting to yell at him,' the teacher responds. 'I'm worried that you two will get into a fight and that someone may get hurt. I don't want that to happen, so please come over here and tell me what's going on. Jose, I'll talk to you later.' With these words, the teacher separated the quarrelling students and provided everyone with time to think and assess the situation before deciding on what steps to take next. Gordon (1974) would describe Mrs Smith's approach as an example of the 'No-Lose Method' of conflict resolution in which the goal is to empower students to become more thoughtful before taking action. He advocates the teacher using 'I-messages' when communicating with children. In this type of exchange, the teacher's language: (1) addresses her concerns about the students' behaviour, not their character; (2) presents the problem in terms of its effect upon her; and (3) describes her feelings about the situation.

As she frames the problem in such a manner, Mrs Smith helps Chris to understand that his actions may have unforeseen, unintentional consequences. By the teacher's addressing the effects of his behaviour on herself, rather than judging and blaming Chris in a negative way, the student is less likely to be angry and defensive. Thus his behaviour is more likely to be reflective rather than reactive.

Describing a similar point of view, Ginott (1972) advocates 'congruent communication' in which 'teacher talk' is most effective when addressed to solving the problem, not attacking the student's personality. When confronted with a student's undesirable behaviour, Ginott advises teachers to: (1) describe what they see; (2) describe what they feel; and (3) describe what needs to be done. Based on the writings of both Ginott and Gordon, the following recommendations for effective teacher communication strategies would apply to Chris's situation:

1. Convey respect for students' ideas and feelings in ways that increase self-worth and self-esteem. After listening to Chris's view of the situation, which was to blame Jose entirely for the quarrel, the teacher said, 'I can understand that you got upset because you felt Jose was not sharing the computer with you.'

2. Support students with appreciative praise of their behaviour because it is productive; avoid criticisms of students as persons because it is destructive. Mrs Smith then said to Chris, 'From what you say, it seems that there was a problem about taking turns and I'm glad that you used words to tell Jose how angry you were. Pulling on his chair is dangerous and I can't allow that.' In this way, she communicated disapproval of the student's behaviour but did not ridicule his character. Rogers (1957) describes this as providing 'unconditional positive regard' for the student. The teacher didn't say, 'You've got to be stupid to fight over a computer. You should be ashamed!'

3. Observe the effects of your words on the students. Try to be brief, avoid lecturing and nagging, which are not motivating. The teacher didn't say, 'Chris, I've told you again and again to stop, but you never listen. How many times will I have to remind you?'

4. Avoid disabling diagnosis and prognosis that could result in harmful labelling of the student. The teacher didn't say, 'Chris, if you keep arguing with Jose, the other kids will think you're crazy and no one will want to work with you.'

5. Avoid sarcastic comments that are likely to provoke resentment and invite resistance. The teacher didn't say, 'Chris, stop complaining like a baby. I've seen you hog the computer plenty of times. Grow up!'

6. Resist providing students with solutions, take time to

give students the guidance needed to solve their own problem. Following her talk alone with Chris, the teacher calls both children to her desk. She says: 'Boys, if you get into a fight, you'll end up losing your computer privileges. How else could you handle this?' Mrs Smith spoke in a manner that encouraged their independent decision-making.

'He started it,' said Jose. 'There was another computer open.'

'You took up all the time on the good computer!' Chris responded quickly.

'You came too soon ... besides, I didn't know you were waiting,' retorted Jose.

The teacher replied: 'Hold it, boys! I know that you're still upset, but we want to solve this problem before it happens again. I have faith in you. Take some time and think about it. Go back to your seats and I'll meet you again in five minutes.'

Promptly, five minutes later, the teacher gathered the students back at the computer centre. Chris and Jose resumed the discussion in a more subdued manner.

'I don't want to lose computer time,' begins Chris, looking directly at Mrs Smith.

'Me, neither,' Jose follows quickly.

'Me, neither,' says the teacher, grinning. 'I don't want you to lose computer time, either.' Both boys smile. 'So now that we all agree, what do we do about it?' she asks.

Addressing his teacher, Chris begins again, 'You told us that we could have 15 minutes at a time on a computer. Jose's time was up! How come we don't have to keep a record of when our time is?'

Slightly embarrassed, Mrs Smith replies, 'That's a great idea. I'm sorry that I didn't think of it myself. So you're saying that we should have a schedule where we sign in and out of our time on the computer. What do you think, Jose?'

'Good, and we should have a waiting list so we know whose turn is next,' Jose continues.

'Yeah,' says Chris, looking and nodding vigorously at Jose. 'Another good idea, boys! How about you two designing a possible form and then presenting the ideas to the whole class. What do you say?'

'OK!' The boys 'high-five' each other, slapping each other's right hand above their heads, as a congratulatory signal.

'OK,' says the teacher approvingly. 'When?'

'How about when we come back from lunch,' says Chris.

'Good time for me,' responds Jose.

'Nice work, boys. I look forward to seeing what you come up with,' ends Mrs Smith.

Talking and walking closely together, Chris and Jose return to their seat. During the latter interchanges, the teacher illustrated the communication strategies known as 'active listening' and humour. Active listening is a process where teachers listen carefully to students and then feed back the message in an attempt to show that they understand what students are trying to say. This is a way of operationalizing the concept of acceptance. Humour is a way of relating to others that can be used to ease tension in an anxiety-producing situation, or to make a student aware of a minor misbehaviour. As exemplified by Mrs Smith, humour should be friendly, not cruel or sarcastic.

Ultimately, the goals of effective psychoeducational communications are to enhance the child's ability to learn and perform, to develop confidence and to take the initiative. From her skilfulness during my observation, Mrs Smith was rapidly improving her practice.

Talking with the troubling child

The psychoeducational approach may help children who act up physically or act out their feelings in forms of anger and defiance. Handling children's anger can be confusing, draining and distressing for adults. In fact one of the major problems in dealing with anger in children is how we deal with the angry feelings that are often stirred up in us. Many of us need to remind ourselves that we were not always taught how to deal with anger as a fact of life during our own childhood. Often we were led to believe that to be angry was to be bad and we were made to feel guilty for expressing anger (Ginott, 1965). As an example, I ask my university education students to reflect on an experience that was important in their decision to become teachers. One student remembered when, as a 7-year-old recent Hispanic immigrant, he was driven by a special bus to integrate into a public school in a socio-economic upper-middle-class community. Starting as a second grader, my student had yelled loudly in Spanish at a classmate who had borrowed and broken his only pencil so that it was unusable. As punishment for his outburst, the teacher called his mother to school and humiliated them both by blaming his 'inexcusable' misbehaviour on his 'family upbringing'. His mother had burst into tears of embarrassment. The memory of that teacher's words, accompanied by his feelings of hurt, anger and responsibility, still remained with him. He said to my class, 'Miss Jones taught me what a teacher shouldn't be. I'll never do that to kids.' Strong feelings cannot be denied, and angry outbursts should not always be viewed as a sign of serious problems; they should be recognized and treated with respect.

While all behaviour has its consequences, in dealing with angry children our actions should be motivated by the need to protect and teach, rather than by a desire to punish. Our goal is not to repress or destroy angry feelings in children, or in ourselves, but rather to accept the feelings and to help channel and direct them towards constructive ends. To respond effectively to overly aggressive behaviour in children, we need to have some ideas about what may trigger an outburst and try to identify the goals of the misbehaviour (Dreikurs, 1968). Anger may be a defensive way to avoid painful feelings; it may be associated with failure, low self-esteem and feelings of isolation; or it may be related to anxiety about situations over which the child has no control.

Defiance may also be associated with feelings of dependency, or may be associated with sadness and depression. For example, I have worked with a pre-adolescent boy who was in therapy with me for six months when, just before the summer, he called me a 'stupid jerk'. He said that he was leaving and never coming back. This outburst was unexpected since we seemed to enjoy working together. Though caught off guard, I tried to respond non-defensively that, while certainly capable of acting in a way that seemed stupid, I wondered what I had done to cause the reaction on that day? As we talked, what emerged was his anger at my leaving for a month's holiday and his fears that I would never return, just like his father who had abandoned him. He seemed to think that by taking an aggressive position and leaving me first, he could avoid the sadness and depression which came from being a passive victim of his father's decision. To protect against further hurt, he was doing to me what had been done to him.

Fritz Redl (1959) developed the 'life space interview' as a communication approach that may prove helpful to aggressive students in the classroom. Comparable to problem-solving strategies described earlier, Redl advises the teacher to talk with children in an uncritical, open-ended manner while keeping focused on the immediate issues. He recommends that the teacher help the student to conceptualize and articulate the current problem, to discuss the problem in close physical proximity to the location where it occurred, to reach some form of closure to the problem and to agree upon a course of action which would be put into practice and subsequently evaluated for possible revision.

Expanding the ideas previously discussed, Redl and Wineman (1957) suggest providing students with opportunities to express themselves and their feelings through the academic curriculum. For example, a tragic fire in an apartment can become the basis for a general classroom discussion on the value of life and the inevitability of death; having a pet in the classroom can focus on the need for care and the role of the 'caretaker' in a dependency relationship. Similarly, reading a book to the class about an immigrant family can stimulate discussion about being a newcomer, help the children explore their own family roots and help children from other cultures feel that they are valuable members of their new community. This strategy is known as 'bibliotherapy' (Ouzts, 1991).

Use encouragement to foster self-acceptance and trust in others. Children need to learn that we're not going to give up on them. We want to help children realize that it is all right to be themselves even if they are different from everyone else. Individual differences should be celebrated, not minimized or ridiculed. The teacher can encourage the class to look at the many sides of issues, allowing them to share opinions and information. When students see that their thoughts count it engenders feelings of importance and power. Both of these feelings are vital for human growth and development.

Try to respond appropriately when under stress. Teachers who remain in control of their feelings and behaviour provide an example from which the children can learn. Children identify with and imitate significant adults in their lives. Teachers who are respectful, organized and accepting of individual differences and opinions foster similar feelings and behaviour in their students. When teachers display calm and control they provide children with a feeling of safety. When children feel safe they can accept interventions that change their perceptions, feelings and subsequent behaviours.

The teacher as a person: the importance of self-awareness

Clearly a large part of psychoeducational teaching effectiveness depends on the professional qualities of the teacher. However, how teachers develop as persons is often inseparable from the choices they make in the classroom. Past and present merge in the decisions that we make; yesterday's beliefs and experiences shape today's expectations and behaviour. Therefore, I'd like to use a personal perspective from my own history to illustrate a significant problem that often interferes with the ability of teachers and children to relate appropriately to each other. My past experiences as a new teacher make clear the concept known in the psychodynamic literature as 'transference' as it applies to classroom life (Weiss, 2002).

I began my career as a teacher with no formal training for the job. I had graduated from college with a liberal arts psychology degree and faced being drafted into the armed services. Since the New York City Board of Education was then (as now) having difficulty finding qualified teachers, I learned that I could maintain my student deferment by becoming a teacher in what is referred to in education jargon as a 'hard to staff inner city public school with substantial minority student enrolment'. Thus I was able to receive an emergency teaching credential because public schools located in the Harlem section of Manhattan desperately needed anybody (better said as any 'body'), to teach 36 undisciplined third grade African-American and Hispanic boys, all of whom had been 'left back' the previous year. Some children carried informal labels, such as 'nuts' and 'retard', but no official diagnostic evaluations had ever been done.

I had never taken a course in education. The only qualification required to teach these boys seemed to be my physical strength and athletic ability. Although I had attended a New York City public elementary school, my experience was as a child who learned to read in kindergarten, had been promoted directly from first grade to third grade because of intellectual ability as measured on standardized tests, was expected to wear a white shirt and tie for school-wide assemblies on Friday or face the principal's wrath, and had obediently learned to raise my hand to be recognized before speaking. I had little understanding of my students' socio-cultural environment, having myself been raised in a lower-middle-class, Eastern European family living in a primarily white neighbourhood.

When I began teaching I assumed that children should and would learn directly from teachers, just as I was supposed to have done as a child. My image of good teachers, as presented to me by my family's values, was that teachers were fountains of knowledge and paragons of virtue whose word was law. Therefore, in my adult view at that time, a good teacher told students what to do and they would obey without question. Consequently, when the children didn't listen and didn't learn what the school administration told me that they should know, it meant that I was a failure. This devastated me. Within a brief time after arriving, I agreed with the boy in my class who wrote in his notebook, 'School Stinks'.

Although I am focusing on my history of minimal preparation for the job, all teachers bring their particular background of professional knowledge and skills with them to the classroom, and these qualities shape their decision making. Although less discussed in the education literature, but at least equally important, our judgements about how to teach and relate to children are also influenced by our personal experiences as children with teachers, as children with other children, and as adults with children. This highlights the concept known by psychotherapists as 'transference'. Transference means that we project our attitudes and beliefs from the past on to present situations, which may cause a distortion in the way we view our current interactions and relationships. Thus I transferred attitudes based on remembrances of my own childhood learning experiences to my work as a teacher. I did to the students what had been done to me in elementary school. This was not what they needed.

To complicate matters, children also bring their personal life stories, filled with experiences, memories, beliefs and feelings into every classroom situation and transfer them to the teacher. By the time the children in my class reached third grade they had had many experiences with failure in a school that was not a place of physical safety or emotional security for them. Teachers had already labelled them negatively and often inappropriately. When I arrived and started teaching in the fifth week of the autumn term, four teachers had already come and gone from the children's classroom and thus from their lives. Understandably, the children felt that teachers were not to be trusted and transferred those feelings on to me. Since I did not possess the skills to help them learn, I was perceived as just another adult who made them feel inadequate and, therefore, damaged their self-esteem. Thus their transference was reinforced.

The climate in my classroom when I began teaching could already have been described as a war zone, where learning activities were viewed as a series of power struggles. It got progressively worse after

I started. I viewed the children as opponents rather than partners in the learning process. When the children did not meet my standards or benefit from my strategies, I assumed that they were being 'bad' or 'dumb' rather than examining whether they, or I, had the skills and knowledge required to become successful. When the children failed a test or had social behaviour problems my reaction was to label or punish them rather than question my assumptions about teaching. This is an approach that has been called 'blaming the victim'. What I did not understand then was that the children saw *me* as the enemy! When the activities I presented did not help the children to learn, *they* felt like losers. Conversely, they could gain some power by making me feel the way they did: worthless. In that they were immensely successful. I came close to quitting several times. I felt alone, in a 'sink or swim' position, without knowledge and skills to guide my practice and without anyone to help me think about my behaviour. In my frustration, I went back to my own elementary school and talked with Mrs Reick, my trusted fifth grade teacher, who stood out favourably among all my other teachers as I grew up. At my request, she understandingly shared her own trials and tribulations as a beginning teacher that I had never known as a child in her class. She also sensitively reminded me of the time I had been caught cheating on a spelling test. Instead of sending me to the principal's office, we talked about how my parents' divorce was affecting my studies and how fearful I was about doing poorly in school. Knowing how much I enjoyed athletics, Mrs Reick encouraged me to come to class early, at the time when she arrived with the morning newspaper, and to use the sports section to focus on learning to spell the names of my favourite baseball players. I got pleasure from the activity and my spelling improved overall.

I recognized then why Mrs Reick had become my favourite teacher. She formed a caring connection with me emotionally and cognitively. She treated me as a whole person with strengths and limitations. She taught by building on my interest in sports as intrinsic motivation to learn, rather than by trying to change my behaviour through the punishment of removing gratifying physical education activities from my school schedule.

It was as if a light bulb went off in my head after my visit to Mrs Reick. Her reflections led me to try to become more aware of my students' reasons for behaving as they did. Rather than depriving the boys of the gymnasium as punishment for misbehaviour, I used our mutual pleasure in athletics to learn to relate to them more effectively. We studied the New York Yankees baseball team as a vehicle for learning reading, mathematics and history. We wrote fan letters to our favourite players. The excitement and enthusiasm grew when the players sent us pictures and letters in return. It was not always fun; frustration on all our parts was common. However, I learned important lessons from my work with the children that continue to inform me as an instructor with adults: a good teacher is willing to learn and to change, and our students are often the best teachers of what we need to know.

Regrettably, scenarios such as the example of my own early teaching days are being played out with unfortunate students even as I write today. While not everyone may be able to seek advice from a favourite teacher or mentor, or have a psychotherapist to consult, what I have learned over the years is that effective teachers learn to subject themselves and their work to regular thought and analysis, both their own and their colleagues'. We call this becoming a 'reflective practitioner'. It is through a regenerative process of: (1) thoughtful planning of decisions ahead of taking action; (2) honest self-observation and decision-making during the course of our actions; and then (3) analysing, evaluating and rethinking our behaviour and feelings after taking action, that we learn how to refine our skills and what more we need to know (Schön, 1983).

Understanding and applying the concept of transference is critical for teachers to use effectively the psychoeducational techniques described in this chapter. Everyone acts automatically and unconsciously, based upon assumptions growing out of past experiences. Transference issues are ubiquitous. Over time, those automatic behaviours become ingrained into ourselves. If we become self-aware and understand how concepts such as transference influence our ways of viewing the world, then habits, even unconsciously, can support our creativity as well as efficiency and can be productive. On the other hand, to the extent that we as teachers make assumptions without self-awareness and fail to consider the needs of individual children or the different ways in which learning and behaviour take place, then our teaching habits risk becoming rigid and harsh and can interfere with our effectiveness in communicating with students.

A commonly held belief has it that 'experience is the best teacher'. That adage is true only if we are in the position of being good learners. From the psychoeducational perspective, being a caring and capable teacher means being a constant learner who strives to be self-aware, as well as open to new knowledge and new ideas, and who works at this with open-minded colleagues.

CHAPTER 20

Promoting emotional literacy: Its implications for school and classroom practice

Adrian Faupel

Emotional literacy is a candyfloss concept. It looks and tastes very sweet, occupies a lot of space but maybe is without much real substance. It is the product of a lot of hot air – and yet it is also a symbol for happy, sometimes nostalgic, childhood and holiday times. Despite that, I am proudly part of a Southampton LEA which was the first and is still one of the few LAs in the UK to have emotional literacy as one of its top three educational priorities, consciously linked to issues of inclusion and equal opportunity.

It is perhaps important to stress at the outset that emotional literacy is not a 'new' concept, though its formulation may be expressed in new language. We describe it in terms of skills and competences that are underpinned by a set of ethical and moral values. An emotionally literate person is one who can:

- *recognize* one's own emotions and the emotions of others;
- *understand* one's own and others' emotions;
- *handle* one's emotions to develop and maintain wholesome relationships;
- *appropriately express* emotions.

Daniel Goleman, who popularized the concept of emotional intelligence (1996), suggests five essential dimensions to emotional literacy: self-awareness, self-regulation, motivation, empathy and social skills. It is, as we will see, quite meaningful to describe not only individuals (pupils and teachers) as being more or less emotionally literate, but also classrooms, schools and LAs.

Cutting through the floss to get to the candy, the significance of emotional literacy is that it reflects a concern that schooling has fundamentally lost its way. Traditionally, we have distinguished between the head (thinking), the heart (feelings) and behaviour (actions). It seems we have lost sight of that essential human wholeness in embracing a narrow view of what education (schooling) is all about, focusing exclusively on academic and behavioural aspects of human development. Schools, the major instrument of education, are measured, weighed and therefore valued almost wholly in terms of academic outputs: SATs, GCSEs and A levels. A poor second comes behaviour – but the outcomes here are crude, easily observed measures such as attendance and exclusions. There is some lip-service in the present government to other issues but, until recently, little evidence of action but see, for example, the impressive SEAL (Social and Emotional Aspects of Learning) curriculum recently made available to all primary schools in England and an improved framework for Ofsted inspections. If this emphasis on academic and behavioural outcomes were simply being imposed upon an unwilling populace that would be bad enough – the real problem, and possibly the cause of governmental lack of courage, is that these policies substantially reflect the view of the majority of 'Middle England'. It is, of course, absolutely correct that we should be concerned about 'raising standards', but the real issue is *what* standards? The primary focus of schools is for teachers to teach and pupils to learn – but teach what, learn what?

Emotional literacy is about recognizing the crucial importance of that third 'dimension' of human development – the feeling or affective aspects of our being. There are cogent arguments to suggest that physically, psychologically, socially and economically it may be the most important dimension of all (Salovey and Sluyter, 1997; Damasio, 2000). To neglect it, to ignore it, to demean it as being pinky leftish 'psychobabble' may be turning us into a herd of Gadarene swine heading for disaster.

For emotions are about survival (LeDoux, 1998). Physiologically, they relate to a very important part of our brains (called the limbic system) which we share with our evolutionary ancestors; hence that part of our brain is sometimes called the 'Reptilian' brain. To survive, those organisms had to be able to sense danger or threat and deal with it. Fundamentally, a hard-wired system led to three possible 'automatic' responses when threat was sensed: to fight, to flee or to freeze (play dead). To survive, the species also had to reproduce, so similarly there were hard-wired automatic responses to sensed opportunities for sexual activity.

We still have vestiges of these fundamentally important biological systems, except that now our brains have developed powers of reason, planning, problem solving, language, etc., using structures in the neocortex. Emotions are concerned about the here and now immediate responses: they push or pull us into action into doing something *now*. Rationality (problem solving) is interested not just in the pulls and pushes of the now, but in the longer-term consequences, weighing up pros and cons, considering alternatives and acting on the basis of the best bet. There is tension but not contradiction between emotion and rationality – but, because emotion involves physiological arousal, it can easily hijack reason and take over. The more physiologically aroused we are, the harder it is to be 'rational', to take the longer-term view. We have to *learn* to regulate our emotions, that is, to rule them in the sense of using them to achieve our longer-term objectives. It can be argued that achieving this balance between reason and emotion is *the* task of the human being. If true, it becomes, therefore, an essential task of schooling and yet it does not seem to figure prominently alongside literacy and numeracy and all the other subjects that we teach in school. What is being advocated in the Southampton LAs' focus on emotional literacy as a priority target is a new balance between thinking, feeling and behaviour. To achieve this balance a shift in the emphasis and understanding of the purposes of education is required.

There is a long tradition in human thinking and practice that what distinguishes us from the rest of nature is our drive to community. Maslow (1987) recognized that we share fundamental needs with lower organisms and higher primates – the need for food, shelter, warmth, safety, etc., and any threat to these will trigger 'emotional' responses. But he went further to suggest that we have higher needs of belonging, self-esteem and self-actualization. These are our specifically human needs and any threat to these has the same significance as a physical attack on us. We respond with similar physiological and psychological 'survival' mechanisms – physiological arousal preparing us for violent action accompanied by subjective feelings of anxiety (flight), and anger (fight) and depression (playing dead). The need to belong – longing to be – is essentially bound up with our individual and collective survival.

This need to feel that we play a significant part in our immediate and wider human environment can be summed up in the need for *community*. Community is an interesting word. It derives from the Latin, *com* meaning 'with' and *unit* meaning 'one'. Community is therefore essentially about *becoming one with*. It is the ethical, moral and philosophical basis of inclusion where each individual is recognized as having a dignity and value not dependent on what the individual does, achieves, looks like, believes, but simply because he or she exists as a human being. We seriously question, for example, whether the current emphasis on academic standards in a competitive ethos of examination results and league tables is not giving an anti-inclusive message to young people that worth and value depend on what a person can do, on the standards that they achieve. That seems to be the antithesis of community and fundamentally violates a principle of inclusion, namely that human worth does not depend on what we do but on the fact that we are!

Becoming one with other people involves a giving and receiving – a sharing – on a basis of a fundamental equality of value and worth. Community can only be achieved by 'communication'. It is the development of language, the only way we establish and maintain communication; it is what appears to be specifically human.

Communication is, itself, essentially a sharing, a two-way process of dialogue, conversation (turning towards each other), a speaking and a listening. It is, as is a sense of belonging itself, something we first of all *receive*: we enter the human community not by first learning to speak but by being listened to. It is our parents who communicate our fundamental value, worth and dignity to us by listening intently to what we as newborn infants are trying to communicate, what our needs are. Being listened to is how we psychologically develop that sense of value and it is the only valid passport to the human community. It is something given to us and not earned. Not being listened to is the most fundamental attack and threat to our psychological survival. It triggers all the emotional consequences of anger, of anxiety or depression. Not being listened to by our parents or significant others, including teachers, is emotional ab*use*, in other words, where people are used as though they were things. Not listening to people is to demean them: to deny them meaning, significance or belonging.

If the longing for community, for belonging, is our basic human need, it is also our basic human task. If education is about helping people to develop all aspects of their humanity (their potential), it would appear that teaching young people the values, skills and competences for establishing and maintaining community must be at the very heart of what schools are about. We all personally have to learn how to maintain, preserve and enhance our own sense of unique value, worth, lovableness and, at the same time, maintain, preserve and enhance the dignity and worth of other people. This is no easy task but it is crucial to our individual survival and the survival of our species.

Emotional literacy focuses precisely on these issues. It deals with those values, skills and competences that are essential to maintain our own and others' sense of belonging, dignity and value and our place in the human community. Emotional literacy is not therefore an optional extra, tagged on to an already overcrowded curriculum. All the rest of the curriculum, our literacy and numeracy, our science and technology, our geography and history only have significance as a means of promoting our own access to the human community and as tools for advancing its welfare. Knowledge, science and technology can be used to promote or destroy human community. Which of these rather important consequences they lead to will depend crucially on how emotionally literate we are and our children become.

Emotional literacy in the Southampton LA had its origins in its commitment to inclusion. The reduction of exclusions and particularly permanent exclusions became the first, pragmatic task to operationalize this commitment. In four years, schools reduced the number of permanent exclusions from 123 to 21. This 'concerted effort to tackle behaviour problems and drive down exclusions has been spectacularly successful, if not without pain for schools' (Ofsted, 2001). It is to the credit of the Southampton Psychology Service, then led by Peter Sharp, that the 'bad' behaviour which is the trigger for exclusions was construed as primarily emotional (angry) in origin (Faupel *et al.*, 1998). One of the main interventions to reduce exclusions was to focus on those pupils at risk by offering small anger management groups (typically for six to eight pupils over six to eight weeks) delivered by the psychology service alongside teachers. Well over 100 of such groups together with social skills and self-esteem variations have been running with direct educational psychologist involvement and using cascade principles, now increasingly being run by teachers and emotional literary support assistants (ELSAs).

Anger management groups for pupils at risk was a pragmatic response to a symbolic antithesis of inclusion, namely permanent exclusions. Before any such groups were run in the school, a precondition was that there should be at least a twilight session, and more usually a half-day in-service training for all staff, teaching and non-teaching. This was an attempt to ensure that the problem of angry pupils was not construed as being their problem alone.

When people do not belong, or feel as though they do not belong, they behave badly. A basic tenet of emotional literacy is that poor behaviour is an attempt by the individual or groups who are behaving badly fundamentally to try to meet legitimate needs. Such needs include the need for attention, for stimulation and variety, for resources, for choice. The ends, or functions, of most bad behaviour are usually good: it is the strategies, the methods used to try to achieve these ends, that are usually bad. This is primarily because alternative prosocial ways are not psychologically available to the person due to lack of understanding or relevant skills. This is a very non-judgemental stance in the face of serious behaviour problems and leads to a teaching response rather than punitive attempts to control deviant behaviour. (Incidentally, a great threat to a sense of belonging are judgemental condemnations of the *person* rather than *behaviour*.) Such behaviours are now seen as attempts to fulfil legitimate needs. Only when a person has a choice of alternative responses do we have a chance of developing 'responsibility'. Responsibility exists only when there is a choice of more than one behaviour available. Such choices are made available by teaching and not by punishing (or rewarding for that matter).

However, even given all the above, there is a strong tendency in the face of bad behaviour to pathologize the individual. Such pathologizing again is the antithesis of genuine inclusion. We have seen this in a number of circumstances, including, for example, bullying where, consciously or unconsciously, we blame the victim and subtly give the message to the bullied child that it is he or she who needs to change by being less provocative, more assertive, etc.

An allegory, which I am entitling 'Lessons from Southampton', reminds us that, by focusing on the responsibility of individual pupils and their lack of skills and competences, we may be missing the point.

The loss of the *Titanic* was to Southampton what the destruction of the Twin Towers has been to New York. That is not an exaggeration. It is said that there was not a street in Southampton nor a family which did not have a relative who went down with the *Titanic*. The ship sailed from Southampton, its home port. A number of the officers lived in Southampton, as did nearly all the engineers and the stewards, cleaners, etc. When the *Titanic* struck the iceberg at 11.40 on the evening of Sunday 15 April, there were 2,208 passengers and crew on board. Only 711, less than a third, survived and almost 1,500 people were lost. But this was an accident – in an accident one might think that people had an equal chance of surviving, but that simply was not the case.

Women and children had much higher rates of survival (74 and 52 per cent respectively) than men (only 20 per cent). Even though an unforeseen accident, these figures reflect human decisions and the commitment on the part of men that women and children should be treated preferentially. That is where the good news ends. When we look at social class, nearly 63 per cent of first-class passengers survived, 41 per cent of second class and only 25 per cent of the third class. As with practically everything else we can measure (longevity, rates of health, housing and educational outcomes), those who *have* (in terms of wealth and access to resources) do better than those who have less. The *Titanic* disaster was no different. The news gets even worse when we look at who among the crew survived. Two out of every three of the deck crew survived. These were the officer class. Compare that with the 22 per cent of the engineers, which is understandable in view of the location of their job, and with the group that suffered most grievously and included by far the largest number of people (nearly 500), who belonged to what were known as the Victualling Department – the unskilled stewards, waiters and cleaners (most of them from Southampton). Less than 20 per cent (one in five) survived. There are clearly human factors at work in the grossly unequal chances of survival based upon class differences. It is quite clear that the *Titanic* was not a very inclusive society!

What might have made a difference in the distribution of who survived from the point of view of equal opportunities?

Whether a person could swim or not (a personal skill or personal deficit) might in the individual case have made a difference. To be in the water for longer than a few minutes meant disaster, but if you happened to be able to swim you might have had the chance of getting yourself on to a piece of floating wreckage. If you could not swim even that option was not open to you. So in terms of who survived and who did not, and in terms of how many survived, the personal skill of being able to swim was very marginal.

In such a disaster as this, one of the very important factors is the ability to keep your head, not to rush around aimlessly, to know where you are going and how to get there. There is evidence that emotionally well-adjusted people are less easily hijacked by panic and fear. To have this rather wider personal skill of being able to problem solve under stress is almost certainly more significant than being able to swim in favouring a person's chance of survival – and had there not been so many people panicking and rushing around the number of people who survived might well have been greater. However, absolutely speaking, remaining calm in a panic would not have been of major significance.

It is known there were problems with the lifeboats, but also that, even if they had all been in good working order, the lifeboats would still not have been adequate to get all the people off the ship. In reality there simply would not have been time, even with perfect organization and no panic, for this to be achieved. Nevertheless, it is true that more working lifeboats would certainly have made a significant difference to the numbers of survivors.

What would have made a huge impact, both to the absolute numbers of survivors and to a more equal distribution in terms of social class, would have been if the ship had been designed differently in the first place. We are not talking about design in terms of seaworthiness but in terms of its 'social' design. It is instructive to see photographs of the first-class accommodation: huge amounts of space on the upper decks, the safest part of the ship, laid out in fabulous luxury, occupied by only 325 people, less than 15 per cent of the total ship population. Had the third-class passengers', stewards', waiters' and servants' accommodation been on the upper decks, far, far more people would have been saved.

What then are the lessons from Southampton involving the loss of the *Titanic*? And what are its implications for emotional literacy?

First of all, that belongingness (and remember that bad behaviour is related to the lack of a sense of belonging) is a matter of *systemic* issues rather than one of personal skills and competences (cf. Sharp, 2001; Weare, 2004). The social redesign of the ship was probably the most important cause of *how many* survived and *who* survived. That is not to say that personal skills and competences are irrelevant, but simply that government, schools and teachers often fail to see the wood for the trees. They focus, as we did initially in Southampton, on trying to help pupils behave better by teaching them anger management and social skills, etc. Such initiatives are not a waste of time, and certainly not for some individual pupils (as the ability to swim and not to panic was for some individuals on the *Titanic*), but the effects of allocating even very large resources *at this level* are likely to be marginal and, in the total picture, hardly measurable.

The second lesson from Southampton is that human systems are inevitably designed by people who have power and resources: people who belong. Emotional literacy is not primarily something for the *have-nots* but for the *haves*. There is an analogy here with what has been learned in the prevention and reduction of bullying. The most effective way of reducing bullying is not to work with the bullies, nor indeed with the victims, but with the *bystanders*. It is changing the 'apathy' of the bystanders that has the greatest impact on rates of bullying and who gets bullied. It is, then, the 60 per cent of the population (the haves) who need to change and to see that it is in their own best long-term (more rational) interests to prevent the bad behaviour of those who do not feel as though they belong by genuinely sharing in the context of the whole community. 'Middle England' needs to learn to be more emotionally literate, and that involves not grasping for and protecting inflated lifestyles at the expense of others. Professor Sir Michael Rutter (1991) has shown that it is relative poverty which is crucial in the development of 'not belonging' and low self-worth. We ask these questions: Why do we have the highest percentage of males in Western Europe in prisons? Why do we likewise have the highest rates of teenage pregnancy in Western Europe? What is the relationship between these facts and that we have the highest percentage of children living in poverty (3.8 million at the last count) and the highest number of households in Western Europe where no member of that household is in gainful employment? Despite the rhetoric, the reality is that the gap between those who have and those who do not have is becoming progressively wider.

The third lesson from Southampton is that when we establish and maintain community everybody tends to benefit. Not only would the social class distribution of survivors have been far fairer had the *Titanic* been designed differently, but there would probably have been far more survivors in total.

The last lesson comes not from Southampton but from Martin Luther King, Jr, who had a dream. The design and building of the Twin Towers were the work of people who had done extremely well at school and achieved very high examination marks and professional qualifications. So were the jets that crashed into them. Academic, technological and scientific achievements crash to 'ground zero' when, for whatever reason, people do not feel as though they belong. 'We have learned how to fly to the moon, but we still have not learned how to walk hand in hand as brothers and sisters.'

Emotional literacy is fundamentally about a dream, a vision – and old men and women need to dream dreams, and young men and women need to see visions.

CHAPTER 21

Communication
confidence through art

Dominique Wilson-Smith Anderson

As soon as young children learn to express themselves in words they seek to record their ideas. Picking up a pencil or paintbrush they swirl around and produce pictures that reflect their thoughts and feelings. Although they may mean nothing to the adult eye, they are precious possessions for the child. Pictures are forever present unless destroyed and are not as spoken words that go in one ear and out the other with often only a fleeting impression. Thus drawings and paintings, although sometimes meaningless to others, have great significance for the artists. They represent the imaginary world of the mind and are an important act of communication with oneself and with others.

Antoine De Saint-Exupéry's story *Le Petit Prince* (1999) exemplifies the differences between the child and adult mind. *Le Petit Prince* begins with a little boy having heard tales from nature and how creatures feed off one another. He then produces a drawing of a boa constrictor eating an elephant as in the picture below. One swallow and the boa constrictor took the elephant inside him to digest later.

'What a lovely hat,' the adults exclaimed. Painfully, the little boy embarked on his second representation ...

The adults were appalled and told the boy to fill his mind with matters of consequence such as geography and history. The boy

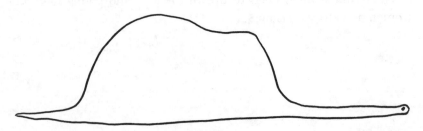

Figure 21.1

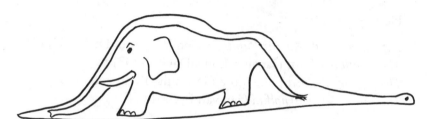

Figure 21.2

resolved never to confide in anyone again. He grew up silent and self-contained.

When the boy finished his education he became a war pilot and one day flew his plane over the desert, where it crashed. He was repairing the engine (as you do!) when a little prince appeared. 'Please draw me a sheep,' the little prince begged. The pilot drew several pictures but the prince complained that the sheep were wrong. Exasperated, the pilot tried his drawings 1 and 2 on the little prince, who responded crossly: 'I don't want a picture of a boa constrictor eating an elephant, I asked you to draw me a sheep.'

Valuing what others create demands an imaginative response as we try to understand what the representation means. So often we view art only in terms of its ability to present a real image. This is probably a relic from the times when painted pictures were the only way of recording people and events. Since then photographs and film images have fulfilled this need, allowing painting to move away from conventional forms and become more abstract expressions of the artist's mind.

Modern art moves beyond reality and presents images that are so unreal they are often difficult to fathom – just like the pictures of a young child. Help is needed in their interpretation if we are to communicate successfully with the artist and share their thinking and broaden our reflections.

Thinking moves from classifying ideas according to set criteria to making comparisons, analogies and then inferences. Our power to infer underpins our ability to bring together a set of ideas and make sense of them. Art is an enormously important activity in helping us shift from simple sorting to complex imagining. It is a vital stimulus to the development of our thinking and was the way of expressing feeling and facts before verbal language developed.

Experience of teaching many different age groups how to think and express themselves more fully has led to a belief in the import-ance of art appreciation in our educational and life experiences.

Pictures such as:

Experiment with An Air Pump (Joseph Wright of Derby, 1768)
The Death of Marat (Jacques Louis David, 1793)
The Raft of Medusa (Theodore Gericault, 1819) and
The Marriage of Arnolfini (Jan van Eyck, 1434)

not only tell a story of the social history of the time but show in the detail of the pictures the views and values of the artist. All these pictures tell a story that illuminates the way the world works and how humans cope with it.

Representation through drawing, painting or sculpture, therefore, is at the centre of our culture and a process by which successive generations are brought into the narrative of life, a story of which we are all an important, vital part.

Art encourages us to take risks and it produces strong images, narratives and impressions, which develop conversations around the dilemmas of life. Experiences of looking at the art of others and experimenting with our own interpretations can only strengthen our collective future and facilitate our communication and confidence. A thought is only half a thought until it is expressed, so that sharing our ideas is a vital part of the visualizing, verbalizing and thinking process.

CHAPTER 22

Using EI as a leader in schools

Judith Mullen

Highly developed emotional intelligence (EI) is vital for effective leadership in schools. I believe that a leader's task is emotional. A leader is a group's emotional guide. The prime task for a leader (teacher) is to draw together the group's emotions and to use their range in order to ensure that people can do their best regardless of their role.

As emotions are essentially contagious, leaders are therefore in a privileged position and should recognize that emotions spread outwards most strongly from the most powerful people in a group. We have all seen it: if someone comes into a meeting upset or angry and that emotion is not dealt with it can spread quickly. More positively, a person with a good sense of humour can quickly relax a roomful of people. The power and disarming effect of the smile should not be underestimated.

Think about the effect you have on your colleagues simply by the way you greet them in the morning. Without our always being aware of it, the impact we have by being rushed, dashing from our car through reception and simply 'not seeing' or interacting with a colleague will sometimes affect them for perhaps the rest of the day. They will wonder what they have done to offend you.

Think about the confrontational behaviour some adults engender when talking at – not to – students. Should we be surprised when young people respond in the vernacular? As a school principal I wondered many times why some adults chose to work with young people, as to all intents and purposes they did not actually seem to like them. In fact they seemed to go out of their way to respond negatively and critically, thus souring any potential relationship.

The leader's moods and behaviour drive the moods and behaviour of everyone else. A cranky and ruthless boss creates a toxic organisation. (Goleman, 2002)

In discussing the potential impact EI has in the leadership of schools perhaps it would be useful to offer to define leadership by postulating what it is not: it is clearly not management. Management might be seen as the technical aspects of a task or role, which might be completed without reference to other people. For example, it would be possible to complete a school improvement plan, a timetable, or review the teaching of a colleague in a technically efficient way. However, for each to become effective, active engagement with people is required. A key transitional phase in the movement from management to leadership is the recognition that rational structures and systems do not necessarily secure engagement and commitment. They are undoubtedly vital but systems and structures alone do not maximize our greatest asset, people. Therefore, if leadership is seen to be moving people from compliance to commitment, from acceptance to active engagement and from task completion to professional involvement, then leading through emotional intelligence is the vital medium. The work of Daniel Goleman (1997, 2002) in *Working with Emotional Intelligence* and in particular in the practical interpretation of that in *The New Leaders* stresses that the most effective leaders have highly developed emotional intelligence.

I believe that it is impossible to conceptualize any model of leadership that does not have emotional intelligence as a key component.

If we accept the premise that we are all leaders and that leadership should be distributed, then no matter what your role it is how you fill it that counts. Effective leaders are aware of their emotional impact and how their leadership styles can be used to create a climate where all can do their best.

The demands of schools and the dynamically changing global environment reinforce the importance of relationship-based leadership. Responses are derived from perceptions and perceptions are real to the perceiver.

At a lecture on the emotionally intelligent school in April 2003 at the National Council for School Leadership, Professor John West-Burnham defined EI as: 'the authentic range of intuitive behaviours, derived from sophisticated self-awareness, which facilitate effective engagement with others. These are behaviours rooted in the integrity of the individual'.

Currently in the UK there is almost a preoccupation with leadership. Tony Blair, the UK Prime Minister's drive for 'world-class leaders', particularly in the education sector (where the government wants to improve education standards in every classroom and for every household in the country through the crusade launched under 'Education, Education, Education' in 1997), along with the socio-economic attainment gap and a demoralized and overburdened teaching force, are causing huge concern. This high-profile and continuing focus on leadership was even more apparent throughout the 2005 electioneering process, where high-quality leadership in education was promoted as the most fundamental aspect of the raising standards agenda.

The national remodelling initiative, reworked national leadership programmes concentrating on high-level leadership attributes and qualities (not simply competence based) and a recognition that new leaders need to be skilled interpersonally are bringing about a new direction for the leaders of our schools.

Charles Clarke, the former Secretary of State for Education, stated that: 'The grit in the oyster … is leadership. We need leadership at all levels – from the top schools to every teacher and to every member of the school team in helping every pupil get the best out of their time at school'. However, the day of the hero leaders has gone. 'Super-heads', who disappeared into telephone boxes and emerged with their underpants on top of their trousers, flying off to save the world are not the way forward. The cult of the leader as hero is inappropriate today. A head may well be a super Chief Executive Officer (CEO) but which company expects its CEO to take responsibility for finance, information technology, human resources, marketing, customer relations and productivity? The day of the EI leader has arrived.

Emotionally intelligent leaders lead their organizations through effective teams where the taking of responsibility by individuals throughout an institution brings about a positive climate. A school, team or department where fingers are not pointed at others but at oneself is more likely to move forward. Organizations that rely on trust as their principal means of control are more effective, more creative and more fun. Those relying on an undercurrent of fear with hugely hierarchical control systems do not encourage participative leadership. Instead of defining roles by positions in the hierarchy that are difficult to change for practical or historical reasons EI leadership would create new patterns of organizations based on distributed leadership.

The most important thing for the leader first and foremost is to know themselves. Then to know their learning styles; to understand their leadership styles, where Goleman's leadership styles might well be the starting point.

We need to ask ourselves what our strong suits are. How others perceive us. How we can plug our gaps as leaders and how we build teams with a range of skills and attributes. A starting point would be to audit our individual and team strengths in a spirit of openness and trust.

EI leaders do not appoint clones who think and act as they themselves do. They encourage diversity of opinion, creative challenge and questioning. They look for both complementary and opposite learning and leadership styles within their teams. The EI-aware leader will recognize the potential of both transformational and dispersed leadership and will exploit the diversity and strengths within a team.

If we are to encourage transformational, life-changing leadership we have to acknowledge that it will not happen by itself. It is deliberate and necessary and must concentrate on learning and attainment. All have to take responsibility as any transformational activity must impact on classroom experiences, otherwise there is absolutely no point in undertaking any initiative. We must look to impact on students' life chances.

Transformation that needs to be reflected in the work culture of the school is led by vision, moral purpose and example. Leaders involved in transformational practices live what they believe and lead by example. Without radical alternative ways of working schools will not transform, they will only shift; they will merely be adjusted, modified and rebranded time and time again.

However, a 'one size fits all' international best-practice model does not (nor should it) exist, as cultural sensitivities and local context must be acknowledged and reflected. The role of the school is to give a common culture and purpose and to create an environment where innovation and ideas thrive and progress is natural.

International examples of EI-aware leaders have surfaced through the evaluation of the International Placements for Headteachers' (IPH) advanced leaders programme administered by the British Council on behalf of the National College for School Leaders (Mullen, 2004). The majority of participants in the programme stress their observations of effective leadership from countries as varied as Brazil, Thailand, Uganda and Finland. The comments relate to the EI awareness of the leader, who more often than not leads an emotionally literate school. Participants regularly highlight their desire to develop their own EI skills as a major target in their evaluation reports.

One of the most difficult things for leaders to lead and manage effectively is change. EI-aware leaders and their organizations do not underestimate the impact constant change has on us all. Some thrive, some feel threatened and some see challenges, while others relish opportunities. Change needs to be embraced by all staff and not seen as an imposition. Schools will thrive if they can create, share and apply knowledge well in a climate of trust. Change is a journey, not a blueprint. It should be built and refined as we go rather than adhered to totally as a preconceived vision. Once the vision is established and shared we can afford to be flexible as we move through the process. Change is difficult as it feels that it goes on and on; often it means new structures, but the paradigm that interests me more in leadership is about changing mindsets and behaviours: the EI way.

Professor Louise Stoll of the University of Bath states (2002): 'School leaders must contend with the reality of global change and others' agendas whilst leading their schools to a desired future'.

The danger is when the external drivers take over. EI leaders should also have the courage to assess the climate and say no. They put people first. EI leadership must be purposeful, inclusive and values driven, embracing the distinctive and the inclusive. It must promote an active view of learning and be instructionally focused. The whole school community needs to be involved as a learning community, built where the leaders are the lead learners. A culture of action research with teacher researchers working with the community bringing about within- and beyond-school innovations and initiatives should be encouraged. EI leadership needs to be future-oriented, horizon-gazing, to see where to go next. It must be strategically driven using experienced and innovative methods supported by a policy context that is coherent, transparent, accessible, systematic, practical and implemented, but above all impact not intention driven.

Schools also need to develop approaches to planning that can encompass both the predictable and the less predictable aspects of their future. But more than anything else leaders have to build and develop capacity from within. Thus capacity building needs to acknowledge and highlight perhaps the most important asset within the EI learning community: students and their families.

Listening to students is something not universally embraced. While there are some excellent practices, lip-service is given by some to ineffective school councils, for example, which look good on paper but in reality are not influential on the climate of the school. Leadership is not just for leaders. Students too have the power to change schools for the better. Up to 90 per cent of the intellectual capital in schools goes unutilized, and the majority of that talent resides in the student body.

EI-confident schools need highly motivated leaders. We know the impact of effective leadership and the powerful potential of dispersed leadership. Those who have embraced this potential have seen the impact throughout their learning community. However, it does take courage and a clear understanding of yourself and your leadership style to encourage and empower others. It can be threatening if you really do encourage the taking of responsibility, innovation and creativity, with the true power to implement dispersed to others. Professor Leo Tan, Director of the National Institute of Education, Singapore, suggests: 'When you empower staff you are not losing control but strengthening your own position'.

In the ideal world we would be talking only of changing culture and mind-shifts, although they alone are challenging enough for some, but in reality we have to ensure that our leaders are emotionally intelligent and can embrace new ways of working. We need to promote EI schools where *smart* working is encouraged through dispersed leadership, shared responsibility and the positive development of leadership teams. If we achieve those goals schools will contain effective leaders who feel empowered to learn and are able to empower others.

If we believe that every child should be in a well-led EI-aware school with every leader a learner and every learner a leader, perhaps the following questions need considering:

- How do we build EI-aware schools?
- How do we alter mindsets and cultures so people are willing to embrace change without fear?
- Can we encourage innovation and risk taking when it could lead to a drop in performance?
- How do we make the shift from heroic to distributed EI leadership?
- How do we redress the balance away from the blame culture?
- Should we perhaps be questioning schools' traditional functioning cognitive, custodial, behavioural, social and qualification sorting? Are they, with their multifunctions, the best way to deliver education?
- How do we encourage the student voice within our schools?
- How do we learn to listen?

CHAPTER 23

John's story: Episode 4

Strategies for coping?

'John' and Paul Cooper

P: So these teachers who you got on with. Did they teach you anything?

J: 'Cos I was in lower sets as well, for some things, there used to be less people in them. So they used to help you anyway. Most of the time it was just helping you. Not getting frustrated, but helping you.

P: How do you mean?

J: Like when you're doing some work and they help you and they don't get frustrated 'cos you're not doing it right. They were patient. They helped you and you got through it a lot quicker. There are worst teachers, average teachers and good teachers. There were three or four good teachers. I think they were good for everyone.

All in the time I was there – I was there for about three years. All of the time I was there I got suspended about 15 times, at least. And that's when my Mum started telling me I'd got this AD/HD. And I started to use this as an excuse. That's not a good thing to tell someone. If you start to believe all the hype that's involved. [You say] 'Yeah. I can't help it. And I've got an excuse now.' That's what it used to be like. I used to say, 'I can't do that, 'cos I've got AD/HD.' I'll admit it, I used to tell the teachers that. But any kid wants to get away – most kids don't want to work.

My Mum thought that that [AD/HD] was the answer to everything, right? All the problems I had, she thought that was the answer. And that was the main cause. And then she started getting involved in voluntary help. And it got worse because she started to believe it. And she started to assume she knew what I was feeling like. And she started taking me to the psychiatrist, and things like that. They used to ask you questions – and because – I was restless anyway. I did have an attention problem. I really didn't like sitting down and listening to other people; especially when I'm not interested in what they've got to say. I just started answering [the psychiatrist] – and I think a lot of other kids who have this problem do it too – I just answered yes, yes, yes, to whatever questions they are asking you. You just want to get out of there.

... My Mum's shown me a lot of programmes where these children have been helped. But I don't think they are. They're getting hindered because I can tell, from my experience, that they're just trying to say 'Yes, yes, that's right. That's how I feel.' It's not something you can feel – this disorder as my Mum calls it. You can't feel it, like it's cancer or something, like it's something you can't control. They think it's like that. But it isn't. It's not like that at all. You can control it. But it's hard to. It's not like everyone else – they think about what they say sometimes. It'll just come out of your mouth. You can't help it. You just did it.

P: What? So, if you felt like saying something, you just said it?

J: Yeah ... it's a sort of automatic thing.

P: So what do you think about this AD/HD thing?

J: I don't say it don't exist. But I think that a lot of the problems that people have with this is that a lot of parents don't give them [their kids] the right discipline they need from an early age. 'Cos when you look back, on other kids in the past – you can't say it's just appeared out of nowhere. Other kids must have suffered from it when they was younger, but, maybe 'cos their upbringing was different. I mean, schools didn't really recognize it then. Now there's so many special schools – to me that's just another way of isolating people. If you put someone in a mental hospital and you keep them there for a while, they'll end up mental, because everyone else around them is crazy. So they're just going to end up crazy.

... I didn't mean it when I was young really – over my behaviour at home.

CHAPTER 24

Music and personal growth

Rosemary Duxbury

Introduction

This chapter is written from a personal viewpoint. I am a composer and am lucky to have been immersed in music all my life. To me, music is an intrinsic part of who we are; it is our heritage, our nature, and is a way of discovering our authenticity. My aim as a composer is to write music that is uplifting, connecting us to a greater reality. I would like to share some ideas of how I see this great resource of sound.

This chapter is about how music relates to the development of 'self' through personal growth. The word 'self' is a complex term with multiple interpretations. By referring to 'self' I mean to imply broadly 'what is inside us' and specifically 'what is at the heart of us – our being or essence'. The chapter is organized in three sections, each of which has three subsections:

A. Introduction
B. Three areas of discussion to show how I feel music can contribute to personal growth, with the main headings also dividing into three:

1. Music as a central resource in knowing Self:
   - music as part of our nature
   - knowing self
   - how music can contribute.

2. Music to be available as a resource:
   - through listening
   - participating
   - creating.

3. Working with music in a conscious, nurturing way:
   - music in our environment

- radio, recordings, etc.
- how a conscious choice of music can benefit our lives.

C. Conclusion

I use the symbol ▣ as a 'key' for inviting you to 'open a door' of the idea, perhaps to explore an experience, and to see what other 'doors' open for you.

First, I will start by explaining what music means to me. I use *italic* to indicate words that build a cyclical process (see Figure 24.1) that contains the theoretical underpinning for the chapter.

I see music as a *creative* force that *awakens* a response in us. It *expresses* feelings, emotions, ideas and so on, leading to greater *understanding*. By *experiencing* music for ourselves, the process of understanding develops what we *assimilate* and *recognize* as part of ourselves. We can then start to *live* that inner creative pulse that in turn *awakens* us, makes us want to *express*; we *understand* through this process. Examples of work I have composed in this quest include 'Atma's Flight' (1990), a cello sonata; 'Awakenings' (1992), for piano solo; 'Passage' (2000)' for piano solo and 'Angel Whisper' (2003), a choral triptych.

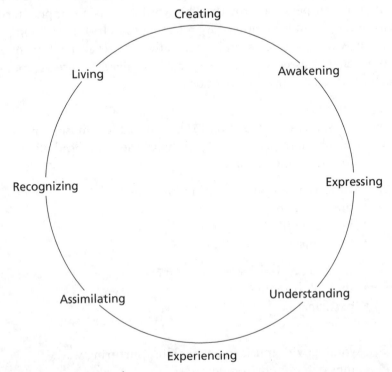

Figure 24.1 *Creative cycle*

I believe that music, especially if worked with in a conscious way, helps us to recognize more of who we truly are, and the more we understand and help ourselves, the more we can help others. The more we know who we are, the more we know what we are about and what we want to say or communicate. If we do not have language we cannot say what we feel, and if we feel but do not know what it is we feel we cannot express it. Therefore, the more we understand who we are, our 'self' (what is going on within), the more we can recognize a way of expressing that and music can be a tool for reflecting and communicating that need.

I believe music is a central resource for those working in areas of communication, emotion and behaviour in the way it not only promotes greater skills and communication abilities, but also enhances the very fabric of who we are, opening us up not only to know ourselves as physical, emotional and mental beings but also to know our spiritual and creative dimensions.

1. Music as a central resource in knowing self

Music as part of our nature

Here are two examples of how music is recognized as part of our nature. The first example is in an instinctive and tribal setting; the second in a scientific and educational context.

> When a woman in a certain African tribe knows she is pregnant, she goes out into the wilderness with a few friends and together they pray and meditate until they hear the song of the child. They recognise that every soul has its own vibration that expresses its unique flavour and purpose. When the women attune to the song, they sing it out loud. Then they return to the tribe and teach it to everyone else.
>
> When the child is born, the community gathers and sings the child's song to him or her. Later, when the child enters education, the village gathers and chants the child's song. When the child passes through the initiation to adulthood, the people again come together and sing. At the time of marriage, the person hears his or her song. Finally, when the soul is about to pass from this world, the family and friends gather at the person's bed, just as they did at their birth, and they sing the person to the next life.
>
> In the African tribe there is one other occasion upon which the villagers sing to the child. If at any time during his or her

life, the person commits a crime or aberrant social act, the individual is called to the centre of the village and the people in the community form a circle around them. Then they sing their song to them. The tribe recognises that the correction for antisocial behaviour is not punishment; it is love and the remembrance of identity. When you recognise your own song, you have no desire or need to do anything that would hurt another.

A friend is someone who knows your song and sings it to you when you have forgotten it. Those who love you are not fooled by mistakes you have made or dark images you hold about yourself. They remember your beauty when you feel ugly; your wholeness when you are broken; your innocence when you feel guilty; and your purpose when you are confused.

You may not have grown up in an African tribe that sings your song to you at crucial life transitions, but life is always reminding you when you are in tune with yourself and when you are not. When you feel good, what you are doing matches your song, and when you feel awful, it doesn't. In the end, we shall all recognise our song and sing it well. You may feel a little 'warbly' at the moment, but so have all the great singers. Just keep singing and you'll find your way home. (www. healthynewage.com/alancohen.html)

Richard Morris, chief executive for the Associated Board of the Royal Schools of Music, reports (2002):

There is a consensus amongst brain scientists (as recently expressed at a public forum at the Royal Institution in London) that 'music is not only part of our culture; it is part of our nature' and that 'music experiences and skills are universal in all societies'. It is the mission of the Associated Board and its examiners to encourage the development of that inherent musicianship throughout all 85 countries where we work.

The first extract illustrates that we have moved a long way from being connected to nature, but both extracts suggest that an important key in being 'connected' to our nature is indeed through music.

- Can you think of a time when music connected you to a sense of well-being?
- Maybe you would like to experiment with singing a healing word. If so, you might like to try singing the word 'HU'

– pronounced 'hue' (see HU; Klemp, 2006) – which can open your heart to more love is an ancient name for God and is recognized in various cultures around the world. It is a name we carry with us as hu-man beings.

Knowing self

To know our nature, we must endeavour to know who we are. Most people believe they are a physical being that is emotional, has a mind and possibly a spiritual dimension. However, consider the inversion of this: that our true nature is a spiritual dimension: a Soul who *has* a physical body, a personality, emotions, a mind. The rest of this chapter adopts the second perspective.

Here are a couple of examples where individuals are working with the notion that 'self' is (1) beyond personality and (2) beyond emotion. One is personal from within the jazz world, the second an example of research into emotions:

1. Jazz pianist Keith Jarrett refers to a need to know our 'centre', something beyond personality, in order to be free (Jarrett, 1987).

Personality is something we've chosen [to surround our essential nature] and are attached to.

Without personality, essence can be revealed.

2. US research by physicist and engineer Lester Levenson, resulted in a technique called 'The Sedona Method' (Dwoskin, 1991), which provides simple ways to allow one to recognize and experience emotions within, but gives one the chance to transcend the emotion so that we learn we do not have to be controlled by it. Knowing that, it can become a choice whether to continue experiencing an emotion or not. It also allows for the fact that it might be necessary to continue experiencing the emotion.

The spiritual dimension, or Soul, is denied its true nature when the other 'faculties' take precedence in our attention, become disturbed or out of balance. To illustrate this, I offer the following analogy.

A string quartet wishes to play music. All four players need to work together so that the music can be brought through successfully. They all need to be in harmony with each other, playing at the same tempo and to be in tune with each other to express the music.

If one player, say the emotion, is out of tune, the sound cannot be brought through as well as when they are in harmony.

Each player in the string quartet of ours has its needs, is searching for balance, and wants to be heard, healed.

◙ You might like to review your responses from the perspective that from a spiritual viewpoint you have a body, a personality, a mind and emotions. How does that change your perspective on life?

How music can contribute

I see music as a way of connecting us with our inner being, touching our true nature. It reminds us, connects us with who we are, beyond the physical realm.

Each 'player', or aspect of our 'self', has a separate identity and will respond to music in a different way:

- music allows us *physically* to move, dance, march, etc.;
- *emotions* can be reached, nourished, recognized, balanced;
- *mental faculty* can be satisfied, ideas understood, explained, knowledge assimilated;
- *spiritual* or *soul* can experience freedom, creativity, an open heart, greater capacity to give and receive love.

Hazrat Inayat Khan, musician and Sufi master and friend of Debussy, expressed it thus:

There are five different aspects of the art of music: popular, that which induces motion of the body; technical, that which satisfies the intellect; artistic, that which has beauty and grace; appealing, that which pierces the heart; uplifting, that in which the soul hears the music of the spheres. (Reported by his son, Inayat Kahn, 1979)

◙ Maybe you would like to examine what types of music you are drawn to and ask what part of yourself is responding to that?

2. Music to be available as a resource

Listening

Such a wide range of sound can constitute what we understand music to be, especially since the development of electronics in the twentieth century and a greater exposure to world music (music of different cultures). We have all probably experienced a relative from a different generation saying that our favourite contemporary piece is not 'music', certainly not melodic in the way it used to be in 'their day'. Maybe we say it or think that ourselves now!

Even classically and in jazz, tastes and styles vary enormously, but often it is how we perceive, it is our viewpoint, our perspective, our consciousness that recognizes or does not recognize what we determine *is* 'music'.

Being part of the Leicestershire Schools Symphony Orchestra, I was fortunate enough to be exposed to experimental music early on, yet when reaching college to study music the tutor did not acknowledge the work of a composer I had played and I encountered a student who felt anything later than Wagner was not really music!

Although this chapter is not about detailing all the sorts of music, I would like to encourage exploration of different types of music, with the proposal that perhaps this helps us to understand the different components which make up the world we live in and also to know the different responses we, as individuals, have. The aim of this identification is that once we know what the repertoire of music available to us is, we can then work with it in a prescriptive sense.

> You might like to examine your responses to different types of music. Draw or write a response, or discuss it with others.

Participating

Singing or learning a musical instrument allows one to participate in music making – that vital step in giving the individual *expression*, *understanding* and *experience*. It is necessary to find the right instrument or style of music to suit the individual and these days there are many options as to styles of music available, e.g. folk, ethnic, jazz, popular, as well as classical.

Let us take a moment to look at some skills and benefits that come from participating in music, for example from learning to play a musical instrument:

- multitask ability
- right brain/left brain balance
- reading
- listening
- interpretation
- discrimination

- confidence
- socializing – can provide a positive, creative, sharing context in which we have the freedom to express ourselves
- expressing in a way words cannot
- tapping into universal expressions
- joy
- recognition
- success
- relaxation
- stimulation
- discipline
- motor skills
- finding our personal voice, i.e. finding we have something to say
- communicating
- a way of learning about the past
- develops imagination
- and as discussed: helps in knowing more about who we are.

🔲 Maybe there are other skills and benefits you can think of that can be added to this list?

It seems that music offers one of the most holistic forms of education. It can form a good basis for all our education.

I was fortunate to have experienced just such an approach through the Leicestershire County School of Music, founded by Eric Pinkett (see Pinkett, 1969). In 1948 he pioneered the provision of instrumental teaching in schools for all, with opportunities to play in county orchestras. Certainly in my primary school every child was encouraged to learn an instrument. Music was central to our school life, equal to English and mathematics in study. It gave me a sense of community, teaching me how music can be part of everyday life, central to our well-being and a natural expression of life.

Creating

As I am, so I see. Use what language we will. We can never say anything but what we are. (Emerson, 1844)

As a language, music is a living way of expressing who we are and what we feel and think, especially when we create the music ourselves. Expressed through intervals, shape of melody, rhythm, tone, scales, tonality, music has a vocabulary for pretty much every condition. A basic example is the use of a major scale to convey happiness compared to a minor scale suggesting sadness. Jazz scales offer further variations working with modes (a different combination of tones and semitones), and Indian ragas with their quarter tones traditionally would be chosen for not only a mood but also for a specific time of day.

When creating music, as in improvisation, for example, if we are going to communicate we need to have something to say, but it also allows us to explore the medium and discover what is inside waiting to be said, reflecting back what is within. Through exploration we can find out what it *is* we want to say. Keith Jarrett, a leading improviser in the world of jazz, believes his process of working with music can provide 'A way of remembering ourselves'. By being *creative*, we can be *awakened*, starting the process of the creative cycle I outlined in Figure 24.1.

Creating music also provides a way of sharing with others, sometimes in a social context where we can speak soul to soul. It is a language beyond words, which connects inner experience with outer expression. Music is fundamental to who we are; it is our instinctive language – it is 'pre-word'. Music can say things that speech cannot always articulate, offering an alternative and often a far more profound expression. It also provides communication where speech may not be available, or there may be a reluctance or fear to communicate in words.

3. Working with music in a conscious, nurturing way

Music in our environment
So often music is played randomly, we listen without consciously choosing to do so, but it is still having an effect on us. For example, we go into a restaurant and a heavy beat may be on; do we want to listen to this while making quiet conversation, or eating our favourite food? Does it affect how we feel, or disrupt our balance? Sometimes I go into a shop and cannot make a clear decision of what to select because of my sensitivity to the background music.

⧉ You might like to examine your own responses to music in your surroundings. How does music affect you in such contexts? Do you find that some kinds of music are experienced very positively and others perhaps negatively? Have you felt music has uplifted or energized you?

Radio, recordings, etc.

The media of computers, radio and television provide a range of music and technology readily giving us an abundance of access to music via CD, MiniDisc, MP3 and iPods, etc., but how often are we conscious of what we listen to? Are we aware of the words and meanings in songs that we listen to or sing along with? Language can often have a hypnotic effect, drugging or dulling the consciousness; for example, repeated expressions of 'I can't' or 'I always fail' can reinforce the belief.

The more awareness we have of all that impacts on our being or 'self', the greater the choice we have as to whether and how to express our feelings (*Awakening* leading to greater *expression* – see Figure 24.1).

How a conscious choice of music can benefit our lives

In contrast, we can choose music to enhance our well-being. Music can change a mood instantly and can be used for creating an environment of our choice. Moods and emotions can be balanced and uplifted by selecting the right music for our needs at any given time. We become more empowered if we make conscious selections of music that benefit us.

Maybe sometimes what we need is silence.

Studies on the effects of music on physiology, emotions and behaviour reveal further benefits. Researched worldwide, this makes a huge topic. For those wishing to explore this further I would recommend visiting www.prs.co.uk/powerofmusicreport to read *The Power of Music Report* (Performing Rights Society, 2001). Professor Sue Hallam of the Institute of Education, London University, has reviewed evidence of the beneficial effects of music as the result of a worldwide literature review of authoritative articles that address the strength of music's influence on our lives.

As an example, results of tests carried out at the Chelsea and Westminster Hospital in London (see Morris, 2002) have shown how live music (classical, jazz or folk) diminished the stress levels of three out of four patients, and pregnant mothers reported lower blood pressure. Since then Bittman, managing director of the Mind–Body Wellness Center, in Meadville, PA, has reported that recreational music making has the potential to reverse stress on the genomic level (Bittman *et al.*, 2005). This has also been written about by DeNoon (2005) and Nieves (2005).

🔳 You may have heard of the Mozart Effect (see Raucher and Shaw, 2005), which controversially suggests children's intelligence is affected by the music they hear, but experiment for yourself. Mozart might not be the music for you, or maybe it is! Maybe one particular piece of Mozart suits you? Take control of what you listen to – bring sound that you choose into your environment – play music at some point in the day – examine why you chose that piece of music, and ask how it makes you feel, how does it change your environment?

Conclusion

All of us as human beings need to communicate, have emotional needs, live and behave in a social context; therefore hopefully all of us as individuals can benefit from recognizing the value of music in the context outlined above (whether it be through listening, participating, creating, or by having a greater awareness of music in your life). I hope this chapter encourages you to see the potential of music as a resource for all in education, and maybe sparks some ideas that will help those working with children with social, emotional and behavioural difficulties. Perhaps you can envision a way of working with music in a conscious and selective way, improving, most of all, the quality of *your* life.

The more we live with an *understanding* of who we have become as the result of conscious *experience*, the more we are able to *recognize* ways in which we may not be fully 'connected' to our self. *Recognition* is an important step in being able to make a change creatively, working with what we have but taking us to a new level of *living* (see Figure 24.1).

The more we are able to function as individuals in an authentic manner, i.e. be true to our selves, the more we are able to guide and nurture. We have tapped into a resource and strength from which to give. We can better integrate with others knowing who we are: safe in who we are. Sound and music, as our 'note' within, will start to find its *voice*, we will begin to *hum* in our 'beingness', will *sing* our story, *play* with others, have the confidence to *improvise* creative solutions, *conduct* our lives with *rhythm* and *harmony* and ultimately engage in a more joyful *symphony* of life.

Acknowledgements

With thanks to Morag Hunter-Carsh for encouraging me to write in words as well as in music; to Professor Andrew Colman for being a 'sounding board' in matters of psychological definitions of 'self'; to Barbara Battey for sharing her inspirational email; to author Harold Klemp for his teachings on the 'Light and Sound' and spirituality; and to Dr Mike Duxbury, who knows my song and sings it to me.

CHAPTER 25

Music therapy

Shiroma de Silva

As far back as 531 BC there is evidence of music being used for therapeutic purposes. The Pythagoreans reportedly began the day by singing and playing the lyre to energize themselves and ended it with music before they went to bed to rid themselves of their worries (Storr, 1993). This chapter describes how emotions can be explored and communication and behaviour problems might be improved through music therapy. Examples from two case studies will be used as illustrations.

The emotional effects of music are universally recognized. Most people would acknowledge, for example, the role that film music plays in adding colour and dramatic depth to the storyline; or think about sacred choral music, which can seem almost to link the human and the divine; or songs sung at sporting events that give supporters a communal sense of identity and involvement. These are only a few examples of the ubiquity with which music is treated as an emotional vehicle through which feelings can be expressed and communicated. There can be little doubt that music can reach into the heart of a person, and of its ability to have powerful effects on mind and body. Music can change our mood, develop and improve muscular movement and even enhance the functioning of our immune system (Moranto *et al.*, 1993).

Music therapy in Britain has been developing for the last 50 years or so and is now considered to be an allied health profession. Music therapists are registered with the Health Professions Council and, as a clinical practice, are established in a wide range of settings including hospitals, hospices, the prison service, day centres and educational establishments.

Music and sound are central to music therapy practice; they are fundamental to developing the relationship between client and therapist. It is through the development of interactions between client and therapist that positive change might be brought about.

The process of engaging in improvisation with the therapist can provide clients with a sense of containment and facilitate them in exploring problematic areas of their lives.

Music therapy is not prescriptive. There are no set ways of working. A therapy session is very much tailored to the needs of the individual. The client largely determines the course the therapy takes and the changes that occur within the therapeutic process. At the heart of music therapy practice is the belief that musical responsiveness is innate and remains intact regardless of mental or physical disability or illness:

> We make and experience music because we have bodies which have pulses and tone, tensions and resolutions, phrasing of actions, burst of intensity, repetitions in developments. Music gives us, in short, access to a whole world of experience, bodily, intellectually, emotionally and socially. (Ansdell, 1995, p. 8)

Our many natural rhythms include breathing, walking and the beating of our heart. We are able to recognize people and their moods from the speed and intonation of their voices. Research on mother–infant interaction (Trevarthen et al., 1998) reveals rhythmic and emotional synchronicity between the two. There are similarities between the way a mother uses her voice and body to respond and build on sounds and movements made by her baby and the way in which a therapist uses improvised music. The music therapy setting provides a defined and boundaried space. In the containing space of the music therapy setting the client is able to project difficult and sometimes chaotic feelings on to the therapist. Music therapy provides an opportunity to express difficult experiences through musical improvisation.

> ... the therapist can accept the chaotic alarming experiences and feelings which the patient cannot or dare not hold on to and which rob him of any continuity in his world of experiences. The therapist accepts these experiences, mentally digests them and then returns them to the patient in a form which is more bearable and understandable. (De Backer, 1993, p. 38)

The potential of music therapy to bring about a radical transformation in the behaviour and emotional interaction of a client is demonstrated in the case of Adam, a 7-year-old with a diagnosis of autism. Adam's classroom teacher suggested that he attended weekly music therapy sessions. His behaviour in the classroom was becoming unmanageable and it was felt that music therapy might help Adam to express and channel his anger and frustration as well as addressing his communication needs. Three members of staff carried Adam to his first music therapy session. He was screaming. His teacher reassured me that this behaviour was quite usual for Adam and that if there were any problems I should pull the alarm cord in the room. I made an attempt at an opening greeting song through Adam's screams and then presented him with a large drum and a beater. He immediately took the beater and began to play. At the start of the session his beating was loud and relentless. He seemed to be building a wall of sound. I was on the outside and he was deliberately shutting me out. There were parallels between this pattern of behaviour and his interactions in other environments. I moved to the piano and tried to support and contain his sounds. Adam seemed to look at me with curiosity when I matched his loud playing in intensity. After several minutes I could sense the beginnings of a growing trust. He maintained the loud playing for a while but then his playing began to become increasingly quiet and I could sense him observing me to see if I would do the same.

The first few sessions consisted of extreme contrasts between loud and soft improvisations. After a few more weeks, Adam moved from drum to xylophone and when he played, I matched, mirrored and extended the sounds that he had produced. Our improvisations together began to have a more reciprocal quality as he began to imitate sounds and rhythmic fragments back again. The sessions seemed to bring out a mood of buoyancy in Adam and he left seemingly more alert. Staff noticed that he was much happier and calmer after the sessions and far more open to learning within the structure of the classroom setting. After one year of individual music therapy sessions Adam started to use the instruments to describe situations in which he felt uncomfortable. One of his first improvisations of this kind involved him moving very fast between the cabassa, shaker and the guiro. He described this as 'people looking with itchy eyes'. I imagine that the use of the word itchy reflected his own discomfort at being looked at. I feel that music therapy provided Adam with a safe emotional outlet and allowed him to externalize difficult emotional feelings within a boundaried and containing therapeutic relationship. Improvisation seems to enable an engagement in which personal (rather than musical) aspects of the personality are exposed (Pavlicevic, 1997). In Adam's case our improvisations together seemed to enable him to express himself without having to overcome the barrier of words and later allowed him to articulate feelings, which formerly he had kept repressed.

One of the most important aspects of being a music therapist is the ability to 'tune in' to the client. This is something we do naturally on a daily basis when we communicate with other people, for example the way we pick up on non-verbal cues and adapt our body posture and voices according to whom we are talking. It is not enough, however, for the music therapist merely to imitate sounds produced by the client. The therapist's response needs to be connected to the client's playing, and the client in turn needs to be aware of the connection that is being made.

The case of Annabel offers another example of how music therapy can assist a client in expressing emotions and feelings that have been repressed, often for very long periods of time.

Annabel, a woman of 42, was referred for music therapy by her GP. He was concerned because she was displaying symptoms of depression and he felt that music therapy might help her get in touch with and express repressed feelings. The weekly sessions lasted for one hour and took place at a community and mental health resource centre. Annabel arrived early to her first music therapy session and was very keen to begin. She was very well groomed, immaculately dressed and extremely polite. It later became clear that she was not only controlling of her outward appearance but that she was also keeping a tight rein on her emotions. She was extremely exacting of herself. Annabel informed me at the start of the first session that she could not touch the instruments for fear of 'doing it wrong'. We listened together to the opening of a slow movement of a Mozart piano concerto before Annabel reached forward and pressed the off button. She told me that it made her head hurt and refused to expand on how she was feeling. The following week I offered her a choice of instruments to play (half expecting her to refuse). Interestingly, she chose instruments with gentle ringing timbres. Her playing of these was very quiet. We discussed her choices and the possibility of expanding the dynamic range of our playing. Annabel then told me: 'I can't. I think I'd better tell you I'm afraid of loud sounds.' She chose a chromatic glockenspiel and began to play very tentatively. I tried to support and encourage her playing from the piano, but found it impossible to connect with her. Annabel's playing was very introverted and stilted. She seemed oblivious to my presence. Moreover, her playing seemed dissociated not only from me, but also from herself. She later told me that she was afraid of playing the wrong notes and that she had been trying to pick out the notes of a favourite song.

There is a reassuring predictability in the structure of familiar songs. After this session I felt that Annabel probably needed the reassurance of more structured activities in the session and continued to work in this vein.

In the sessions that followed our improvised playing seemed to adopt a 'leader–follower' format. Annabel always managed somehow to slip into the role of follower. After a few seconds of being leader she would exclaim: 'I'm following you!' I remarked on this to Annabel and after some discussion she said that leading made her feel 'vulnerable like a child' and that she needed me to be 'in control'.

During our eleventh session I felt that Annabel might be ready to play more freely. I introduced her to the pentatonic xylophone (a wooden, mellow-sounding instrument, tuned to the notes of a major scale but with the fourth and seventh notes omitted). It seemed less likely that she would attempt to pick out well-known tunes on this, and that because of the impossibility of producing extreme discordance on this instrument she would be more inclined to play freely. Annabel began the improvisation tentatively, but quite quickly her playing began to gain momentum. I supported her playing at the piano; her playing started to become very energetic and we improvised together for 40 minutes. When the improvisation came to a natural end Annabel began to cry. She said it was the first time she had cried for two years and revealed that that was when she had lost her 5-year-old son to stomach cancer. Her tears had taken her by surprise.

Annabel entered the therapy room for her twelfth music therapy session very confidently. She said she wanted to play a big drum. I gave her a large beater and a large drum and she began to play. Her body language and face seemed to express rage. Annabel played so loudly that the room began to vibrate. I supported and reflected what I felt to be anger in her playing on the piano with harsh atonal, disjointed chord clusters using the whole length of the keyboard. When the improvisation stopped she said she was exhausted and had not realized she could feel anger; she had thought that she could 'reason everything through'. She said she was angry with the doctors who had not diagnosed her son's stomach cancer and also revealed that her former husband had beaten her – something she had not been able to acknowledge openly before. She went on to explain that she feared loud sounds because they reminded her of the abuse she had suffered.

Annabel had clearly derived a sense of empowerment from these sessions. We only met for a few more occasions before it seemed appropriate for her to be discharged. Music therapy had evidently assisted her in confronting and coming to terms with her grief and also with the abuse she had suffered at the hands of her ex-husband.

The sessions were all audio recorded. For our final session we listened together to extracts taken at particular stages during her period of music therapy. Annabel listened with enormous interest and spontaneously made connections between her playing and her emotions and relationships. She said that she felt 'a very different person from back then' and seemed genuinely proud of her progress. She seemed empowered, somehow, and appeared to be more aware of when she was connected to and disconnected from her feelings. Annabel was now more willing and able to explore and understand her emotions.

Annabel was aware that the pain caused by the loss of her son would not disappear. She missed him desperately and was dreading spending Christmas without him. But, as Annabel pointed out, she was now able to talk about this in a way that would have previously not been possible.

These two abbreviated case studies are very short summaries of the clinical work undertaken. They attempt to illustrate some of the ways in which music therapy provides opportunities for overcoming and working through difficult emotions. By forming a relationship through music, both Adam and Annabel were able to explore new ways of relating and expressing themselves in a way that allowed them a greater sense of freedom. It was vital for Adam and Annabel to feel sufficiently safe and confident in the music therapy room before they could fully express their emotions. They also needed to feel that the therapist and they themselves would not crumble under the intensity of the emotions they expressed. Music is a powerful medium through which an individual's isolation can be penetrated and surmounted.

For reasons of confidentiality identities have been changed.

Note

For further information on music therapy see Alvin (1968), Bunt (1994) and Heal and Wigram (1993).

CHAPTER 26

Dance: The empowerment of the inner self

Albie Ollivierre

Introduction

This chapter arises from a conversation with Morag Hunter-Carsch at the Cumbria conference on Wise Minds. The conference was about developing wise minds and my concern was to point out how dance, as an avenue for everyone, can promote awareness of how to make wise choices. While we both recognized that it is difficult to share dimensions of dance through writing, the idea of attempting to communicate my enthusiasm about dance in this way began to take form – and here it is.

I am a dancer and dance tutor. Before becoming a dance tutor I was a choreographer. Before becoming a dancer, I was a graphic designer. Before all of that I was always creating, but as a child I had a struggle to overcome speech and communication difficulties. I became a difficult and non-cooperative teenager. In contributing to a book about working with students who have communication, emotional and behavioural difficulties, I am attempting a less familiar form of creativity for me – that of formal writing. I am also drawing upon personal experience to try to share some of the inspiration that has assisted me in overcoming my own problems. I do so in the hope that this will be of assistance to others – both teachers and learners – in their quest to draw upon the power that can be found within their inner selves.

During my secondary schooling my English teacher, Mr Daniels, provided me with the kind of inspiration that helped me to create my own stepping stones to tackle a severe speech impediment. Mr Daniels read aloud John Steinbeck's *Of Mice and Men*. His Welsh tones blessed and soothed the class with vibrant rhythms – rhythms that made me feel totally involved in the unfolding story. I was already an artist. My gifts and talents started to reveal themselves from within me when I was only 5 years old. I needed nurturing, and listening to Mr Daniels acted as an exciting catalyst and set me on the road to discovery.

Through every minute of my life I have been fortunate in being able to be creative. The key to creativity is improvisation and this is something I have always enjoyed and found easy. However, simply mastering a technique is different from actually sharing and performing something that is both unique and of substance. This is where my own uniqueness comes into play. My beginnings, my roots, come from the Caribbean, and even though I was born in London my roots and upbringing have affected all aspects of my existence thus far. But, in spite of the pain and struggles and being raised amidst violent inner city London, I have managed to do things that other people may only dream of: I have performed on some of the greatest stages in the world, participated in some amazing tours, taught and choreographed works with some of the most gifted people. Trust me when I say that I am no hero – but I am living proof that if I can make it happen – so can you!

The following three sections of this chapter concern, first, the links between composing, dancing and power; secondly, the challenge of promoting the positive in the inner self. The third section connects the individual with others in addressing issues about creativity. All of these matters are of relevance in understanding how best to empower students to draw upon their inner selves in responding to the challenge to become wise humans and to make wise choices.

Composers, dance makers and people power

Both music and dance have evolved to become influential social hybrids. Collaborating harmoniously together music and dance are a complete fusion and synthesis that reflect and render visible the vivid mental and spiritual landscapes of our times. Dance is interpreted differently by people right across the vast global village. Every living creature or being operates and dances in circles, patterns, rituals and journeys. Spirals and angles are brought together by design, timing and destiny.

Choreography influences and defines. Along with musical rhythms and patterns, dance kinaesthetically translates, migrates and evolves. Through the use of shape and form it penetrates into all aspects of our lives. Musical pulsations, undulations and vibrations flow and merge through progressive positive rhythms. The awesome power of the arts invades, reshapes, creates pace, moods and space, providing us with the untold, the mythological, the imaginative and the most expressive of experiences. It is important for us to stay in touch with our inner selves – with our deepest thoughts and most sensitive of feelings.

In the twenty-first century the values in life have changed dramatically. Indeed, taken from the contemporary arts point of view, dance, music and theatre have assumed multifunctional roles. Creative avenues of deconstructional perspectives such as architecture, design, film and technology have also made remarkable advances. Still, the power of nature remains the most beautiful holder to the key of life. The circle of life evolves and adapts to the changeable spirit of nature.

I am a dance maker. Working with dancers, we create, inspire, motivate – the dancer-performer and the audience – to reach and share in alternative states of being. We reach inside ourselves to find expressive and emotional platforms from which to communicate and exist. The root source of our life stimuli is to invigorate and elevate, to touch and move and to transform people's lives. It is my belief that, no matter what age or level of ability, almost anyone can learn to act, sing or dance.

By providing people with the right opportunity and environment we can help to support and develop the correct tools of positive encouragement. Using the correct sense of focus and nurturing, once we begin to relax and enjoy, we gain confidence. With confidence comes both inner resolve and strength. We are all capable of achieving virtually anything. However, it is important to keep an open mind and to do this we need to allow our inner self to be revealed to us and to strip away any hidden preconceptions, to dispense with any self-opinionatedness and negativity. Tags and labels are not very helpful ways to define what it is to be spontaneous, creative or original. Yet it remains the case that we have the choice to surround ourselves with a sense of purpose (i.e. to create this state) or to create our own obstacles and barriers.

As dance makers or creative artists, we are privileged to combine and actively juggle many guises; for example, we can assume the role of impartial diplomat, challenging risk taker, a trusted partner or an invaluable friend of the people. Also, being avid communicators who bridge the void between a kind of 'no-man's land' and the shared-spiritual-common ground, we can act as magicians or grand illusionists; always controversial – but unique – as leaders and instigators of movement and style. If, by chance, you recognize anything familiar here, you are probably 'a creative' (person) and you may not yet have allowed yourself to flow or gather the right impetus and momentum and to be placed in the right positive direction for self-discovery of your creativity or even to find your direction.

The question then is, 'In what direction should we lead or follow?' This question centrally affects our recognition of our values and the direction in which we are travelling, collectively. This is where 'people power' comes into the equation. We live in a consumer society context, one in which we have practically devoured and consumed everything. With the advent of so-called reality TV, countless chat shows, computer games, fantasy films, food and shopping obsessions, all the goalposts have shifted. In order to prevent our vibrant cultures and global villages from becoming completely bland, new, positive and creative pathways need to be shared among the young who constitute our future.

Yet we must not forget the inspiration from the past. All the best and most memorable pieces of music or dance appear to be the simplest. Yet what may appear to be easy can often become the hardest to define or realize. As the saying goes, 'Climbing the mountain, reaching the summit, always seems like a good idea at the time!' However, alas, in reality simply staying there and placing down positive foundation stones can be a lot harder than we first think it will be.

Promoting the positive inner self

Interaction=Reaction=Inclusion=Consolidation=Communication=Concentration=Motivation=Foundation=Passion=Creation=Connection=Love

Seventy per cent of learning and performing dance is in the mind. As for the rest, some of it comes in the physical form that effortlessly links with our spiritual ('vibes') and essence. As with any sense of expression, drama, vocal or dance movement, it needs a certain level of inspiration. That is what the spiritual dimension is about. With dance, the thinking is not purely on a cognitive (intellectual or academic) level. Learning a dance style or technique is about collecting and gathering an energized intensity, a dynamic vibrancy, and being involved in inventions which may be spontaneous. In relation to performance, there is the well-known comment 'You are only as good as your last show'. If the dancer tries too hard to please the audience, the audience can quickly 'lose the plot' since performing only feels right when the dancer can remain truthful to his or her inner self.

By learning other art forms we can become less restricted, constrained or 'boxed in'. We can become limitless sources of life through nature's enrichment. We can empower and become aware of the natural freedom of harmonious expression. By dancing, all of us can stay in touch with the natural elements: Earth, Fire, Wind, Water. To these I add the essence, 'Spirit'. All of these elements inspire musicians, artists, all of us, alike.

Another question we need to consider is, 'What attracts and sustains our attention?' What is the direction of our response – is it taking us in a constructive or destructive direction? Humans seem to seek new forms of worship, new 'faiths', new recreational diversions, 'drugs', new realms of 'voyeurism'. Their behaviour often involves watching and assimilating, copying, consuming and desiring each other. We love ourselves and we aspire to particular lifestyles. While love of self may be all right in small doses, if we are surrounded by an atmosphere that promotes images of indulgence, which surrounds, invades, manipulates us, we can end up with decreasing levels of positive growth and awareness. This can impact on our attention span and further deplete our overall concentration levels and our ability to explore our creative minds.

The loss or depletion of a sense of inner self can result in loss of positive growth and awareness. It is suggested that in our highly visually distracted culture, whether children are playing at home (e.g. on computer games) or involved in various school activities, they lose concentration. It just dips or falters. This prompts film makers to increase the ingredients of action, suspense and humour and to repeat or dynamically accent by including stimulating events approximately every 15 minutes.

This seems to be reflected also in the auditory context, in popular music, in which the same 'rules' (and prescriptions) are operated through the use of sound effects, multiple repetitive beats, melodies that play with and on our senses. In this way many images attach themselves and become embedded in our senses and subconscious inner states.

In this context, the question that is uppermost must be, 'How can we possibly create, support, harness, enrich and improve ways of empowering the inner self?'

Within young people and adults alike there are countless abilities and avenues through which to study and learn. This learning should also recognize and remain responsive to the significance of the creative arts in influencing all aspects of development. We might ask ourselves, 'Who will be the new spokespeople, leaders, working collectives; writers, poets and philosophers; world-class actors/musicians/athletes/film makers; scientists and educators; where are they all going to come from?' The creative feed the wise, the wise feed the inspired, and the inspired include those who escape through the net.

The point is that development of interpersonal skills, good citizenship, life-enhancing experiences come from our ability to create new vocabularies, themes and positive ideas through communication with each other. How can this infrastructure for positive thinking be both maintained and sustained?

Here are some of the options and suggestions as to why movement, music and dance are important and essential aids in providing an organic platform on the pathway of self-discovery:

- for social inclusion of everyone; sharing in thought-provoking moments, feeling and communicating together on shared common ground; becoming more aware of a constructive sense of focus and purpose; generating themes and ideas that allow us to sustain positive aspects of our lives, dreams and passions and exploring and tackling relevant social issues in a safe and shared environment, thereby empowering our interpersonal skills;
- recognizing the significance of melody, rhythm, harmony; development of movement vocabulary, raised awareness of the social and traditional art forms; improvement of coordinative and motor skills; improvement of kinaesthetic and motivational skills;
- for problem solving, especially when facing what is difficult and dysfunctional; by combining music and dance therapy within the structure of social inclusion;
- for further development of learning and communicative skills; use of dynamics, timing, contrast, expression and interpretation;
- for the promotion of positive role models among young people and for raising levels of realistic achievements, presentation and performance – that remain independent of the competitive edge;
- for evoking, inspiring and building upon progressive cultural stepping stones and for promoting spontaneity, originality, creativity – among everybody.

Collective pathways of originality

Originality=Nature=Grasping hold of the challenging and unknown=Revealing that which yet is undefined and undiscovered=Collective knowledge=Wisdom=An inert sense of Being=Dreams and fantasies=Change and diversity=Life and existence=Projected visionary landscapes=Continuous development of the spontaneous spirit.

Both collectively and individually we are all unique – totally original. It is not just in the composition and blueprint of our DNA, but kept within our 'root-source-foundation'. It is a bit like, one day, being blessed by a personal revelation or turning point and seeing that most powerful light of 'enlightenment' and inspiration. The truth being told. Originality can come to us in many different shapes and forms.

Check out the genius of Pelé, Muhammad Ali; the brilliant uniqueness of Stevie Wonder, Sarah Vaughan, David Bowie, Marvin Gaye, or the superhuman pace of Michael Johnson; the bizarre and visual worlds of Pablo Picasso or Salvador Dali; the inspirational humility of people such as Mother Theresa, Martin Luther King, Jr, Nelson Mandela; the remarkable presence and dynamics of Rudolph Nureyev, Mikhail Baryshnikov, the Nicholas Brothers, Gene Kelly; the creativity of Mozart, Bach, Schoenberg, Stravinsky, Miles Davis. Why not start to create your own list? As an experiment, try composing your own list of things, moments and people that have shaped, changed or inspired you to take new pathways. If you take a careful look at the names of the people already mentioned you might see that nearly all of them have evolved to overcome barriers and boundaries, adversities, struggles and prejudices which surrounded them.

What about the future 'creatives'? Where will the 'original ones' come from? Where will our next inspirational voices exist? In the age of the opportunist, corporate takeovers, ozone and mineral depletion, rising crime, violent sub-culture and 'Generation X' – what next? Perhaps the key is shared positive thinking, and how might we achieve this?

Being creative or original cannot simply be defined by privilege, colour, age/gender or background. We have a natural ability to learn from our mistakes and how to persevere and become more focused and determined to coexist positively in our multicultural, global village. Vitally, it is also about how we show that we feel and care. And for the dance of life – well, given the right set of circumstances, the right chances – and wise choices – we can do anything our imagination wants. What are you waiting for?

Acknowledgements
With thanks to the organizers and colleagues at Cumbria's Wise Minds Conference and to Morag Hunter-Carsch for the encouragement to widen my modes of sharing the message of the value of dance and the recognition of its vital contribution to human communication and potential for learning.

CHAPTER 27

John's story: Episode 5

Reflections

'John' and Paul Cooper

P: So what do you think schools and teachers should do?

J: I think they shouldn't treat young kids like they are china dolls. 'Cos a lot of kids are being expelled from school now from kindergarten. I think that's just silly. What's the point in that? You don't achieve anything by that. And the kids just go on worse. And I think this AD/HD is not as big a problem to it as the way everyone else treats you. I think it makes the problem a whole lot worse. I think the AD/HD is a small problem that is made a lot worse by other people. I don't think it has a major effect on someone's life if they never knew they had it ... like the pills they used to give you. They never used to do anything for me; they used to make you feel sad ... they used to make me feel depressed. My Mum thought it was helping – it wasn't. So she put me on this other one. Then I went – I got expelled. I went to a different school. A special school. Which I hated, School L. I hated it, completely. They were racist again. They were all shouting all the time. I was never that bad – like aggressively bad – throwing chairs at teachers – swearing all the time. I wasn't doing things like that. I just kept myself to myself. So my Mum thought it was working, but it wasn't. It was just a different school. But she doesn't seem to understand that, she just thinks I was lying to her about the pills. She wanted to hear that, so I told her. I was on medication 'til I left school. My Mum insisted that it was helping. So I just used to say, 'Yes, it is.' 'Cos when you're a kid, you really don't want to hurt your mother's feelings by saying it's not true. I don't think you do it knowingly. You just do it as a child – to your parents. You don't lie to them intentionally. You just don't tell them.

I think the problem for me at school was racism at Z to begin with. But I think in general schools just suspend kids for silly things. And I mean for really silly things. I mean they just suspend kids for no reasons any more. I had one friend who had an aerosol in the class, and he was spraying it when the teacher came in. She had asthma. And she started to accuse him of 'aerial assault'! And she tried to suspend him for 'aerial assault'! Things like that are just silly! What do you need things like that in school for? 'Aerial assault'! That's rubbish! Like he did it just to annoy her. They all loved doing these things to her. But she picked on me.

I'm sure if I hadn't been given the attention I was given, when I was doing the things I was doing, I wouldn't have behaved badly. And I see these kids, and see their mothers picking them up – they just leave them, go. They're going to come to you anyway. They're not going to run off. But you're making the problem a lot worse because you're going back, and they're seeing that. And when you're a kid you know that that's the truth – that any time you cry your Mum's going to come and get you. Any time you cause a fuss, you're going to get some attention. Some kids just grow up like that.

It's also the culture where you grow up. 'Cos I never really lived here when I was younger. 'Cos I was mixed race. It was a big problem. Around where I lived I had a couple of friends but it was a big problem. Around here black people are still treated different. They are still persecuted. For definite. Half-castes and black people are just persecuted for no reason. 'Cos they got a bad rep[utation] from everyone. See what I mean? I think it's where you live as well. You have to take into account where you live. A lot of kids that grew up in poverty really – maybe they're bad there. Maybe they're bad at school sometimes, and when they get home they're all right. It all depends on how you're brought up.

My Mum – she didn't bring me up like that. She wasn't rich, she wasn't poor. She never really tried to give me the kind of attention other parents give to their kids. When I came here, I could see that for definite. I never really experienced that many black people before in my life. I think that was the difference. I never used to see my family on my Dad's side. But she used to blame him for that. I ain't too sure. There's blame on both sides there. But I think that affected me in a lot of ways.

P: So how did this lack of attention affect you?

J: I think it made me greedy.

P: What sort of attention did you want?

J: I used to complain a lot to my Mum. And she used to just give in. I knew she'd just give in, in the end. She wouldn't just say, 'Hush your mouth!' or something. 'Keep quiet!' she'd say, 'Shut up, John. Shut up! Shut up! Shut up!' But she was still talking to me, so I knew she was still listening. If you just switch off, and let the child run around, and say, 'Make all that noise, make all that noise. I don't care!' she never used to say things like that. She'd say, 'It causes so much stress!' But a lot of parents, when they try that, they don't really do any favours for the kid. They do make the kid look stupid. You don't want to make your kid look stupid when you're doing it. You just want to make him see that he's doing wrong – not laugh at him while he's doing it. A lot of parents do that – I've seen it on these shows – while they do it they're laughing at the kid. That ain't going to help the child no more, by just laughing at him, and saying, 'You're just being silly.' You should just let him go on and say, 'Go on, just be stupid, then' and sit down – and he's having the temper tantrum over there, sort of thing.

P: So it's all about discipline then?

J: Yes. I think so. 'Cos where my Dad came from, the Caribbean – [they had a] strict upbringing in Jamaica, when he was younger. He came here when he was 10. So for all of his infant life, really, he knew what it was like. And discipline was a lot different then. So you can tell by other people's generations that school was a lot different then as well.

I saw on some TV show the other day that they're trying to do something now about more advanced kids, that they're not going to do GCSEs. They're going to do A/S levels. And I think that is unfair, that they should be allowed to do A/S levels. It's like saying that everyone who doesn't do A/S levels are stupid. They have to do the second GCSE course. And if they aren't doing A/S levels, their parents are going to start thinking – 'cos parents do pile pressure on to their kids, and say, 'Why aren't you doing A/S like your friend?' or something. D'you know what I mean? And I think schools – and I think from maybe when you was younger – since then schools have never got better. They've just changed things. And they've taken away things. And that's what's made school how it is today. I still don't believe they should have the cane. But the way school used to be was a whole lot different to how it is now. Even tho' they used to use the cane. But I still think that if they treated the kids the way they did back then, things would be a lot different.

P: So do you think there should be a more disciplined environment in schools?

J: Yes.

P: So did you behave differently with your Dad?

J: I used to be pretty quiet with my Dad. I used to be a bit loud. But I was usually pretty quiet.

My Mum used to cuss him all the time. Every time I used to go there she used to ask me, 'What you been up to?' Say, if I said something like, 'Oh, we went out somewhere,' she'd say, 'He's got all the money!' Things like that. So I didn't really want to talk about things like that. But it's a hard thing to realize, and my Mum doesn't realize all the things she used to say – all kind of pressure that puts you under, or how it makes you feel. My Dad never used to speak to me that much. He was just quiet. He never used to speak to me. He used to just pick me up and give me some money. So we never really used to be that close.

I think that all these things that go on around you – I've seen these programmes like *How to Build a Human*. You can never have a child how you want it to be. 'Cos how it grows up and what it experiences changes a child. And this AD/HD I think it exists, but it's not as big a problem as –. I think it sets things off, and it sets things in motion. It's like a wave. It gets higher and higher, and it just splashes; makes a big wave.

P: So does that mean that having AD/HD made it easier for you to get into trouble?

J: Yes. Definitely. When I found out I had it I could just use it as an excuse.

P: Did having AD/HD make it more difficult for you to resist misbehaving?

J: Yes, I think so. Really, 'cos everything to do with attention – 'cos that's what it's about, losing your attention. If you're bored you want attention. That's what it used to be. Like I said,

I still think that's all it is to do with. But I think other things happen, with teachers and other things in your life, parents. It just changes the way you are. I think that makes other kids aggressive. When you grow up it makes other kids aggressive. The whole condition. But then they start treating everyone the same. They start treating everyone as if they are the same. And they cross-reference you with other people and start thinking, 'He's the same, he's the same, he's the same.' And when parents watch these shows they say, 'Oh, my kid's just like that.' And they'll tell the kids, 'You're just like that.' And that doesn't help them, does it? That makes it worse, I think … and when you get all the psychiatrists and all that, that's when it's a bad thing. And they start explaining to you what it is.

P: Does that put you under pressure to behave?

J: Badly! 'Cos otherwise they don't believe that you got it. I start thinking, 'Well, if I can't help it, I might as well just do it.' I don't think that helps anyone. Like when I went to the special school, it was like being treated like a little kid. For being good you got gold stars. I don't see why any kid should get a gold star for being good. That should be compulsory – that you have to be good. There's a lot of things I understand now that I didn't understand when I was younger. But I can see that everyone had to be good at school. You don't get a gold badge for doing it. Or a silver badge. Rewarding kids for bad behaviour doesn't help them. It puts them in a kind of false security. If you surround them with everyone the same – it's like segregation. And when you go to college you have the dumb group of people, and you still have your next group of people. And they all start to pair off, and it starts and it gets worse through their life. A lot of people like that suffer from depression when they get older. A lot of them just kill themselves. 'Cos they've never known what it's like to have integration. When I went to that special school some of them [other pupils] had never been to [mainstream] junior school. They'd only ever been past infant school – they'd been suspended. They were all acting bad and they never thought it was wrong. They didn't have no other kids for an example. To set an example. They didn't know. So they just thought it was all right to behave like that. But it wasn't. Special schools don't help you. They pull you back. 'Cos they start giving you work that ain't of a high school standard. How are you going to help someone by going slower? 'Cos they're going to be like that forever. It's a horrible chain. I hate to say it, but I think that special schools should help kids learn quicker not slower. It's putting them further behind other people, 'cos when they come out they ain't got any qualifications. When I went there it had only been open about two years. When I left I think I did only one GCSE. Science syllabus. I got 'F'. We never really did any maths that was kind of challenging enough. We used to get these textbooks that you did in Year 7. I remember doing it in Year 7 at School A. We did it in Year 10 and 11 [at the special school]. And kids were struggling. I remember doing it easily. And kids were struggling. But what Mum said was they wouldn't accept me in any other mainstream school. So I don't believe in any kind of segregation for any kids. 'Cos I think for segregation the pros are well outweighed by the cons. I mean in later life. Everybody's talking about the present but you want to worry about your kids later on in life. But parents don't seem to look at that sometimes. They need to focus on what's best for their kids in the future; not just what's going on now. 'Cos when you're a kid a lot of things will help you, but in the end there's those things that will let you down. Like kids with disabilities in general should go to mainstream schools. I think for kids who can't do anything for themselves, maybe that's different. Maybe there might still be bullying, but that's going to occur anywhere. I think the only way to eradicate it is to stop segregating people from other people. When you do that you make the world a whole lot worse place. 'Cos if people start building judgements out of crowds. 'Cos if you grow up with one crowd they look at other people differently. 'Cos you're not all together. 'Cos kids with disabilities get treated like that – like they're always like that. And I think a lot of people with disabilities, they can't help being like that 'cos you've treated them like kids anyway. If you treated them a lot different then they might be different. They might still have that disability but they might be different. They might be human. Sometimes they feel like they don't get treated like humans. They should just get treated like everyone else. Some of them die so early they missed out on everything. 'Cos they been treated like a kid for so long they missed out on loads of things they could have done when they were younger. Especially like kids who can walk when they are young but have got a deteriorating thing – their parents make them stay in.

P: Is it the case that although having AD/HD can have an influence on your behaviour, in your view kids' behaviour in school is affected most by the way in which they are handled?

J: I think most kids with AD/HD – a lot of the kids I knew – they could help the way they were. Things set them off a lot easier because of the ways they were segregated and put into the same schools. Everyone else around you in normal school has got a certain level of patience. If no one else around has got the same amount of patience as them then there's going to be riots, ain't there? There's gonna be fights – disruptive. If you put a whole lot of people together with the same kind of thing – with attention problems – you're going to have a lot worse because everyone's going to start. It's like have too many of them in one place. It's a hard thing to say. I don't believe in special schools. But then if you start putting everyone in the same schools then they start expelling everybody. People don't go to school. It's hard to say, but I don't think the way the system works now works at all. I don't think it helps any kids. Just making more special schools makes it worse. As you see more people get segregated every day.

I do believe there is such a thing as AD/HD but I think the hype around it makes it a lot worse than it should be. There's a lot of psychiatrists around; they assume they know what you are feeling. But they don't. And you don't really want to tell them. It's not until you get older you have reasons. When you're younger you don't seem to know why you have to tell anyone. When you get older you feel, 'Oh, I can tell them now.'

CHAPTER 28

Drama and role-play in learning

Neil Kitson

Introduction

Drama and role-play can help all of us, if we choose to explore its potential. It may enable us to acquire the confidence, clarity and conviction that we need to break bad news to others, give a presentation, manage a group or run a meeting. It allows us to reduce the gulf between 'us' and 'them', between the givers and the receivers, by acknowledging the potential in drama and role-play for ourselves and others.

In this context we are not talking about drama as a staged play, but as an event in which we can act out various roles in order to perform better in future, similar situations. Doctors can be put in the consultant, patient or relative roles to achieve understanding of the different feelings and emotions that accompany the breaking of bad news to others. It enables them to try out words and actions in a safe environment, one where they can gain feedback on their performance.

Drama, therefore, is active learning where the people involved are urged to take courage and experiment, receive advice and learn by reflection. It has been used since the 1960s with mentally ill patients as well as with children achieving poorly in schools. Mime, movement and improvisation were found to produce encouraging results. Since then, drama has developed as an important activity in the training of those who are learning personal skills for their jobs.

Why drama and role-play?

Whatever the context and composition of a group, two factors always apply:

1. Drama increases confidence and improves a range of skills in simulated experiences that are based on real events.

2. Participants can find a sense of community, security and support within the drama and role-play experience.

They may explore, take risks, increase their understanding of 'self', build confidence and make relevant changes to their behaviour. Creative drama and role-play in a group setting can be the means of finding out about the unknown while, at the same time, having an equal value in reinforcing the known.

Structure of drama and role-play

Social psychologists have observed that we organize our lives in a dramatic structure or framework. We can view others and ourselves in a series of scenes and episodes, some of which have a consciously predictable structure, such as the way we organize a meeting, presentation or celebration. Such scenes have a conscious 'text' and usually the 'roles' are prescribed. The scenes within this framework will have their key 'actors' and 'supporting cast'. There will be a series of events leading to a predictable ending. There are other scenes, however, which do not appear to be predictable – meetings that occur by chance, informal gatherings and daily interactions with family or colleagues at work. On examination, however, we find that many of the scenes have predictable elements including a sub-text, roles which may be flexible or inflexible, as well as an inevitable ending.

Roles

There is a reluctance to admit that we constantly engage in role-play in the events of our lives. Perhaps the use of the word 'play' makes us feel that what we are doing is not for real and therefore not important? Or is it that being in a role somehow implies that we are not being ourselves?

We cannot escape, however, from adopting a variety of roles in the situations in which we find ourselves if we want to be successful people. This capacity to role-play develops very early – at about 10 months of age. Becoming 'mobile in character' is more important initially than becoming 'mobile in body'. It is an essential feature of behaviour that allows us to play a part in what goes on. If we fail to develop this skill, our ability to communicate and cooperate is completely stunted. Our role-playing ability develops right through childhood and adolescence and is shaped by the family and our contacts in the world outside. By the time we reach adulthood, each of us has embraced a huge variety of roles, which form a role repertoire to relate our internal and external worlds.

Sometimes individuals find difficulty in making connections between these internal and external facets. Others may develop rigid and fixed roles in early life or inappropriate roles may have emerged through inadequate or faulty modelling. Drama and role-play help us to come to terms with everyday life and facilitate exploration of our inner selves. Role-play also enables us to transcend ourselves and go beyond our daily limitations and boundaries.

Using drama and role-play activities helps us to:

- *expand* the limits of our experience;
- *stimulate* our artistic and aesthetic sense;
- *uncover* the predictable structures that trap us in unhelpful behaviours and find creative alternatives;
- *redevelop* appropriate roles through practice and remodelling until they become natural and less conscious;
- *encourage* the extension of our role repertoires in different situations;
- *create* new possibilities for experiencing scenes in unusual ways;
- *discover* ways of connecting internal responses with external behaviour and vice versa.

The basic premise for drama and role-play is that we all have potential for some change in our feelings, thoughts and actions if given the right opportunity and support. There are three distinct types of focus that can be identified:

1. *Creativity and expression*
   The emphasis here is on creative development and aesthetic experience and can include mime, movement and improvisation. Participants may be encouraged to produce something for sharing with a wider audience. Such activity provides stimulation, encouragement and a heightened experience of self. Confidence is developed from imagination and the use of undiscovered potential. Communication and cooperation are improved.

2. *Tasks, skills and learning*
   The behaviour and skills of daily life can be rehearsed, refined or modified through the medium of role-play. Skills acquired may include simple communication or training in the use of non-verbal behaviour. Initiating conversation and improving conceptual skills such as problem solving are important outcomes of this

approach. Participants gain experience of decision-making and negotiation. They develop autonomy as well as cooperative skills. This type of drama is very goal specific and the facilitator is often a role model. The training of doctors, teachers, magistrates, social workers and others includes this type of role-play activity. Playing out a doctor–patient consultation, a class lesson, a court scene or a counselling session in order to develop the relevant skills and evaluate behaviour is a vital part of training that targets personal development and performance.

3. *Self-awareness and change*
   An 'insight-type' group is set up in order to explore feelings and relationships in a safe way. Unconscious processes may be given creative expression by enacting scenes from the past, present or future and recreating experiences. Self-discovery and change are the aims and the group involved represents life. Participants are encouraged to reflect on their own experiences and changes can be explored through the medium of role-play.

Drama and role-play are not just a set of techniques but a creative process which taps experience at a deep level and reflects on it with regard to future performance. Role-play must make use of the real experience of the participants. If you are asked to role-play a Victorian, for example, this might be impossible because of a lack of knowledge or experience of this historical period. Role-playing registering as a hotel guest is easier if we have done this before or are acquainted with the procedures by someone else. Any involvement in role-play must include a 'de-rolling' process, such as shutting eyes and picturing in the mind's eye the character just played and visualizing them walking away, turning a corner and waving before being lost to sight. This done, participants can open their eyes and share with each other what it felt like to play the role. This helps individuals become themselves again and leave the group with their own identity.

Creative drama, as just described and experienced by the participants in this session, is an adventure, and as with all adventures has inherent risks and dangers, as being someone else can be disturbing for someone who is not comfortable with their own identity. Drama and role-play can, however, be a powerful way to learn new insights and develop personal skills. Take a risk and reap a rich reward!

CHAPTER 29

The art of influence

Ian Jones

Introduction

Our ability to influence people lies at the heart of selling ideas to others and is the basis of successful communication. The concept of 'persuasion' is germane to this process and can be broadly defined as human communication designed to influence others by modifying their beliefs, values or attitudes.

Definitions, however, can be troublesome things because they are treated as providing sharp distinctions about what is or is not the character of the object so described. So, for example, if one defines 'persuasion' in such a way as to distinguish cases of 'persuasion' from those of 'manipulation' by requiring that in genuine cases of persuasion the persuader acts in good faith, then some will object that such a definition is too narrow. Including 'manipulation' as an instance of 'persuasion', however, will produce objections from those who think it important to exclude instances of sheer 'manipulation' from the definition of persuasion.

It is possible to clarify a concept without having to be committed to a sharp definition by focusing on the shared features of paradigm cases of the notion. These paradigms are the sorts of instances that most people would agree are circumstances of the concept in question and provide straightforward, uncontroversial examples. One can achieve a sense of the central application of the idea, therefore, without the necessity to be confined by sharp definitional lines.

Common features of persuasion

What sort of shared features can be observed in applying the idea of influence or persuasion? There are six obvious ones.

First, when we say that one person has persuaded (influenced) another we identify this as a successful attempt. The notion of success is embedded in the concept, as in saying: 'I influenced him'. One can say: 'I tried to influence him but failed', which does not make any real sense.

Recognition that influence is connected with success leads directly to the next two features: the presence of some criterion or goal and the existence of some intent to reach for them. To speak of 'success' is to imply a standard of success and that the one who does the influencing intends to achieve a goal. If I said: 'I persuaded Neil to vote for Jon', I am implying that I intended to obtain that effect.

A fourth feature, shared by cases of persuasion, is a measure of freedom (free will, free choice, voluntary action) on the part of the one doing the influencing. Being induced by a television appeal to make a donation freely to a good cause is in direct contrast to a thief who takes a victim's money under circumstances where threats have been made. Here, the persuadee's freedom is minimized and it would be questioned whether 'persuasion' or personal influence is involved. The persuadee's freedom is not clear-cut, as in the example.

Next, cases of influence are ones in which effects are achieved through communication, especially through the medium of language. That is, influence is something achieved through one person communicating with another. My physical dragging of you by the scruff of the neck to come shopping with me is something quite different from my talking you into accompanying me so that you can choose what you fancy for supper. What distinguishes these two instances is that communication is involved in the latter case but not in the former.

Finally, cases of influence involve a change in the mental state of the persuadee as a precursor to a change in behaviour. Some ordinary cases of influencing may be described as involving only a change in mental state, as in: 'I persuaded you to go to the Doctor'. But even when behavioural change is involved as in: 'I persuaded Ruth to go running', there is normally presumed to be some underlying change in mental state. Ruth has been influenced to think that her general fitness is poor and that she needs to take up running to improve this.

Thus even where a persuader's eventual aim is to influence what people do (to influence how people vote, or what products they buy), at least in cases of persuasion that aim is ordinarily accomplished by changing what people think (e.g. what they think of the political candidate or what products they buy). That is, persuasion is generally conceived of as involving influencing others by influencing their mental states rather than by somehow influencing their conduct directly.

In literature about persuasion and influence the relevant mental state has most commonly been characterized as an attitude, and that attitude change is the goal of such a process. Even where a persuader's ultimate goal is the modification of another's behaviour, that goal is typically seen to be achieved through a process of attitude change – the presumption being that attitudes are precursors of behaviour.

These shared features can be strung together to produce a definition of persuasion and influence: a successful intentional effort at influencing another's mental state through communication in a circumstance in which the persuadee has some measure of freedom. Such a definition leaves open to dispute, however, how much 'success' is required and how 'intentional' the effort should be.

In spite of such shortcomings, the features just described help us to achieve a sense of the central core of the concept of persuasion and influence. What brings about persuasion is the matter of the following sections. Three ideas are considered, which help to explain the activity. These are rapport, relationships and recall.

Rapport

When we begin communicating we have to open up the channels before the information can be passed through. We do this initially by greeting each other, which produces a warm feeling and a sense of belonging. After this there might be some 'small talk' such as: 'lovely weather we're having', which acknowledges the other person's existence and helps to dispel the discomfort of the initial contact, when people are wondering how to get the dialogue going.

Harmless, trivial remarks unlock the gates so that conversation can flow. The next phase in the process would be to identify oneself in a brief introduction and this ritual takes place in order to find out whether you can get on with the other person and make a social link. Much of our communication, particularly in leisure hours, is of this nature and is known in the textbooks as 'phatic communication'. Although some despise this 'small talk' as inessential comment because it is chat rather than serious conversation, it is nevertheless vital for starting relationships.

Relationships

These are established through social interaction that continues long enough so that we become linked to another person by a relatively stable set of expectations. The reasons we commit to a relationship with someone else are various. It may be to seek comfort, feel wanted, or to find a framework for fashioning our behaviour. At the very least a relationship will be founded on self-interest, and successful relationships depend on both parties gaining something from the experience.

Successful relationships encourage and require the exchange of personal information and report of feelings. Levels of disclosure may need to be high in order to identify with each other's concerns. Relationships are defined in terms of how close you feel to the other person, how you expect to act and others to act towards you. Differences in authority will dictate how you act with another person. Teacher–student, parent–child, boss–subordinate are all relationships which imply that communication will take place along dominant–submissive lines. Other relationships are based on equal authority patterns as between friends, colleagues or clients, where you cannot force the other person to change their behaviour but could influence them by appealing to their needs. For example, someone could be persuaded to buy a new cleaner if they were told that it saved them the valuable time and effort that was an important issue for them. Roles, therefore, play a crucial part in setting expectations and providing the framework for successful relationships.

Recall

All of us have had the experience of revisiting a place where, for example, we went to school or on holiday and found that a particular sight, smell, sound and touch brought back a flood of experiences thought to be forgotten. The ability to recall and reproduce memory images is vital for successful performance. Memories influence how we react and act in new experiences based on our recall of similar activities and our ability to learn from them.

The Greeks so worshipped memory that they made a goddess out of her – Mnemosyne. It was her name from which derived the current word mnemonics, used to describe memory techniques to help learning. Long before we had discovered the physiological breakdown of the functions in the right and left hemispheres of the brain, the Greeks had intuitively realized that there are two under-lying principles that ensure an effective memory.

Imagination and association

In present times, most of us are actively discouraged from using our imaginative abilities. Consequently we learn very little about the nature of mental association. Quite simply, if you want to remember anything, all you have to do is link it with some known fixed item that calls upon your imagination. This we have attempted to do in this presentation. The picture *Escargot*, by Matisse in the Tate Gallery, is the link for the three ideas rapport, relationships and memory as seen in the presentation at the end of this chapter. This picture uses blocks of shape and colour to represent a snail (*escargot* is the French word for snail) and is a useful framework on which to hang the core ideas of this chapter.

The rules for recall developed by the Greeks fit in with information discovered about the left and right brains. They realized that in order to remember effectively you have to use every aspect of your mind. The left brain is attuned to verbalizing whereas the right brain is attuned to visualizing and these processes must integrate. In order to recall you must include in your associated and linked mental landscape the following:

1. *Colour*: vivid colours (as in the *Escargot* picture) improve your recall by about 50 per cent.
2. *Imagination*: the more vividly you can imagine, the more easily you can remember. Sub-areas within imagination include:
   (a) expansion: the more enormous the mental images the better;
   (b) contraction: imagine your picture as very tiny and you will recall it well;
   (c) absurdity: the more ridiculous your image the more outstanding it is.
3. *Rhythm*: vary the rhythm in your image and it will weave into memory.
4. *Movement*: moving images are memorable.
5. *Senses*: involving all senses in your image: taste, touch, smell, sight, sound, strengthens recall.
6. *Sex*: as the strongest drive is a powerful image maker.
7. *Sequence and order*: categorizing and organizing allows easy retrieval.
8. *Number*: using number aids in different ways helps recall (e.g. blocks in *Escargot*).
9. *Dimension*: using the right brain to visualize in 3D makes the image real.

In each memory system there are key words (such as rapport, relationships and recall) and these provide the pegs on which to hang other items that need to be remembered as in the detail about the topic.

Thus recall is about connections and these need to be as easy as possible:

- crashing things together
- sticking things together
- placing things on top of each other
- placing things underneath each other
- placing things inside each other
- substituting things for each other
- placing things in new situations.

For example, if you wish to remember the French word for 'rabbit', which is *lapin*, imagine a white rabbit in your lap!

The systems of memory, worked out by the Greeks and for nearly 2,000 years regarded as mere tricks, were in fact based on the way in which the human brain actually functions. The Greeks realized the importance of *words* – order, sequence, number – now known to be the functions of the brain's left side; and of *imagination* – colour, rhythm, dimension and daydreaming – now known to be right brain activities. Put together verbalizing and visualizing and use both parts of the brain together for the secret of success in thinking and communicating.

Mnemosyne was to the Greeks the most beautiful of all the goddesses, proved by the fact that Zeus spent more time in her bed than in that of any other goddess or mortal. He slept with her for nine days and nights and the result of that coupling was the birth of the nine Muses – the goddesses presiding over love, poetry, epics, hymns, dance, comedy, tragedy, music, history and astronomy. For the Greeks, therefore, the infusion of energy (Zeus) into memory (Mnemosyne) produced both creativity and knowledge.

They were correct. If you apply these recall techniques correctly your creativity will soar and your ability to communicate and influence others expand and develop. In the process you will be synthesizing the left and right sides of your brain and allowing your entire mind to influence your performance. This presentation uses the image of *Escargot* to illustrate the art of influence – a process that you must understand and remember if you are to be a successful communicator and a successful person.

Backgound

Ian has been the director of Mindskills (www.mindskills.co.uk), a training organization that focuses on the processes of learning. He was originally a senior member of staff at the Hendon Police College but a serious car accident forced him to retire from the Police Force. Since then, he has worked with Tony Buzan, the well-known 'mind' guru. He has been a frequent presenter on radio and television and was a consultant to the very successful Harlow On-Line Learning Initiative. Ian has had clients from all over the world – even from royal families! He has been a special award winner in the Human Communication International Awards for Communication and impresses everyone with his ability to communicate his knowledge in a fun way!

CHAPTER 30

The University of the First Age and study support schemes

Chris Comber

This chapter seeks to explore and assess the effectiveness of two innovative approaches that set out to be complementary to, but different from, mainstream approaches to education. They focus on the interaction between social, emotional and cognitive dimensions and are relatively informal by nature. Research findings arising from these initiatives are examined and considered with regard to their application to the classroom.

In the present climate of emphasis on End of Key Stage assessment results and league tables, the measurement of a pupil's progress through the (National) curriculum plays a key role in the education process. Test-oriented teaching requires the application, marking and interpretation of specific procedures in order to track pupil progress. In order for this to be a reliable indicator of attainment, even assuming that the tests are effective and appropriate, it also has to be assumed that:

- what is being measured is a valid indicator of 'progress';
- the battery of tests is fully comprehensive;
- all children present 'progress' in the same way.

It can safely be accepted that some tests provide indicators of 'progress' in certain areas of certain curriculum subjects (e.g. reading age scores) but it is by no means as certain that the majority of these tests address all indicators of 'progress' (such as levels of self-esteem, confidence, decision-making), nor that they are capable of demonstrating that all children have made progress in the same way. It could be argued therefore that the requirements of these tests have, for many, resulted in a system whereby what, how and when something is taught (and learned) is dictated by the perceived need to drive up results. Assessment relies heavily upon testing procedures and 'achievement' is charted accordingly. A child's recorded success (or lack of it) is directly related to his or her scores from those tests.

What happens to those pupils who do not present gains in a way that can be measured by these tests? Is it to be assumed that a pupil whose scores show little, if any, improvement on standardized measures of attainment is actually making no educational progress in any area? Either way, the result is that there are children for whom praise and celebration of progress are rare events. Expressed another way, there is a need to examine and redefine our criteria with regard to what is meant by 'progress' and how we, as educators, set out to achieve it.

To this end, this chapter looks at findings of research conducted on two innovative approaches used in Leicester:

1. the New Opportunities Fund (NOF) sponsored University of the First Age (UfA) Summer Learning Programme, July/August 2001; and
2. the Leicester City Football Club Study Support Centre activities, 1999.

Both approaches were made distinctive by their relative informality and their provision for the necessary interaction between social, emotional and cognitive dimensions.

The UfA programme provided a variety of learning experiences based on a series of challenges given to its participants. Its stated aims were to:

- improve student confidence in learning and motivation to learn;
- develop teacher skills in an area of 'learning to learn', in the development of learner resilience and the teaching of thinking skills;
- develop a curriculum planning framework leading to the development in learners of knowledge and understanding and skills and competences;
- promote a portfolio-based system of student progress.

Each project took the form of a learning challenge, including activities that ranged across the curriculum (e.g. sport, art) and beyond (designing team events, making promotional videos). The notion of a learning team is of particular importance to the UfA model; therefore in addition to teachers those involved were drawn from support staff, parents, governors and local community members. The students were encouraged to regard themselves as part of the team, for example by contributing to the development and evaluation of the programme or becoming 'peer tutors' – in other words, being included at all stages, with the aim of developing skills, confidence and abilities, a concept central to the UfA approach to learning.

Without exception the UfA challenges were regarded as a success by those involved. Indicators of that success were provided by a number of observations. The level of enthusiasm from both pupils and staff was high throughout the time the scheme was running and this was borne out by the fact that many pupils went on to join after-school study support clubs. There was a high level of conflict-free collaboration and teamwork, combined with learner independence and autonomy, with children of different educational abilities and social backgrounds working together effectively. Work produced was of a good quality, children clearly demonstrated confidence in presenting their efforts, and parents were impressed by the achievement of their children. Finally, staff and helpers found the experience of working in this way both rewarding and stimulating, more than one going so far as to say that it represented 'what they had come into teaching for' far more than the regular curriculum. The overall picture is one of strong endorsement of the projects on the part of the participants at all levels.

The Leicester City Football Club Study Support Centre scheme project, a joint venture in partnership with the city and county education departments, formed part of a wider, government-inspired initiative, 'Playing for Success' (PfS), and aimed to assess the impact of attending the scheme on levels of literacy, ICT competence and pupil attitudes. It targeted KS2 and KS3 children deemed to be underachieving or in some way disengaged from learning. Through the provision of a stimulating learning environment, it aimed to:

- raise the aspirations and achievement of pupils;
- design curriculum materials intended to enrich and extend literacy and numeracy skills;
- encourage development of ICT capability;
- promote learning as a positive endeavour;
- improve motivation, social skills and self-confidence.

As with the UfA scheme, children were encouraged to work collaboratively on a variety of different tasks, typically in groups of six or seven working on various word-processing tasks or internet work. Groups moved around after about 30–40 minutes, though there was choice and tasks other than 'set' activities were available. It was intended that children would receive a high level of individual support during the sessions and though the pupil/mentor ratio was higher than intended, it was still, at around 7:1, a better ratio than that found in the typical classroom. Again as with the UfA scheme, there was a high level of engagement from the pupils for sustained periods of time, all the more remarkable when it is considered that the sessions ran for two hours after a full school day. Pupils enjoyed what they were doing and there was rarely any disruptive behaviour.

The two schemes had several crucial common elements. They both provided a challenge-led curriculum with a variety of tasks, with both personal and group progress-led learning. Both provided for a high degree of student autonomy, choice and involvement with mentoring and partnerships central to the ways of working. Both were more informal than school in nature, with many staff and pupils on first-name terms, and both provided more staff (sometimes in the form of helpers) than school, thereby increasing the opportunity for interaction between pupils and staff. There was movement from one task to another, with frequent breaks and snacks and drinks available. Finally, great emphasis was placed on the celebration of success in any area, non-academic (such as an increase in self-confidence) as well as related to the task in hand. Praise rather than criticism was the norm.

It is interesting to compare these characteristics to those of 'normal' classroom teaching, which is more formal in approach. In school, the learning environment is curriculum led and work tends to be teacher led with dissemination of information from the teacher down. Pupil involvement in the design and application of the learning programme is typically minimal, with progress regarded in the main as academic in nature with a reliance on test scores as indicators of that progress. Work takes place within set periods of time with few breaks (themselves timetabled) and many tasks require the pupil to stay in one place. Progress tends to be centred upon the individual, not the group, in most subjects, and some schools can provide no support other than that given by the teacher.

It goes without saying that this is a generalized view and that there will be schools which differ widely from those described above. However, even in classrooms where group work and discussion-based activities are the norm, the teacher remains the person with main responsibility for and control over the curriculum and its dissemination. It must also be acknowledged that the provisions of schemes such as those described above and those of schools do overlap. Both provide teaching and learning environments. Both possess aims and objectives. Both have structure and use assessment procedures and reward systems. Both will have links between home and school and both will offer visits and special events. So what, we must ask ourselves, is it that makes the schemes seem so much more successful in terms of pupil engagement and enjoyment? Why, in the words of one pupil, are schemes regarded as 'much funner'?

What is required is the identification of those elements that enrich the scheme environment and the application of those elements, where appropriate, to the environment of school. Let us take as an example the notion of student involvement. This was seen as a motivating factor in the out-of-school schemes. Through becoming involved, or being required to become involved, in decisions about their learning, pupils were provided with an element of choice and, alongside it, of control. It provided a baseline for engagement with the learning process that would be lacking were learning to be 'imposed' such as occurs in a more formal setting. Involvement with others through group work and, through that involvement, the gaining of support from peers is another way of engaging a pupil, as is a system of peer mentoring.

One of the main stated aims of both schemes was to affect the way in which pupils view the learning process and, by implication, the way they view school. It is clear that the schemes succeeded overwhelmingly in motivating children to engage in the learning process within their own environment, but what of attitudes to school? It was one major and disappointing research finding that although an out-of-school activity takes its participants from a school community, the two environments can remain separate, that what succeeds in the out-of-school schemes is not automatically communicated to the classroom, even where, in some cases, the same staff members are involved in both. The cause of this is unclear and could be due to a number of factors such as lack of staff training, lack of scheme/school coordinators, lack of time or commitment on the part of staff whose workload and obligations leave them little time for dissemination of new ideas. Whatever the cause, if the link between scheme and school remains at best tenuous, how are the pupils expected to make the connection? If a pupil's success in the scheme is not noted and celebrated in school, why should they change their view that the scheme is somewhere 'you can do lots of things, meet nice people and learn lots of stuff' and that school is a different place entirely? Perhaps one solution would be to make elements of the school learning environment appear more like a learning opportunity presented by a scheme. In this context and in that of national guidelines, the 'challenge-based curriculum' of the scheme would become the curriculum-based challenge of school.

With regard to issues of self-esteem and confidence, ways of working such as peer mentoring and collaborative group work (in which all had a part to play) proved highly effective and popular. These and other strategies that are more commonly observed in out-of-school schemes are already regularly used in some schools and have been for some time. It is not suggested that schools can – or would wish to – abandon a 'standards'-based approach entirely. Neither is it proposed that schools return to the (albeit somewhat mythical) 'progressive' educational principles of the 1970s. Nevertheless, there is plentiful evidence that out-of-school-hours schemes can be highly motivating and positive experiences for children, and incorporating some of their principles and practices into the more formal setting of the traditional classroom has, we suggest, considerable potential.

Applying the 'sharing' principles to this, one could suggest that a school that does work in this way should mentor one which does not, disseminating information and sharing good practice. Staff training should be provided if possible, but at the very least managers should ensure that all staff recognize the validity of such things as an increase in ability to work collaboratively or a gain in self-confidence as indicators in assessing progress.

The informality of the schemes was another major factor in their success and its application to mainstream education should be considered. A more flexible timetable could perhaps be intro-duced for at least part of the day. The common system of using one member of staff to teach one subject for a whole year to a particular group should be challenged. Would it really be beyond the time-tabling capability of a school to use staff more imaginatively, with – for example – staff sharing responsibility for each group, resulting in more variety of approaches for children and a wider variety of groups for the teacher? The use of support staff and other helpers, such as appropriate volunteers, would also help provide a better staff:pupil ratio.

Some school staff, managers and teachers alike, will require tangible evidence to persuade them that it is worth the effort and time to try to make full use of the transferable gains made as a result of involvement in out-of-school activities and it is a challenge to develop user-friendly testing procedures suited to that purpose. It is important, however, that potential improvements to be made as a result of amalgamating scheme and school approaches should not be seen as a means of driving up test results.

There are gains in terms of pupil engagement, learning and enjoyment to be derived from both the challenge-based curriculum and the curriculum-based challenge. The two learning environments are certainly not mutually exclusive and have clearly been shown to enrich each other. What is required now is the will and the funding to instigate real efforts to amalgamate the two approaches in order to provide a learning environment for all pupils that draws upon best practice from both and to evaluate thoroughly the impact of such initiatives.

Professor Tim Brighouse, Chief Education Officer of Birmingham and founder of the UfA, summed it up when he said:

> Giving young people more time, to do more of the same, in the same way, with the same people is not going to raise standards of achievement dramatically upward – we need to seize the opportunity to do something radically different.

CHAPTER 31

Patterns of effective provision for pupils with emotional and behavioural difficulties: the English experience

Ted Cole

Introduction

What are the key constituents of effective provision and practice for pupils with SEBD? Between 1995 and 2002 the University of Birmingham SEBD research team conducted a series of projects suggesting answers to this question. Our work included: a national study of English SEBD schools (Cole *et al.*, 1998), an investigation into good practice in mainstream schools for pupils with SEBD (Daniels *et al.*, 1998), establishing patterns of provision made by LAs (Cole *et al.*, 2003) and a longitudinal study of young people permanently excluded from schools in ten LAs (Daniels *et al.*, 2003). This chapter draws on data from these and others of our projects, as well as a wide study of the literature on SEBD.

The use of the term 'effective provision' should not be construed as indicating an acceptance of simplistic notions of 'school effectiveness' or 'improvement' (see Cole and Visser, 1998). I use the term to denote more than schools responding to the headline effectiveness factors (see Cooper *et al.*, 1994), relevant though these usually are to most educational settings for pupils with SEBD. I associate effectiveness with educational communities that value and respect children with SEBD which work in a holistic, collaborative manner within and across the school or unit's boundaries. In these settings, staff understand and address the social, educational and, sometimes, the biological/genetic reasons for these young people's often challenging behaviour (Cole *et al.*, 2002; Daniels and Cole, 2002). The pastoral is stressed and interwoven with the pursuit of the academic to an extent that is not realized in too many English schools (e.g. Cooper *et al.*, 1994; Powers, 1996). Here, the pupils with SEBD generally *feel* wanted and included. In a continuing imperfect world, these are *only sometimes* mainstream schools (Daniels *et al.*, 1998).

This chapter first describes the range of provision where 'effective practice' can be found, while estimating the numbers of pupils involved. It then describes some of the key ingredients of effective provision, irrespective of physical location.

Numbers in/range of English provision

Estimating the numbers of pupils with SEBD is problematic given difficulties of definition and inadequate government statistics (Cole *et al.*, 2003). However, our research indicates that most pupils with SEBD and/or disaffection remain in mainstream schools (perhaps between 3 and 6 per cent of the population) (see Cole *et al.*, 2003; Daniels *et al.*, 2003) for England; Kauffman (2001) suggests a similar range for the USA. These pupils with SEBD may spend all their lessons in mainstream classes or, more likely, some or all of their time in forms of 'on-site unit' (e.g. 'learning support units'). In 1998 a small number (about 0.3 per cent of the compulsory school-aged population, i.e. *c.*20,000 pupils) attended SEBD special schools or PRUs. In that year, about 11,400 pupils attended SEBD schools (estimate based on DfEE figures). By 2002 the numbers of pupils attending PRUs had grown to nearly 10,000, although some of the young people in PRUs could be described as more disaffected or perhaps delinquent than 'SEBD'. In addition, in 1998, there were about 6,500 pupils sometimes with attendant moderate learning difficulties placed in MLD schools registered with the DfEE to accept pupils with SEBD (Cole *et al.*, 2003). There are also unknown numbers, possibly thousands, of young people, aged under 16 and who might be termed SEBD, now receiving education and training full or part time in further education (FE) colleges. Boys heavily outnumber girls in all types of provision.

Our research clearly indicates that effective provision, appreciated by the young people with SEBD, can be made in mainstream or special schools, PRUs or FE colleges. LAs are wise (as most are) to maintain a range of options. This allows the better matching of the young person to appropriate provision and for movement of the young person from one setting to another in response to his or her changing needs (Cole *et al.*, 2003; Daniels *et al.*, 2003).

The ingredients of effective practice

No matter where the physical location of the provision our studies indicate patterns emerging from the data. Effectiveness clearly relates to 'whole-school' provision as well as to interventions designed to address an individual's specific difficulties. Writers of an older generation talked of 'environmental' or 'milieu therapy' and 'life-space intervention' (see Cole *et al.*, 1998). Trieschman *et al.* (1969), cited in Cole *et al.* (1998), called their classic US text on working with 'disturbed' young people 'the other twenty-three hours'. They argued that the culture of the environment the young person inhabited for the greater part of the day, i.e. the physical and psychological 'life-space', was of critical importance. It was of more help to the child with SEBD than an hour's weekly or daily counselling from a trained mental health professional delivered in a clinic or special room. Our research supports this. Creating a receptive, understanding and encouraging whole-school or unit

Population
- Children/young people: violent or disruptive behaviour not allowed to undermine the maintenance of a safe, caring school environment.
- Parents: the support of parents/carers should be won and sustained.

People
- Leadership: energetic and proficient head and senior management team.
- Teachers, LSAs, careworkers: with appropriate values base, empathy, skills and knowledge; commitment to pupils; able to offer a broad and balanced curriculum and quality group and individual care.
- Professional support: commitment and practical support from governors, LEA or proprietors, educational psychologists, education welfare service, local CAMHS and other agencies.

Provision
- Policies: comprehensive whole-school policies on education, behaviour and care, 'owned' by staff and pupils, implemented and regularly reviewed.
- Programmes: individual education/behaviour and/or care plans addressing pupil's short- and long-term affective and educational needs. Efficient assessment, implementation and review. Pupils active contribute to their own programme planning and monitoring.
- Time for talking and listening: in one-to-one and small group situations.

Place
- Physical plant: 'the home that smiles, props which invite, space which allows' catering for individual, group and whole-school/unit needs.

(Adapted from Cole *et al.*, 1998, p. 147)

Figure 31.1 *Effective provision for pupils with SEBD*

or college environment has to be a prime priority. Within this supporting, caring ethos, the needs of individual young people should then be targeted, involving the resources and skills of the setting's own staff but also drawing on effective support from professionals not working directly for the setting.

Effective provision for pupils with SEBD, whatever the setting, can be summarized under the headings of *population* (pupils and parents); *people* (the staff working with them); *provision* (policies and programmes); and *place* (the physical environment) (see Figure 31.1).

Client population

Clearly the collecting together of children with SEBD on one site can create volatile situations. Nevertheless, Cole *et al.* (1998) and Ofsted (1999) reported on calm, well-controlled classrooms and wider communities. To achieve the latter, clear admission and placement review policies are necessary and the opinions of senior staff on the suitability of potential entrants to their schools, units or FE courses should be heeded (Cole *et al.*, 1998). However, given that a change of environment often removes the catalysts for some of a child's difficulties, it might only be when a young person has been in a school or unit for an extended period that a truer assessment can be made of the suitability of the placement. Reviews of the placement should occur at regular intervals. Exclusion of young people from special schools should be kept to an absolute minimum, but it is crucial that special settings are not prevented from arranging the planned transfer of a few young people when the physical or emotional health of other pupils is seriously threatened.

Educational settings for pupils with SEBD must be proactive and have the resources to spend time and effort in building positive relationships with the families of young people with SEBD. Our various research projects indicate the acute difficulties in the children's home circumstances. Further, their caring parents have often developed negative views of teachers and other professionals after negative experiences. The staff of special schools and PRUs break through these barriers through home visits, telephone calls, sending certificates home and other trust-building approaches.

Staffing

Marjorie Franklin (1945, p. 14) did not think 'that it can be too much emphasised that in planned environmental therapy the staff are the most important factor'. Half a century later, commentators hold the same view (Cooper *et al.*, 1994; Cole *et al.*, 1998; Ofsted, 1999). The quality of leadership, particularly that of the headteacher but also of deputy heads, heads of care and senior teachers, is crucial. Without it, as Ofsted reports have shown too often, the safe, orderly environments stressing education and addressing emotional needs cannot be created and sustained. Recent senior teacher – and other staff – recruitment difficulties present a worrying challenge to the achievement of effective provision, openly recognized by government (DfES, 2003).

Under strong and effective leadership, children need to be in the daily daytime care of sufficient numbers of skilled and committed teachers, supported by learning support assistants (LSAs). In residential establishments, in the evenings, the same applies to care staff. Cole *et al.* (1998) report staff views on the characteristics of effective teachers of pupils with SEBD. They are not thought to need special qualities but rather ordinary abilities and aptitudes displayed with more consistency and depth than teachers working with pupils without SEBD. They should be well organized, consistent, fair, have a good sense of humour, an even temperament, be adaptable and stimulating. Importantly, they must understand, empathize and respond to individual needs, having a close knowledge and relationship with the child with SEBD. They need resilience and stamina. Further, as Ofsted (1999) consistently emphasize, they should be confident exponents of the subjects they teach. The same qualities should be present in teachers working in all other settings for pupils with SEBD (see Daniels *et al.*, 1998).

A variable and unsatisfactory situation has to be reported in relation to the degree and quality of other agency support offered to staff working in schools, units and colleges. It is clear that the staff in many settings receive only limited support from other professionals (Cole *et al.*, 1998; Ofsted, 1999). Resource pressures, additional statutory responsibilities, alterations to funding contribute to the 'under-lapping' of services in many areas rather than the 'joined-up' model required by successive governments. It is to be hoped that recent government initiatives will move provision to a more holistic approach, which manages to reach different parts of the ecosystem of the child with SEBD.

Provision

Educational settings for pupils with SEBD must have clear and comprehensive policies covering all aspects of education and care curricula, behaviour management, health and safety issues and other legal requirements. Much thought, based on a sound understanding of both theoretical, legal and practical issues, has to go into the writing and application of these. Personnel beyond the senior staff must be involved in their construction and regular review. In effective provision, these policies are 'owned' by staff and pupils and seen as useful aids, giving direction to practice.

Some mainstream schools are more successful than others in balancing the academic and pastoral (Cole *et al.*, 2002) and consequently in minimizing SEBD. These effective schools are communities with an underlying value base of collaboration and inclusion. Approaches are used that build self-esteem and the emotional resilience of particularly the 'underachieving'. Academic standards are valued but there is a flexibility and breadth of curricular approach, particularly for Key Stage 4 pupils, that plays to pupils' strengths and avoids reinforcing pupil failure. There is ongoing staff development in relation to recognizing and addressing pupils' affective as well as their cognitive needs. Pastoral systems, working closely with special educational needs provision, devote considerable time and energy to supporting pupils identified as having SEBD.

Ofsted, in the 1990s, expected the primary stress to be on *teaching* in SEBD schools (and, to a lesser extent, PRUs). The change to this view, still not universally accepted, had been gradual. Laslett (1977) saw the addressing of personal and social needs as the priority. Wilson and Evans (1980) stressed the importance for children deemed maladjusted, of:

- a 'normal education' as a therapeutic tool;
- addressing their pronounced educational underachievement;
- building pupils' self-esteem through successful achievement;
- working through closer personal relationships to ameliorate emotional and externalizing behavioural difficulties.

Stressing emotional and social education at the expense of delivering a broad, balanced and 'normal' school curriculum was not acceptable to Ofsted. The schools visited by Cole *et al.* (1998) judged by Ofsted to be sites of effective practice suggested staff stressing education and addressing emotional needs, with personal and social development tending to permeate school or unit life.

To create safe environments, lessening SEBD in all educational settings, there need to be regular routines and structured systems both in and out of class. Fritz Redl talked of the 'great ego-supportive power of traditionalised routine' (cited in Cole *et al.*, 1998). To increase the happiness of pupils with SEBD, to help them feel secure and to form beneficial relationships, they need the well-ordered communities observed by the Ofsted inspectors in 'good practice' schools (Ofsted, 1999). Behaviour might be an external expression of inner, unresolved turmoil and needs to be handled sympathetically, but respondents to Cole *et al.* (1998) did not think it sensible for staff to adopt an overly permissive stance. Rather there should be forgiving and easily recognized 'rubber boundaries' (Amos, in Cole *et al.*, 1998). Sensible and flexible controls from without can promote the 'controls from within' of which Redl and Wineman (1952, cited in Cole *et al.*, 1998) talked. Many senior staff in SEBD schools found systems of rewards and sanctions (e.g. points systems, tokens and other extrinsic rewards to promote prosocial action) useful. However, appreciation of a behaviourist-learning approach was mixed with cognitive approaches that sought to adjust pupils' skewed patterns of thinking, encouraging their internal locus of control and promoting their self-esteem (Cole *et al.*, 1998).

Given that pupils with SEBDs' commonly underachieve in basic literacy and often numeracy skills, a stress on remedying this is clearly good practice. Beyond this, many of these young people want to experience the same core curriculum as their peers, leading to some national accreditation, although perhaps reduced in quantity. Cole *et al.* (ibid.) found that in general senior staff in SEBD schools supported the framework and breadth of the education that was prescribed by the National Curriculum. However, staff and pupils clearly believed that certain aspects of the latter were more useful and motivating than others. Many pupils with SEBD clearly enjoy and find satisfaction in sport and creative subjects. The greater the range of educational experience on offer, the greater the chance of providing esteem-building success for every pupil.

Our studies suggest pupils with SEBD respond well to skilful, differentiated teaching that achieves the following:

- pays attention to where the child is at
- guides the child to the logical next step within his or her grasp
- uses a small-step approach punctuated by frequent positive reinforcement
- understands the pupil's learning style
- avoids humiliating public criticism of pupils in front of their peers.

Skilled teachers help to build pupils' self-image and confidence through successful classroom achievement, helping young people to view themselves in a different and improved light.

The capacity for independence of young people with SEBDs' usually grows from a firm base provided by a healthy dependence on reliable adults (Greenhalgh, 1994). Teachers and support workers in mainstream settings, SEBD schools and PRUs can become 'significant others' for their pupils and provide that essential base. The pupils come to rely on the staff's capacity to 'be there' for them even when the children's behaviour is challenging and anti-social. Relationships develop between young person and staff as they regularly share the same 'life-space', both in and outside the classroom. This provides chances for talking and listening as adult and child do activities together over extended periods, often months turning to years. Many staff in special schools and PRUs gradually earn the trust and respect of children with SEBD in a way that is difficult in large secondary schools with acute time pressures and basic staffing levels. Special schools and PRUs are able to structure the school day and, in residential schools, the evening care hours, to maximize the time staff have available for individual listening and talking to a far greater extent.

Place

The physical environment can clearly foster prosocial behaviour and pupil well-being. It is therefore important to create and maintain a pleasant, attractive, homely and well-equipped provision that allows for individual and group needs. Violence can increase in confined spaces such as cramped classrooms. Dilapidated buildings encourage a lack of respect for property. Redl and Wineman's plea (cited in Cole et al., 1998) for 'a home that smiles, props which invite, space which allows' summarizes what is required and is an accurate description of some schools and PRUs observed by our research team. Yet government inspectors (see Cole et al., 2002) too often have to condemn the decaying 'prefabs' and neglected accommodation observed by them (and by our research team) at many SEBD schools and units.

Conclusion

This chapter has highlighted some of the major patterns emerging from our research on the constituents of effective provision in mainstream and alternative settings. If, as Cooper et al. (1994) argued, mainstream schools could realize in practice more of the principles described above, then the need for so many places in special, unit or further education colleges would reduce – but history suggests that some 'alternative' places would still be required.

CHAPTER 32

Assessing the social and educational value of AD/HD

A brief critical review of the literature

Paul Cooper

Introduction

In this chapter consideration is given to the medical diagnosis of AD/HD. The nature and origins of the condition are described and approaches to its management are discussed. A central concern of this chapter is the controversy surrounding the social and educational value of the diagnosis. Attempts are made here to bring clarity to some of these debates and to assess the potential contribution of the AD/HD diagnosis to promoting the social and educational inclusion of children and young people who may attract the diagnosis. This exploration in turn requires examination of the relationship between biological and psychosocial explanations of learning, emotional, social and behavioural difficulties.

The nature, effects and history of AD/HD

Nature

Attention deficit/hyperactivity disorder is a diagnosis formulated by the American Psychiatric Association in its *Diagnostic and Statistical Manual of Mental Disorders* (DSM, APA, 1994). It describes behavioural symptoms of inattention, impulsiveness and hyperactivity that are presented to a degree that significantly interfere with a person's family and peer relations as well as their educational and/ or occupational functioning. There are, according to current APA diagnostic criteria, three main sub-types of AD/HD:

- the mainly hyperactive/impulsive sub-type
- the mainly inattentive sub-type

- the combined hyperactive-impulsive/inattentive sub-type.

International prevalence rates vary between 3 and 6 per cent of school-aged children and young people. The incidence of AD/HD applies across social and cultural boundaries, with males outnumbering females by a ratio of 3:1 (Tannock, 1998). Current estimates place the prevalence rate in the UK at between 3 and 5 per cent for school-aged children (NICE, 2000). This estimate accords closely with US prevalence rates (APA, 1994). This makes AD/HD the most prevalent of childhood disorders. Furthermore, although considered for many years a disorder restricted to childhood, it is now believed, by researchers and clinicians, to be carried forward into adulthood by between 30 and 70 per cent of those people who present the symptoms in childhood (Weiss and Hechtman, 1993; Hinshaw, 1994). The developmental course of AD/HD usually begins between the ages of 3 and 4, though some children show evidence of the disorder in early infancy, and others not until the ages of 5 or 6 years (Anastopoulos, 1999). The APA diagnostic criteria requires the presence of symptoms before the age of 7 years.

Effects
The effects of AD/HD are seriously debilitating. Individuals with AD/HD are more likely than the general population to experience social isolation, motor accidents and psychological disturbance (Tannock, 1998). People with undiagnosed AD/HD are often dismissed as incompetent, disorganized, aggressive, disruptive, lazy, untrustworthy, neglectful, selfish, accident prone, anti-social and/or asocial. There is strong evidence to suggest that school students with AD/HD are likely to perform at far lower levels academically than their scores on standardized tests of cognitive ability predict (Barkley, 1990; Hinshaw, 1994). In the UK Hayden (1997) found the symptoms of hyperactivity to be one of a range of predictors of formal exclusion from school among children of primary school age. Other studies have found the symptoms of AD/HD to be associated with serious relationship problems, marital breakdown, employment difficulties (Hinshaw, 1994) and imprisonment (Farrington, 1990; Weiss and Hechtman, 1993). In addition to these problems AD/HD is found to co-occur with a wide range of other difficulties at rates of between 25 and 60 per cent, including specific learning difficulties (SpLD/dyslexia) (Richards, 1995), conduct disorder (CD), oppositional defiant disorder (ODD), depression (DD) and anxiety disorder (AD) (Barkley, 1990; Angold *et al.*, 1999). The emotional

and behavioural 'co-morbid' disorders (CD, ODD, DD, AD) tend to emerge during the adolescent years, giving rise to the hypothesis that these are socially induced problems which occur as a result of the misunderstanding and mismanagement of the primary AD/HD symptoms (ibid.). Having said this, current research has been interpreted by some to suggest that the high rates of co-morbidity between AD/HD and CD/ODD may indicate the existence of an additional major sub-type of AD/HD and an acting-out behavioural disorder (Angold *et al.*, 1999).

History
It is important to note that the AD/HD diagnostic criteria is the most recent formulation in a series which has developed over many years (BPS, 1996). The English physician George Still is widely credited as publishing, in a 1902 issue of the *Lancet*, the first account of a congenital 'defect of moral control' bearing many of the hallmarks of current conceptualizations of AD/HD (Barkley, 1990; Anastopoulos, 1999). However, recent scholarship has identified the work of a Scottish-born physician, Alexander Crichton, whose account of 'morbid inattentiveness', published in 1798, is proclaimed as an earlier account of a condition bearing close resemblance to the current DSM criteria (Palmer and Finger, 2001).

In the twentieth century attempts to describe the condition have included minimal brain dysfunction and hyperactive child syndrome. In 1968 the APA produced the first standardized criteria of hyperkinetic reaction of childhood (DSM II). This gave way in 1980 to attention deficit disorder with hyperactivity (ADDH) (DSM III, 1980), and was revised in 1987 to attention deficit disorder (ADD) (DSM UIR, 1987). These changes in nomenclature are significant in that they reflect changing conceptualizations of the nature of the condition. The DSM II criteria mark a shift away from an emphasis on causation to a continuing emphasis on behavioural symptoms as the defining characteristics of the condition (Anastopoulos, 1999). This shift is reflected in the alternative diagnosis of hyperkinetic disorders (HD), which is a diagnostic category of the World Health Organization's *International Classification of Diseases* (ICD 10, WHO, 1990). The ICD 10 criteria for HD is almost identical with the APA criteria for AD/HD in terms of content. However, the WHO criteria is more restricted in its scope, requiring a higher proportion of potential symptoms to be present before diagnosis can be made. This includes a requirement that impulsiveness is always present, whereas this is not the case for the APA criteria. Also, there is a requirement in the WHO criteria that symptoms are generally pervasive, whereas for the APA criteria pervasiveness across only two situations is required. The WHO's classification system also places greater emphasis on the need for the diagnosing clinician to observe symptoms, while the DSM allows greater reliance on reports of symptoms (Barkley, 1990; Anastopoulos, 1999; Munden and Arcelus, 1999). The consequence of these differences is that the diagnosis of AD/HD is more inclusive than that of HD, with the latter producing prevalence rates in the UK of between 1 and 2 per cent of the childhood population (NICE, 2000).

Causes of AD/HD: a biopsychosocial perspective

The precise causes of AD/HD are not known in any definite sense. Having said this, AD/HD has become one of the most widely researched of all disorders of its type in the psychological and psychiatric literature. Tannock (1998), in an authoritative review of international research on AD/HD, identifies three major areas of theoretical exploration of this subject: cognitive research, neurobiological research and genetic research.

Cognitive research

Cognitive research has increasingly focused on impulsiveness as the central feature of AD/HD and the possibility that a dysfunctional response inhibition system is the neuropsychological mechanism, located in the physiology of the frontal lobes of the brain, underlying this problem. This means that children with AD/HD can often be characterized as experiencing significantly greater problems than most in inhibiting or delaying a behavioural response. The nature of the dysfunction in this system is described alternatively in terms of a failure of the inhibitory control system to become activated, or as extreme delay in the activation of this system. Barkley (1997) proposes a model which suggests that neurologically based problems of response inhibition lead directly to problems in four major 'executive functions' of the brain which are essential to effective self-regulation. The first executive function is 'working memory', impairment of which makes it difficult for individuals to retain and manipulate information for purposes of appraisal and planning. The second function is that of 'internalized speech'. It is suggested that self-control is exerted through a process of self-talk, during which possible consequences and implications of behaviours are weighed up and internally 'discussed'. The third executive function is that of 'motivational appraisal'. This system enables us to make decisions by providing us with information about the emotional associations generated by an impulse to act and the extent to which the impulse is likely to produce outcomes we find desirable. The final executive function is that of 'reconstitution', or 'behavioural synthesis'. The role of this function is to enable us to plan new and appropriate behaviours as an outcome of deconstructing and analysing past behaviours.

It should be stressed that this and other models (e.g. Sonuga-Barke et al., 1992; Sergeant, 1995; Van der Meere, 1996) apply almost exclusively to the hyperactive/impulsive and combined sub-types of AD/HD. The mainly inattentive sub-type is believed to be caused by impairments in the individual's speed of information processing and their ability to focus or select the object for their attention. This contrasts with the impulsive/hyperactive and combined sub-types, which are believed to be underpinned by more fundamental problems that cause the regulatory functions to fail (Barkley, 1997).

Neuroimaging research

Although there is a variety of cognitive theories of AD/HD most of these theories are based on the assumption that the cognitive dysfunctions are underpinned by neurological problems (Tannock, 1998). The basis for this assumption can be traced through a long line of research dating from the early years of the twentieth century, which repeatedly indicates close similarities between the symptoms of AD/HD and those produced by injuries, particularly in the prefrontal cortex of the brain (Hinshaw, 1994; Barkley, 1997). Other studies suggest a link between neurological damage affecting this part of the brain as a result of toxin exposure and AD/HD-type symptoms (Hinshaw, 1994). Authorities suggest that while recent research has added support to the neurological aspects of AD/HD, such research is far from conclusive, and has been at times inconsistent in its findings (e.g. Hinshaw, 1994; BPS, 1996; Barkley, 1997; Tannock, 1998). It is also important to point out that research on AD/HD that has employed modern neuroimaging techniques, such as computerized transaxial tomography (CT), magnetic resonance imaging and electroencephalography (EEG), has been limited in quantity (ibid.).

With the above qualifications in mind, it can be concluded on the basis of existing neuroimaging research that individuals with AD/HD sometimes exhibit abnormalities in the development of certain brain regions. In particular these studies show that individuals with

AD/HD tend to have smaller structures in those regions of the brain, particularly the striatal regions, which control movement and behaviour (Barkley, 1997; Tannock, 1998). These findings, however, as with EEG studies, leave us with a great many unanswered questions. The main problem is that the studies do not show a direct link between the brain abnormalities and AD/HD. What they do indicate is that these abnormalities have been found to commonly co-occur with AD/HD. The neurological basis for AD/HD, therefore, remains an interesting and promising hypothesis that is as yet unconfirmed.

Genetic research

Tannock (ibid.) reports that there is strong evidence from studies carried out over the past 30 years that AD/HD is more common in the biological relatives of children with AD/HD than it is in the biological relatives of children who do not have AD/HD. The problem with these studies is that it is difficult to control for environmental factors that family members often share and which may influence the development of AD/HD-type behaviours. This problem is addressed through twin and adoption studies that have repeatedly shown a much greater incidence of AD/HD among identical (i.e. monozygotic) twins than among non-identical (dizygotic) twins. Similarly, studies which compare the incidence of AD/HD among children and parents who are biologically related with that of children and parents where the child is adopted have tended to support the heredity argument (ibid.).

These findings are given further weight by molecular genetic research that has identified certain genes as being implicated in the aetiology of AD/HD and AD/HD-type symptoms. In particular there is evidence that points to genetic abnormalities in the dopamine system (ibid.). Dopamine is a neurotransmitter that is found in systems of the brain concerned with, among other things, the regulation of movement (Thompson, 1993).

As the foregoing review illustrates, AD/HD is likely to involve a complex interplay between, in themselves, complex human systems. The above evidence suggests that, for neurocognitive reasons, individuals with AD/HD respond to the world in ways that are different from those of the general population. The consistency and pervasiveness of the behaviours associated with AD/HD are taken to imply that individuals with AD/HD experience the world differently; that is, they have different ways of processing and responding to the external world at the level of their cognitive processes. The apparent level of resistance of these patterns of response to external influence, in the form of normal behavioural correction of the type practised by usually competent and successful teachers and parents, is taken to imply deeper structural underpinnings to these cognitive problems. This leads researchers to the brain and an exploration of the neurological structures that regulate cognitive functions. While the evidence for the relationship between neurological abnormalities and AD/HD is difficult to interpret (Tannock, 1998) there is a small amount of reliable evidence to support an association between neurological abnormalities and AD/HD. Interestingly, the neurological abnormalities can be related to some of the cognitive theories of AD/HD. The fact that the neurological evidence most commonly appears to implicate abnormal brain development rather than brain injury (Barkley, 1997) justifies the increasing interest in familial and chemical genetic studies of AD/HD. Again, these studies appear promising, in that both familial and chemical studies suggest that the risk of developing AD/HD can be transmitted from one generation to another (Levy and Hay, 2001).

Interpreting the biopsychological research

The above account illustrates that one of the shared limitations of the dominant research approaches to AD/HD is their tendency to focus the search for explanations of the condition on 'within-person factors'. That is to say that all of the approaches described above assume that a major reason why individuals with AD/HD behave as they do is located within the individual who bears the AD/HD diagnosis. There is a circularity to this approach. Clearly, automatically to assume that an individual's behavioural problems are a product of characteristics within the individual would be very misguided. Such assumptions would inevitably lead to a misdiagnosis of the nature of problems in many instances. In turn, such misdiagnosis would disadvantage individuals whose behaviour was the product of unsympathetic or harmful environmental conditions. On the other hand, in the face of a growing body of evidence in support of the contention that there are systematic differences of a neuropsychological nature between persons with AD/HD and persons who do not have AD/HD, it would seem ill-advised to automatically dismiss the validity of the AD/HD diagnosis in *all* cases.

Unfortunately, there has been and continues to be a destructive tendency that encourages an unhelpful polarization of views of AD/HD (Cooper, 1997a). In particular there is a tendency to see

AD/HD as a set of problems that are induced by biological factors *or* as problems that are generated by the environment. This crude nature versus nurture argument contributes virtually nothing to either our understanding of AD/HD or our understanding of emotional and behavioural problems in general. It does, however, tell us a lot about the tribalism of competing disciplines and professions (Hughes, 1999).

This situation is compounded by the fact that researchers, including many of those whose work was considered earlier in this chapter, have tended to focus their research on single factors in their explorations of the aetiology of AD/HD, such as neurological structures, cognitive processes or the genetic pathways (Tannock, 1998). This is in spite of the fact that many of these same researchers would claim to view AD/HD as a bio-psycho-social problem (e.g. Barkley, 1990, 1997). That is, a problem which has a biological element to it, but that interacts with psychosocial factors in the individual's social, cultural and physical environment. Clearly once we recognize this consensus view we find that simplistic nature versus nurture arguments are untenable (see Levy and Hay, 2001).

Frith (1992) offers a model that helps us to understand the ways in which biopsychosocial factors may interact in developmental disorders. Frith's model describes biological causes leading to cognitive deficits, which then lead to behavioural manifestations (e.g. the behavioural symptoms of autism). The extent, and indeed to some extent the nature, of the behavioural manifestations are influenced by a set of social and psychological factors, namely experience, maturation, compensation and motivation. Thus the extent to which the neurological problems result in behavioural and social dysfunction will be influenced by the individual's learning and experience, which may, for example, give the individual skills that enable him or her to compensate for cognitive deficits, or provide the individual with a high or low degree of motivation which in turn will affect his or her ability to cope. Clearly the severity of the initial biological problem will vary, as will the nature of the individual's experience and environment. Thus in some cases biology will be more dominant than environment in the aetiology of the disorder, while in others environment will be more dominant than biology. Given that biology is heavily implicated in most prominent theories of the nature of AD/HD, while its precise function is still being debated it seems only sensible to take the biopsychosocial perspective and recognize that in a given case it will always be very difficult to tease out the biological and psychosocial strands.

AD/HD: biological, psychological, social and cultural issues

No definitive clinical test for AD/HD exists, nor is likely to exist in the foreseeable future (Hill and Cameron, 1999). The reason for this is that while there is strong evidence to suggest that there is a biological aspect to AD/HD, the manifestation of AD/HD as a personally and socially debilitating condition is not determined by biology alone, but by a combination of biological, psychological and social factors. Put simply, AD/HD is not 'caused' by biological variation alone; neither is it solely the result of environment and experience.

Perhaps the best way to think about the role of biology in relation to AD/HD is to think about it in terms of creating propensities. That is, the development of AD/HD in an individual cannot be predicted on the basis of genes or neurology alone (Rutter, 2001). Certain genetic and neurological factors, however, when present in an individual, make it more likely that he or she will develop AD/HD than another individual who does not possess the genetic/ neurological predisposing factors. For AD/HD to develop in the first individual, he or she will have to experience what are, to him or her, a set of aversive circumstances. These circumstances are made aversive by the way in which they interact with biological propensity factors and, therefore, are not experienced as seriously aversive by the individual who does not possess the propensity characteristics. Furthermore, biological propensity factors can themselves be influenced by the post-natal environment. Evidence from neurological research indicates that human beings are unique among animals in the extent to which certain aspects of neurological development, particularly in the area of the dopamine and other neurotransmitter systems (implicated in the aetiology of AD/HD), take place after the human individual is born (Ellis and Young, 1988). It is crucial that these (and other) neurological systems receive essential forms of stimulation at critical periods in the early weeks and months of the individual's life in order for optimum development to take place. These critical periods represent opportunities that often will not be presented again, owing to the process by which the brain 'prunes' unused neurones. Having said this, genetic and other pre-natal factors will also play a role here, possibly influencing the extent and nature of stimulation that is required by different human beings. Thus, owing to such predisposing factors, different individuals experiencing identical forms and levels of stimulation may develop differently.

The circumstances in which the individual finds him- or herself and, therefore, the opportunities for appropriate stimulation will, in turn, be influenced by individual factors, such as family composition, the characteristics of parents/carers and other significant individuals (such as siblings) and the ways they interact with the child. Put straightforwardly, the early family (or substitute family) unit plays a crucial role in shaping an individual's behavioural characteristics (Nigg and Hinshaw, 1998). The early social learning that children experience here provides them with the social and cognitive tools with which they negotiate the worlds within and beyond the family. Wittingly or unwittingly carers will reinforce certain of a child's behaviours and, in effect, 'train' the child to perform certain behaviours in order to achieve his or her wants and needs (Patterson et al., 1992). Biological propensities will inevitably interact with the training regime (Lahey et al., 1999). So, for example, parents' efforts to redirect a child's behaviour may succeed with one child but fail with a second child who requires more intensive intervention or a type of intervention that is beyond the skills or resources of the parents. For example, a common feature of children diagnosed with AD/HD is their tendency to require tightly focused and highly intensive intervention.

The role of culture

These individual factors are nested within a further set of influences that are of a structural and cultural nature (Cooper, 1997b; Ideus, 1997). For example, we can think of AD/HD not so much as a disorder, but as a cognitive style that is not well adapted to modern life in the developed world. The child's 'problems' in this context are characterized by an apparent inability to conform to social and procedural rules (in the home and school), extreme difficulty in maintaining effort and interest in school and leisure activities (particularly those involving sustained attention) and problems of overactivity and impulse control that make the individual appear self-centred and anti-social.

These behavioural patterns are rendered problematic in environments where a high premium is placed on methodical rule observance, predictable behavioural patterns and the ability to sustain effort on sedentary tasks in group situations. Throughout the world, where there is mass schooling, these are the qualities commonly required of the student. Also, where there is mass schooling this tends to reflect an approach to economic development which stresses these same characteristics for the mass of the population in the workplace.

These expectations of conformity and self-control go hand in hand with a paradoxical emphasis on early childhood as a period of relative freedom from such constraints. For the child with a propensity to develop AD/HD concerted and intensive early intervention designed to influence the development of internal controls would seem to be essential. This becomes problematic when we place it alongside what some commentators see as the disintegration, throughout the developed world, of the social and familial support networks that traditionally provided support, expertise and resources to fulfil this need (see Rutter and Smith, 1995).

Assessment for AD/HD

Given the complexity of AD/HD it is not surprising that its accurate detection depends upon a similarly complex assessment process. Just as the condition is multifaceted, so is the assessment process, depending for its accuracy on a wide range of sources of information. The crucial aim of assessment is, on the one hand to rule out, as far as possible, environmental and otherwise localized influences on the symptoms as their major causes and, on the other hand, to establish that the symptoms are pervasive across different situations, are a source of serious disruption to the individual's personal development and that they have been present, in the same or different manifestations, throughout the child's life. Failure to meet any one of these criteria usually means that the presenting problems are attributable to something other than AD/HD.

The assessment process is, therefore, complex and multifaceted, requiring the input of a variety of individuals and the application of qualitative as well as quantitative measures. Detweiler *et al.* (1999) describe the following framework for assessment:

Phase I
- a parent interview; a developmental checklist
- the child interview.

Phase II: neuropsychological testing
The next step in the diagnostic process involves neuropsychological testing. Detweiler *et al.* (ibid.) have designed their own neuropsychological instruments for the assessment of the following:
- intellectual functioning
- the functioning of processing strengths and weaknesses (visual, auditory and visual motor)
- achievement levels in fundamental school skills
- visual and hearing ability.

In addition they have developed a computerized test of vigilance and impulsivity. It is only on the basis of results from these tests, when added to the information gathered in the interviews and through the checklists, that a diagnosis of AD/HD may be made by the team physician, in this case a child psychiatrist with many years' experience in working with children with AD/HD and its precursors.

Accurate assessment is crucial in determining the nature of the problem under consideration. In turn, the accuracy of the assessment will influence the appropriateness of the interventions that are selected. It is to the issue of intervention that we now turn our attention.

Intervention

There is a great deal of concern about the use of medication in the treatment of childhood AD/HD (e.g. Baldwin, 2000). It is undoubtedly the case that medication is commonly prescribed for children who are deemed to present clinically significant levels of hyperactivity. In the USA between 2 and 2.5 per cent of all school-aged children are prescribed some form of medication for hyperactivity, with over 90 per cent of these being prescribed the psychostimulant medication methylphenidate (Greenhill, 1998). This has to be compared with the much lower figure of less than 1 per cent of children in the UK receiving similar pharmacological treatment (NICE, 2000), revealing UK physicians to be among the least likely of medical professionals in the developed world to make such prescriptions (Kewley, 1998).

There are a number of important observations about the use of methylphenidate and other psychostimulant treatments for hyperactivity, which are shared by a wide range of informed commentators. First, psychostimulant medications generally, when applied in relatively low and moderate doses, are widely regarded as being highly effective in reducing the core symptoms of AD/HD (Hill and Cameron, 1999). Figures taken from a number of controlled studies indicating significant improvement in between 69 per cent and 75 per cent of cases have been frequently recorded in reponse to psychostimulants, compared with figures of between 20 and 29 per cent in response to placebos (Barkley, 1990; Hinshaw, 1994; Greenhill, 1998). Secondly, methylphenidate in particular is seen as an extremely safe medication, being non-addictive, with for the majority of users' only mild side effects (such as sleep disturbance and appetite suppression), which can be controlled and often avoided through careful adjustment of the dosage after attention is paid to routine and regular reports from users, their parents and teachers (Kewley, 1998). Finally, all of these cited authorities agree that medication alone is never a sufficient treatment, but where it is used it should always be part of a multimodal intervention approach that employs behavioural, psychosocial, cognitive and environmental interventions (BPS, 2000; NICE, 2000).

This multimodal approach reveals a conception of AD/HD as in part a dysfunction of the individual and in part a problem that is created and exacerbated by the environment in which the individual operates. From this perspective medication is seen as creating a 'window of opportunity' that allows social and other influences to be brought to bear effectively. Coupled with this approach is the realization that the behaviour of children with AD/HD is often misunderstood by parents, peers, other adults and teachers, and seen as a problem of motivation and volition rather than an involuntary reaction to stressful circumstances created by the conflict between a particular cognitive style and the cognitive demands of an environment that is geared to the needs of a contrasting cognitive style. By developing an understanding of these behavioural problems in terms of the cognitive and other theories of the aetiology of AD/HD, adults can make more informed judgements about how best to approach and facilitate the positive development of the child with AD/HD. In this way the concept of AD/HD can be seen to help reinforce the widely held view that apparent behavioural problems are often experienced by their perpetrators as reasonable responses to what they experience as difficult circumstances.

This last point should be of particular interest to teachers and educational psychologists, as well as parents and professionals such as social workers, whose job it is to support parents and families. The task that is now presented to these individuals is one which involves both learning and teaching. They need to learn to listen to the child with AD/HD and see the world through his or her eyes. They also need to find points of connection and cooperation with these children in order to provide the circumstances that will help to rebuild these children's often shattered sense of self and to help them develop the emotional strength, self-confidence, trust in others and self-belief necessary to succeed socially and academically.

There is not space here to detail in any depth the kinds of psychosocial approaches that are promising or successful. Stated briefly, preferred interventions include, for the individual: social skills training, problem-solving skills, training in self-activated response delay and reflection techniques. For parents and teachers: behaviour management training and the use of a form of applied behavioural analysis. Hinshaw *et al.* (1998), in a comprehensive review of treatments in which medication is combined with non-pharmacological interventions, found evidence that behavioural therapy was effective in promoting improved behaviour and academic gains and, where used with medication, it was found to lead to reductions in the level of medication required to produce an effective response. Cognitive interventions, such as 'reframing' techniques, are also recommended (Cooper and Ideus, 1996). In the home and school environment distractors are identified and eliminated where possible and careful attention is given to the ways in which social, academic and behavioural expectations are defined and expressed to the child (DuPaul and Stoner, 1994), For example, instructions need to be given in short sequences and in highly direct language, with the avoidance of non-literal illustrations or figurative language (Weaver, 1994). Also, children with AD/HD have been found to learn particularly effectively when engaged in concrete and kinaesthetic activities. Similarly, children with AD/HD benefit considerably from frequent opportunities to engage in structured physical activity (Pellegrini and Horvat, 1995).

Many of these interventions are not only appropriate for children with AD/HD but are beneficial to almost all children. However, for children with AD/HD they are often essential rather than simply desirable. This draws our attention to the often noted but sad fact that the vast majority of children are very capable of 'putting up' with circumstances that are not supportive of positive personal development, but are actually highly negative in their social, personal and educational effects (Neill, 1968; Silberman, 1971; Schostak, 1982). Children with AD/HD differ in that they cannot 'put up' in this way, but rather are the first to 'crack' under the strain of unreasonable conditions that some of us, too readily, take for granted.

The need for an holistic approach to AD/HD

As the foregoing indicates, AD/HD is a complex phenomenon that can be understood in different ways. The emphasis of much of this chapter has been on the role of biomedical and psychological insights and research in shaping our understanding. These are important perspectives that will continue to develop as more research is carried out. As has been already noted, it is hoped that these different approaches to research will move beyond the current tendency to restrict studies to the exploration of single factors and concentrate attention on interactions between them.

In addition to the understanding that can come from sometimes abstract and reductionist research, however, it is also important to listen to the voices of those who, in one way or another, live with the daily reality of what some people call AD/HD. It is not the case, necessarily, that these voices are more important, in terms of their contribution to our understanding of AD/HD, than the research perspectives already mentioned. What is clear is that these voices have things to tell us which are not made available to us through conventional scientific research channels. Perhaps more than anything these voices bring images of human beings to us and so remind us that the value of a concept such as AD/HD is best judged on the basis of the extent to which it has the potential to contribute to positive human growth.

In this regard, one of the important things to emerge from a recent study is the way in which pupils' perceptions of the nature of AD/HD appears to affect their sense of control over its course (Cooper and Shea, 1998). The tendency among some students in this study to adopt a simplistic, biological determinist approach to understanding AD/HD was associated with a sense of helplessness and extreme reliance on medication as the remedy for the condition. Where the participants had a more contextualized view, which related the condition to the demands of schooling and their own plans and aspirations, there was much more of a sense of the students being 'in charge' of the condition and seeing medication, for example, as a tool for helping them achieve their own goals.

As yet there is very little published research of this kind enquiring empirically into the social reality of this medical condition. The indication of this study, however, is that the children themselves need to be much more closely involved in the dialogues and debates about AD/HD. The response of the children in this study to the experience of AD/HD was multifaceted and complex. It indicated, very powerfully, that for them AD/HD existed as a daily reality, having a major effect on their lives. Their need was for a positive and constructive perspective on the issue: one that would serve their need to make their positive, forward way in the world. Commentators who disparage the concept of AD/HD often seem to forget this point and labour under the illusion that somehow they can disinvent the concept and diagnosis. They cannot do that. What they can do is perhaps contribute to the positive development of this 'evolving concept' (BPS, 1996), by helping to place it where it belongs, firmly within a biopsychosocial framework of understanding (BPS, 2000).

CHAPTER 33

John's story: Episode 6

Plans for the future – 'lifelong education? …'

'John' and Paul Cooper

P: What are your plans for the future?

J: At the moment I'm not doing anything really. I'm unemployed. I don't want to be unemployed. I'm trying to change that. I'm looking into something like a trade – a proper trade. Not just a job; a trade. Like electrician, builder. Something like that. I haven't really thought about that since I left school. I didn't think about that. But just recently I started to think about that. The future.

P: So are you planning to go on a course?

J: Yes. Hopefully. Next year.

P: You've just moved into a place of your own, haven't you?

J: Yeah.

P: How's that been?

J: It's all right.

P: You were living with your Mum before, weren't you?

J: Yeah.

P: Was that a bit of a strain?

J: Yeah. Well. It was a strain on her, not on me!

P: So, how's it going?

J: Fine. It's fine.

Acknowledgements

The editors acknowledge, with appreciation, John's contribution as a keynote speaker at an international conference held at the University of Leicester in 2003 and in sharing his original interview through its inclusion in this volume, which seeks to promote a deeper and more empathetic awareness of what it means to listen and what may be involved in 'managing' attitudinal, learning and behavioural difficulties. We also wish to note our appreciation of John's mother's substantial contribution to assisting other parents to share their concerns and come to a better understanding of the impact of both dyslexia and AD/HD on children and families and for working in a multidiscipline approach to try to improve communication about such learning and behavioural difficulties.

CHAPTER 34

Teacher leadership and student behaviour

Bill Rogers

Introduction

In the last 15 years I have worked with many schools as a mentor-teacher. This role emphasizes professional development within a mutually supportive collegial model. The primary aim of such mentorship is to provide an elective, collegial framework within which colleagues can work together in the classroom, team-teaching and using mutual review meetings to raise professional self-awareness about issues of behaviour and learning.

I have worked in many classes where students with challenging (and SEBD) behaviours are present. My colleagues and I team-teach in these classes and then (over serious tea and coffee) use descriptive, non-judgemental feedback to acknowledge and affirm what we have experienced together (often with very challenging students). We use shared feedback to focus on our own behaviour – as teacher leaders – to see where (and if) we can bring appropriate (and at times necessary) change to the way we lead and guide groups and individuals. I have seen many colleagues rebuild levels of confidence and goodwill as they supportively reflect on their own behaviour (as well as that of their students) and develop more consciously skilled approaches to behaviour leadership.

In this mentorship model the mentor is also a coach; inviting their 'mentee' colleague to observe the way the mentor-teacher leads and relates to difficult and challenging students. They also work together in the follow-up of students beyond the classroom context (in counselling and developing individual behaviour agreements with students who present with emotional and behavioural disorders).

In this chapter I have noted some of the key protocols and skills my colleagues and I focus on in our mentoring journey. Our *charac-teristic* behaviour as teacher leaders has a significant effect on the nature and quality of teacher–student interactions. It is the belief that we can change our behaviour in relation to our students that is central to this mentorship model.

Some teachers, in some schools, can go for years without any serious attempt at professional self-reflection. At best, such reflection is ad hoc, incidental, even 'accidental' (Rogers, 2002a). Where mentor coaching is elective, collegially supportive and based in a desire for professional self-reflection, it has a significant on-flow to positive student behaviour and learning. While the aim of such mentorship is to increase teacher confidence and skill in behaviour leadership (Rogers, 2002b), it also has a direct outcome in positive teacher–student relationships. In working with students with challenging and EBD patterns of behaviour, the quality of teacher–student relationships – based in empathy, respect, mutual regard and resilience – is essential to all learning outcomes.

Key protocols, key skills of behaviour leadership

In every school of every kind I have worked with as a mentor-teacher I have consistently noted key protocols of behaviour leadership that significantly affect the behaviour and learning in classroom and school-wide contexts. These 'protocols' describe and delineate aspects, features and patterns of characteristic teacher behaviour that positively affect student well-being, their working relationships with their teacher and the impact on student motivation and learning. These protocols and practices of behaviour leadership are set within a context of shared rights and responsibilities. In any learning community it is crucial that behaviour leadership be exercised within a common framework of rights and responsibilities, for teacher and students alike.

The right to feel safe: belonging

With any age of students the teacher will need to clarify, with the class group, the key rights and responsibilities of a learning community: the right to feel safe at school – psychologically as well as physically. All children want to feel they belong in this big place called school that takes up so much of their life. They want to feel that they can enter the gates of school and not be 'picked on', 'put down' and 'scored on'. The 'need to belong' is a fundamental human need; it is what children often refer to at school and outside of school, when they talk about their friends, their relationships, when they like being at school or like or dislike particular teachers. (Even particular subjects can have their general approval rating go up or down depending on the given teacher that year.)

The right to learn

The right to learn (without undue distraction or disruption) and the right to fair treatment are fundamental and foundational to effective learning communities. All children want basic fairness and just treatment from their teachers – nothing new in that. In those schools where I have seen significant and positive change in students' attitudes to learning and social relationships, I have also seen teachers who develop whole-class student agreements around these central rights. In their first meeting with their new classes teachers will discuss learning and behaviour within these rights and then delineate (with the students) the routines, rules and consequences contingent to those rights. Every schooling context needs to have a clear establishment phase that clarifies the 'whys' and 'wherefores' and expected 'how' of classroom behaviour, even deceptively basic routines such as:

- how we all enter the classroom (25–30 students moving from a boisterous social playtime into a focused learning place is no mean feat for teacher leadership!);
- settling down within an appropriate seating plan;
- fair routines for class discussion and questions (so it does not become a 'free-for-all');
- appropriate noise levels during whole-class learning time (again no mean feat for 25–30 students);
- how to get equitable teacher support during on-task learning time.

Discipline within behaviour leadership

Having positive, fair rights, responsibilities and rules is one thing, *maintaining and consolidating* a learning community based on such rights is another. Effective behaviour leadership requires conscious skill in balancing needs, rights, emotions and language, all within an emotional moment. At the beginning of a teaching year one's behaviour leadership will be 'tested', challenged, many times. Teachers will have to address a range of behaviours that affect teaching, learning and emotional safety and well-being.

In most classes, in most schools, there will be students who butt in and chat away while the teacher is talking; who call out (some with annoying frequency) causing inappropriate noise levels; roll on the carpet seeking attention (I have seen this behaviour in some adolescents as well as infants!); present clowning behaviours, or rudeness, arguing and defiance.

Travis walks into his English class, late again. This is his second lesson (term one) with Mr Smith. He pushes the door open loudly. All eyes stare – why not? Mr Smith quickly, emotively, notes the sly grin, the 'grand entrance', and turns to challenge Travis's lateness. Travis walks to the back of the room (ignoring the teacher) and playfully punches a mate as he says, 'Hi, what's happening Craig?' He has interrupted the flow of the lesson as well as being late. Mr Smith is already finding this class a challenge – they are residually noisy, a number of students call out and butt in, several are task avoiding. He does not need *this*, now, with Travis:

Teacher: Oi ... don't walk away from me; why are you late?

Student: What? [Travis turns, now having reached the back of the room.]

T: Why are you late? [The teacher is (naturally) annoyed.] This class has been going for five minutes.

S: Jeez, people are late sometimes you know! [Travis is half grinning (is he enjoying this *mano-a-mano* as his class peers look on)]

Mr Smith quickly focuses in on Travis's insouciant tone of voice, body language and manner. The lateness is annoying enough but 'how dare he speak to me like that!' is a thought quickly focused on by Mr Smith.

T: I said why are you late! [Mr Smith looks, and sounds, as if Travis's 'cocksparrow behaviour' is a kind of threat to his leadership.]

S: I told yer – I'm late, all right, it's no big deal, OK?

T: Don't you talk to me like that.

S: Like what? – Jeez. I'm late, all right. What's the hassle?

T: Right! [Mr Smith recovers some composure and 'authority' and points to a spare seat.] Sit over next to Daniel and I'll see you after class.

S: No way, Jeez, I sit with Ben and Matt.

T: I said sit there. [The teacher points ... the class watches as the time races entertainingly on.]

S: [Travis feels he has to play the 'hard man'. Folding his arms, brow furrowed, sulky scowl.] Naaa.

T: Right, get out – go on, get out of my class, go and see Mr Davies – now! [Mr Smith has had enough. He feels he has to 'win' in this exchange – it's his reputation he believes is 'at stake'.]

S: [Travis walks off raising his voice en route.] Yeah, well it's a shit class anyway! [Travis marches out of the classroom to the teacher's parting 'shot'.]

T: And you'll be on detention!

S: [Travis calls back from the corridor.] I don't care!

I have worked with teachers (such as my colleague above) who believe it is important to 'win' in such transactions; they define discipline in similar situations as win/lose, when in reality there is no contest and our students are not 'the enemy'. In the example above, Travis is a 14-year-old lad. I am not unsympathetic, either, to the teacher as to what has happened here. Students such as Travis can be really annoying in their behaviour, particularly when they are seeking peer attention (even in episodic lateness). I am not talking about bad-day syndrome either – all of us have bad days. Teacher leadership, however, can significantly affect 'discipline' transactions such as these.

In a different class, a different teacher but a similar context Travis walks in late (second time this week). He scans the room, on show again. Mrs Brown 'stops' him at the door (with a relaxed open hand signal).

T: Welcome – is it Travis? [She is trying to remember his name.]

S: Yeah. [Travis is a bit reserved. Mrs Brown looks relaxed; she does not look threatened. While she has had to stop the flow of her teaching, she is consciously aware she needs to avoid any unnecessary confrontations and keep the focus on the main issue *at this emotional moment*. She is also aware she does not need to address the barely disguised insouciance at this stage – the sigh, the eyes to the ceiling, the gait.]

T: Travis, I notice you're late. [She briefly acknowledges the fact of his lateness quickly adding] I'll have a chat later ... there's a seat over there. [She points at a spare seat, adding an expectant] Thanks.

S: [Travis frowns] Yeah, but I don't sit there, I sit with Nick and Nazim.

T: [Mrs Brown *briefly* tunes in to what he has said and redirects.] I'm sure you do, those seats are taken, Travis; we can organize a seat change later. Ta. The spare seats are there. [She beckons – again – across the room. Her language is *descriptive*, not judgemental and (at this point in the lesson) she does not ask 'why' he is late, nor does she argue about who he sits with. To the class group it looks as if this teacher is relaxed, but still in control (as classroom teacher leader). Not 'in control' of Travis but in control of the context that they are both in as teacher/student and audience of peers.]

S: [Travis saunters off – muttering.] Yeah – sit there, 'spose – no big deal if it makes you happy. [He mutters this aloud.]

T: [By this time the teacher has reclaimed whole-class attention.] As I was saying, class … [She resumes the flow of the lesson that had been interrupted by Travis.]

By redirecting the class and giving Travis some 'take-up-time' she also 'signals' to him that this 'transaction' has ended and she 'expects' and believes that he will see the common sense and natural fairness of what she has directed regarding his behaviour at this point in the lesson. She also *tactically ignores* his sighs, pouts and low-grade attentional gait en route to his seat. She knows that it is important to keep the focus of her leadership on the *primary issue* and the *primary behaviour* at this point, and not get drawn into *secondary behaviours* (sighs, pouts, clicking of tongues, shoulder shrugs, skewed eye contact) or secondary *issues* (such as 'why' he is late). She has learned that 'why' questions – the easy use of the interrogative – is not an effective feature of management/leadership language.

The interrogative ('why' or 'are you?') is commonly used in corrective, discipline, language, e.g. 'Why are you late?' (or, as unhelpful) 'Are you late?' (of course he is late!). When students call out, butt in or talk while the teacher is talking, it hardly helps to ask the student 'if' he is talking or calling out ('Are you calling out?'). My colleagues and I find that descriptive or reminding language is much more effective. A basic example follows.

Two students are talking while the teacher is talking (during whole-class teaching). Rather than say, 'Lucas, Mark, *stop* talking' or 'Lucas, *why* are you talking?' the teacher could more thought-fully say, 'Lucas, Mark, you're talking.' (This *briefly* describes what they are doing that is distracting or disruptive.) This 'description of reality' is often enough to raise behaviour awareness and invite cooperation. Sometimes we might need to add a brief *behavioural* direction, '... facing this way and listening now. Thank you.' Or we could give a clear rule reminder, 'Remember our rule for ... thanks.' This is one, small, example of many that could be given. Of course, the *mere* words are hardly enough; one's characteristic tone, respectful manner and expectation all carry conviction, confidence, expectation or indecision.

While we could say that this teacher clearly has 'high emotional intelligence' she is also conscious that when engaged in behaviour leadership (discipline) she will avoid unnecessary confrontation (or embarrassment, sarcasm, 'cheap shots' or scoring). When she needs to confront – with necessary assertion – she will do so without hostility or verbal or postural aggression. She has learned that she can communicate her frustration, and even anger, without descending into emotionally abusive language. This is not easy – it is a skill that can be learned.

The teacher is also conscious of using a least intrusive approach to corrective language. If a student is reading that 'great' English newspaper the *Sun* during on-task learning time she will not grab it from the student; she will use a directed choice.

Rebecca is idly and surreptitiously reading the newspaper while doing her classwork. The teacher walks over.

T: How's the work going? [She is pleasant – as she makes eye contact with Rebecca she also quickly eyes the newspaper with an 'I-know-you-know-I-know-you-know look.]

S: OK, suppose.

T: By the way, the *Sun* ... I'm disappointed to see you reading the *Sun* ... the *Guardian* maybe. [She winks.] I want you to put it in your bag or on my table. Ta. I'll pop back to see how you're going later.

S: I wasn't reading it. [The girl smiles back with an 'oh yeah' look.]

T: Even if you weren't ... [The teacher *partially agrees* with the student.] I want you to put it in your bag or on my table. Ta.

I'll see how you're going with your work later. [She leaves her with a task reminder.]

At this point the teacher walks off, giving Rebecca some 'take-up time' – again conveying confidence and trust. She *tactically ignores* Rebecca's muttering, later coming back to her table to re-engage her and encourage her. This teacher never calls a student 'a liar' if they claim they 'weren't reading' or 'wasn't chewing gum' (whatever). This teacher will acknowledge and redirect. If the student refuses to put a distracting object away (mobile phone, comic, Walkman, etc.), they will either defer the consequence ('If you choose not to put it away now I'll have to follow this up later') or, if the behaviour is significantly disturbing, they will use a directed time out option. Either way the teacher's leadership approach keeps the 'intrusion' low and avoids any unnecessary confrontation. She is also aware that the 60–70 per cent of naturally cooperative students will support her leadership when the emphasis of her discipline centres on student responsibility.

Some teachers will merely take distracting objets d'art off children's desks (noisy pencil cases, mini-skateboards, keyrings, swap cards): 'Right, give it to me, come on, give it to me.' Compliant children might well hand the object over; other children will 'stand their ground' and make a minor issue escalate into a major one that may see the teacher ejecting the child from the classroom: 'Right, get out, go on, get out! If you're not going to give that stupid keyring to me now you can leave!'

'Primary' and 'secondary' behaviours

It does not help, either, when a teacher quickly and easily focuses on a student's sulky tone of voice or their body language. When addressing student behaviour it helps to keep the focus of the exchange on the *primary issue* or behaviour and avoid getting drawn in or focusing on a student's secondary behaviour. Typical secondary behaviours are pouting, eyes raised to the ceiling, drawn-out sighs, skewed eye contact, tut-tutting.

I was mentor-teaching in a class last year when a young girl continued to annoy her classmate in the next seat with overly ebullient, friendly strangling, to the point where she fell off her chair. Great audience excitement. I called Jacqui over, away from her classmate. 'Jacqui ... Jacqui ...,' she looked up, 'What!' Her voice tone was surly, arms folded, low-grade scowl. She sighed grandiloquently. 'I want to see you over here for a minute or two.

Thanks' (firmly, briefly). I looked away to the other girl, directing her to reclaim her seat. It was on-task learning time. Jacqui slumped back in her seat. I called her over again, 'Jacqui.' At this point I also momentarily chatted with some students nearby to give Jacqui some take-up time. Jacqui sauntered over, stood next to me and said, 'Yes! What'd I do anyway?'

It isn't easy to *tactically ignore* some student behaviour (there are times we feel like verbally maiming!). *Tactical* ignoring is a conscious skill and can enable a teacher to keep the focus of the exchange on the primary issue and avoid browbeating or arguing about sighs, muttering, raising of eyes and other such body language. These behaviours can be addressed at a later stage (one to one) when the emotional heat has calmed.

Following up with students after class

When we need to follow up with an after-class consequence, it is important to emphasize the fair certainty of the consequence without intentional severity.

If (for example) a student has been provocatively rude to a teacher in class the teacher will respond with a brief, firm 'I' statement. 'I don't use that kind of language with you; I don't expect you to speak to me like that.' It will, on occasion, be necessary to direct the student to take some informal or formal time out to calm down and think about their behaviour. Later, when the teacher follows up one to one with the student, the teacher will:

- Tune in to how the student may well be feeling at that point. Some teachers (conversely) will immediately focus on very negative factors in the consequential outcome, e.g. 'Travis – you could be outside now, couldn't you? But now you're in here missing playtime. Why? I'll tell you why – you don't listen, do you? You wasted time all through class – three times I asked you to get on with your work. You were rude, you ignored me – you made no real effort to work, did you? And when I said that if you didn't make any effort, you'd be staying back at lunchtime, you said you didn't care – you're caring now, aren't you – eh?' While all of what the teacher here says may be true (and tempting to deliver!) it will hardly help in developing any sense of repairing and rebuilding. My colleagues and I have learned that it is the *fair certainty of the consequence that will have more 'teachable effect' than the severity of the consequence.*

- Focus on the behaviour or issue (without attacking the student).
- Give the student a 'right of reply' – this is crucial in mediation contexts. There are occasions when teachers will need a colleague to sit in and assist such mediations. Any extended, after-class follow-through between a male teacher and a female student should also include a female colleague 'sitting in' (for ethical probity).
  Right of replies can be verbal or written (Rogers, 1998). Key questions such as: *What happened* (e.g. regarding the behaviour)? *What rule (or right) was affected? What is your account ('your side of the story')? How can you change things? How can I help?*
- Bring the focus of the consequence or follow up back to the right/rule affected by the student's behaviour.
- Focus on the expectations of the consequence; or clarification of future behaviour; or mediation or restitution (as the case may be).
- Separate amicably (without patronizing the student). Some teachers finish such exchanges with a readdressing of the issue/behaviour all over again: '... you speak to me like that again and you won't just be speaking to me after class; I'll be contacting your parents and I'll tell them what kind of ...!'

Colleague support

These few case examples are drawn from typical mentor-teaching (and teachers) contexts I work with. Colleague support – moral and professional – is essential to validating the common struggle, common problems and issues we face as teachers. The behaviour of students is never an either/or: 'their fault', 'their bad home backgrounds and parenting' or 'poor teaching'. There will always be patterns of distracting and disruptive behaviour present in schools. Such behaviours are always affected by a complex mix of factors present in a small room (and a slightly larger school space). 'Rolled round in earth's diurnal course': teacher and students, together, seek to relate as human beings yet also within respective roles where emotional needs, rights and responsibilities have to coexist.

Summary of key protocols of behaviour leadership

With any students in any context – mainstream or EBD – the protocols of behaviour leadership will emphasize:

- Positive corrective language *avoiding* easy use (or overuse) of 'don't, can't, mustn't' (e.g. don't call out, don't butt in). Avoiding easy use of interrogatives, e.g. '*Why* haven't you started work?', 'Why are you being rude to me?' It is more appropriate to say, 'That tone of voice is ... I don't speak to you like that; I don't expect you to speak to me like that').
- Keeping the corrective discipline focus on the *primary* behaviour or issue. Keeping the fundamental dignity and respect intact (even when communicating one's frustration). 'Calmness' is not inconsistent with appropriate assertion.
- Using *descriptive feedback* to encourage students rather than overuse of global praise, such as 'brilliant', 'great', 'marvellous'.
- Giving students 'behaviour choices' within the fair rights and rules.
- Managing students from a least-intrusive stance wherever possible – moving to more intrusive as necessary. When engaged in more intrusive correction, the emphasis is on assertive behaviour (not hostile or aggressive behaviour).
- Avoiding *unnecessary* confrontation (or embarrassment, sarcasm or public shaming). Necessary confrontation on issues such as significant rudeness in student speech, personal abuse, safety or bullying is addressed from an assertive stance with supportive collegial backing in crisis situations. This assertive stance is based in belief, attitude and skill. These skills can be *learned*; they can be taught. The belief that one should lead *from* 'power for' (rather than 'power over') is a belief about the *kind* of leadership we believe is right. The skills of assertion can support and realize that belief.
- When applying *behaviour consequences* the teacher will emphasize the certainty of the fair consequence rather than the severity of the consequence.
- The teacher will give the student appropriate right of reply following a serious discipline incident, and offer support for behaviour change.

These protocols, as noted earlier, necessitate considered attitude and conscious skill. The skills of language and relationships within these protocols are not dependent on personality as such (although an open, caring, naturally confident and supportive personality will help, along with a general liking of children and a belief that one can 'make a difference'). If we focus on personality alone ('Oh well, she can work successfully with challenging students because of her personality') we effectively excuse poor behaviour leadership, implying that it is only about 'whether you can or can't do it'. My colleagues and I believe there are factors and skills of behaviour leadership that can be developed through supportive collegial mentor coaching (Rogers, 2002b).

Aristotle (1953) makes the crucial point about the virtuous direction, and development, of our profession, art, or craft:

> Of every art (we become) good or bad as a result of building well … this makes it our duty to see that our activities have the right characters, since the differences of quality in them are repeated in the dispositions that follow in their train. (p. 56)

So it is a matter of real importance whether our early education confirms us in one set of habits or another. It would be nearer the truth to say that it makes a very great difference indeed, in fact all the difference in the world.

PART III

THE WAY FORWARD?

Chapters 35 to 37 bring together a number of issues: continuing professional development of teachers, the potential of young learners in relation to conflict resolution and, finally, generating a framework for conceptualizing SEBD and intervention practices.

CHAPTER 35

Wise young minds: how schoolchildren model conflict resolution skills

Scilla Elworthy

The big question

The big question that arises is: how do we, as citizens, deal with men such as Saddam Hussein without using bombs, without opposing violence with more violence? This is a valid question in most of our lives, whether the bully is Saddam Hussein, a brutish employer or a bully in the school playground.

The first step is to look at non-violence, at what it is and what it is not. In combat you are risking your life to kill others; in non-violence you are risking your life (if necessary) so that no one else will be killed. This requires rigorous training and deep conviction; the effect it has on violent, cruel or angry people is more powerful than more violence. It affects them at a profound level. It is the force of satyagraha, developed by Gandhi and entirely successful in driving the British out of India. The practitioner renounces the use of force, voluntarily and on principle, and replaces it with determination combined with an appeal to something deep in human nature:

> What Satyagraha does in such cases is not to suppress reason but to free it from inertia and to establish its sovereignty over prejudice, hatred and other baser passions. In other words, if one may paradoxically put it, it does not enslave, it compels reason to be free.

This is the power Martin Luther King, Jr taught and used to vast effect in desegregating the deep South. It is what Aung San Suu Kyi used when she walked unarmed straight up to the machine guns of Burmese soldiers who had been ordered to shoot the demonstrators she led. It is what Nelson Mandela developed during 27 years in jail and used to prevent a civil war in South Africa on his release. It was the power behind the 'Velvet Revolution', which brought down the Iron Curtain.

Tolerance, training and mediation

We need tolerance training and mediation in schools. Today tolerance is beginning to be taught in schools around the world; age-old prejudices and stereotypes are being challenged. Approaches include, for example, in London, LEAP Confronting Conflict, founded in 1987, which has rapidly attracted regional, national and international recognition. LEAP believes that all young people have the potential to be leaders, initiators, creators, mediators and problem solvers. Also in London, Conflict and Change, a programme for peer mediation, is funded by the London Borough of Newham.

In Israel, The School for Peace at Neve Shalom/Wahat al-Shalaam, a Jewish-Arab community, has organized 'encounter' workshops and summer camps for over 16,000 Arab and Jewish children. Non-violent Communication (NVC) training, the brainchild of Marshall Rosenberg, is also being used to great effect in Israeli primary schools, where children learn 'giraffe language' in contrast with 'jackal language'.

NVC training for junior schools is available in the UK from Charles Suggate. He says, 'extending children's emotional vocabulary facilitates a process by which feelings are explored and needs are expressed raising self-esteem and extending a caring attitude, where responsibility for our behaviour lies with ourselves'.

In the USA, more than 50,000 schools use a programme on 'Teaching Tolerance'. Children in Boston public schools learn perspective taking and empathy by writing their personal stories and reading them aloud in class. If peace proves elusive for this generation of adults, these programmes inspire hope for the next one.

Professor Michael Nagler, founder of the University of California Peace and Conflict Studies Program, suggests that the biggest troublemakers turn out to be the best mediators. How odd. 'After his "conversion", one of those mediators told a friend of mine that to be a mediator you have to "check your ego at the door". You are not just in it for yourself, is what he meant. You have to put your own feelings aside. Then he added, still more significantly, "I've always had the skills to be a mediator, but I didn't use them before because I had no one to show me how." Nor is he that special; everybody has this capacity so very few learn to use. 'We're all like hidden gold mines.'

This mediator's statement is like a textbook of conflict resolution condensed into three sentences:

1. You have to 'check your ego at the door', get a little above your own personal feelings. Some kind of spiritual sacrifice, large or small, is the basis of any action that can result in peace.
2. All it would take for most people to get their hands on this skill is a little training.
3. And finally, given such training, we discover a 'gold mine' in every one of us. Children are also teaching their peers.

How do you do non-violence?

Non-violence is different from pacifism, which is usually defined as something we will not do, whereas non-violence starts from a positive statement: 'How can I make a creative, constructive long-term impact on the situation I'm in and, ultimately, on the world I'm in?'

Non-violence is quite distinct from passive resistance. Passive resistance can even have a provocative effect if the people doing it are angry or fearful. Thus the inner quality of the people who practise non-violence is what gives it power. They are moving towards being free of hatred and free of fear.

What you have to do is train. You train as if you were preparing for the Olympics. You train your mind, you train your emotions, you train your body, you open up your spirit. And how do you do *that*? I will offer here a few suggestions, from my own limited experience, and what I know of others'. You may have many more.

1. Mental fitness

One aspect of training one's mind for non-violence lies in learning to distinguish information from propaganda or disinformation.

Relatedly, an important aspect of mental training is to understand the concept of projection, and then to notice it happening. What is projection? Human minds make a split between what we can tolerate about ourselves and what is so intolerable that it has to be repressed into an unconscious area, which some people call the shadow. We hide all sorts of unacceptable tendencies there – the inclination to lie, to steal, to be dirty, to torture – they are buried away from our conscious sight where we think we can disown them. But because these tendencies are repressed, they accumulate energy; they become very significant to us. Since we cannot admit them in ourselves, we begin to notice them outside ourselves, in other people. If another person infuriates or disgusts us, or if we hate them, then it is very likely that that person or those people has/have some trait or characteristic that is actually, secretly, ours. This is projection.

It is mental exercise to wake up daily, even hourly, to the fact that what we criticize or hate *out there* is in fact what we criticize or hate *in here*. What we have to learn to do is to unravel our own angry accusations against others and examine them to see whether in fact we are furious with that person because they are doing something that we secretly want to do. Or because they have a characteristic that, buried deep down, is our own shadowy stuff. It is a painful business, full of awful discoveries: 'Oh NO!' But discovering, *uncovering*, these areas of our minds is a liberation. It liberates our energy for change.

2. Emotional fitness
Everyone feels fear. Everyone feels anger. What is interesting is what we do with those emotions. Only when we stop criticizing and disabling ourselves, and realize how deeply we are loved, can we begin to love our neighbours, let alone love those who hate us.

3. Spiritual fitness
All the great spiritual leaders tell us that peace starts within; that we cannot be effective peacemakers in the world until we find our own peace. *That* is the big challenge, finding our own peace. Peace begins by quieting the mind, learning that the mind is a good servant but a terrible master. Quieting the mind has to be practised, just like learning to play the violin or throwing the javelin.

It may sometimes be hard for us to accept that it is not what you do, it is how you do it that matters: that the quality of being is more important than the quality of doing.

We need to learn again and again to surrender to a power and presence infinitely greater than we can imagine. We must learn to do what we do without an expectation of outcomes. The acid test of non-violence is that there is no rancour left behind afterwards.

4. Physical fitness
This is the easy one, but the one peace activists so often forget. We sit at our desks as if nailed to the keyboard. We drink too much coffee, thinking it gives us energy. Lunch? We grab a sandwich in the office. And all the while what we need is not in here under the

neon lights and the air-conditioner. It is out there, under the trees, in the grass, under the stars. Go for a walk in the woods, come back with a clear head, come back with more energy than caffeine could possibly provide, come back having remembered what it is that really needs to be done.

To be effective peace workers we need well-cared-for bodies. Bodies that are loved and listened to will not let us down when the stakes are high. Our bodies always tell us what they need, if we will only listen.

What would non-violence look like now?

What if there were not just hundreds or thousands of people trained in this way (as there are now) but hundreds *of* thousands, perhaps millions?

What if they were being trained and training others, ready for crisis situations all over the world?

What if Richard Branson were ready to fly them there?

What if the military respected them and learned from them and cooperated with them?

What if their techniques were introduced into schools?

What if awards were given for this kind of courage, the courage to risk your life for strangers, possibly the most extreme form of courage in the world?

Well, it is not so far away as you might think. In three years the Non-violent Peace Force, operating from offices in St Paul and San Francisco, has guaranteed endorsements from seven Nobel Peace laureates, established bases in Europe and Asia and built up a network of participants and potential volunteers from around the world, emphasizing the global South. This new project, if it succeeds, will result in a worldwide peace service capable of intervening in a conflict or incipient conflict more quickly than the UN peacekeeping division and – more importantly – with a different kind of power from that of national militaries.

> While the US government insists there is no alternative to endless war, the Non-violent Peace Force is quietly attempting to institutionalize a proven alternative. If it succeeds, the world will have two kinds of standing army to choose from.

I take myths seriously, and I take modern myths as seriously as ancient ones. If we look at Philip Pullman's prize-winning *Dark Materials Trilogy*, or Tolkien's *Lord of the Rings*, or even J. K. Rowling's *Harry Potter*, what we find is young people, people with powerful values, saving the world from darkness. These unarmed heroes have the qualities we have been talking about: they keep going when things are very bad; they have a vision of how things could be; they believe in themselves; they draw their strength and power from interior sources rather than exterior ones.

References

Niwano Peace Foundation: The Niwano Peace Foundation was chartered in 1978 to contribute to the realization of world peace and the enhancement of culture by promoting research and other activities, based on a religious spirit and serving the cause of peace in such fields as thought, culture, science and education.

Shamvilla Catherina 5F, 1–16–9 Shinjuku, Shinjuku-ku, Tokyo, 160–0022 Japan. Tel: +3 3226 4371, fax: +3 3226 1835, web: www.npf.or.jp, email: info@npf.or.jp.

Rissho Kosei-kai: They found projects with the aim of restoring humanity to society through such social activities as blood donation and charitable fund-raising. Their firm belief is that people of religion the world over, as well as others whose activities are rooted in the spirit of religion, should cooperate in a way transcending sectarian differences to promote such activities from the broad-based viewpoint of social and public well-being.

Megumi Hirota, Rissho Kosei-kai of the UK International Association for Religious Freedom, 2 Market Street, Oxford OX1 3EF, UK. Tel: +44 (0)1865 241 131, fax: +44 (0)1865 202 746, email: rkk-uk@jais.co.uk.

Non-violent Peace Force: The mission of the Non-violent Peace Force is to build a trained, international civilian peace force committed to third-party non-violent intervention. At the invitation of local groups, Peace Force will deploy hundreds of peace workers to protect human rights, prevent violence and enable peaceful resolution of conflict. Peace Force uses *proven methodologies* and has been endorsed by *world and local leaders in peace and conflict resolution*, including seven Nobel Peace laureates. Web: www.nonviolentpeaceforce.org.

Oxford Research Group: Founded in 1982 to research nuclear policy decision-making and the prevention of war, Oxford Research Group is an independent organization of researchers and support staff. Its aim is to assist in the building of a more secure world without nuclear weapons and to promote non-violent solutions to conflict.

51 Plantation Road, Oxford, OX2 6JE, UK. Tel: +44 (0)1865 242 819, fax: +44 (0)1865 794 652, web: www.oxfordresearchgroup. org.uk, email: org@oxfordresearchgroup.org.uk.

Peace Direct: War has many funders, but those on the front lines of conflict who choose to resolve conflicts through non-violent means are rarely supported or in a position to apply for funding. Peace Direct will identify those motivated not to use violence and put them in touch with support groups, initially in the UK, and later around the world. These support groups will be trained and will help to provide those on the front lines with the tools, resources, training and funding to help achieve their goals and build peace in their region. The support groups will also have a great deal to learn from the front line groups.

56 Leonard Street, London, EC2A 4JX. Tel: +44 (0)845 456 9714, web: www.peacedirect.org, email: info@peacedirect.org.

Peace One Day:

Block D, The Old Truman Brewery, 91 Brick Lane, London E1 6QL, UK. Tel: +44 (0)20 7456 9180, web: www.peaceoneday.org, email: info@peaceoneday.org.

Dolphinton Dialogue Centre: A very exciting project is unfolding in Scotland close to Edinburgh airport. On a 30-acre site, a centre of excellence will emerge that will offer a creative space for groups to engage in facilitated dialogue, develop best practice and learn the skills of dialogue for extending it to others. Currently funding is being sought for developing the buildings on the site but skilled facilitators of dialogue are available now to work with groups or organizations.

Contact: Tricia Boyle, tel: +44 (0)131 319 2224 or +44 (0)131 319 2203, email: patricia.m.boyle@btinternet.com.

Newnham Conflict and Change: run excellent workshops for schools throughout the country on conflict resolution.

Chris McDermott, Christopher House, 2A Streatfield Avenue, East Ham, London E6 2LA, UK. Tel: +44 (0)20 8552 2050, email: conflict_change@btconnect.com.

Daren De Witt is a freelance conflict resolution, mediation and non-violent communication trainer who works as part of the education team of Newham Conflict and Change. He can be reached at daren. dw@bigfoot.com.

Pioneers of Change and Common Futures: Pioneers of Change is an emerging global learning community of committed, young people in their 20s and early 30s from diverse cultural, social and professional backgrounds. Together they set up and run community projects around the world.

PO Box 197, Westhoven 2142, Johannesburg, South Africa. Tel/fax: +27 11 624 3704.
c/o Thygesen, Snorresgade 8, 5. tv., 2300 Copenhagen S. Denmark. Email: mille@pioneersofchange.net.

Womankind Worldwide: works internationally to raise the status of women, equipping them with the skills, knowledge and confidence to challenge discrimination and oppression and make positive changes in their own lives – for the benefit of all.

Viking House, 5–11 Worship Street, London EC2A 2BH, UK. Tel: +44 (0)20 7588 6099, web: www.womankind.org.uk.

Non-violent Communication (NVC): is a process of communication developed by international peace builder Marshall Rosenberg to enable people to communicate with respect, compassion and honesty. It leads to being heard and understood, communicating clearly without blame or judgement, and choosing actions that are in harmony with each others' needs and values. NVC offers a range of courses nationwide.

For more information, contact:
Bridget Belgrave, tel: +44 (0)845 456 1050, web: www.LifeResources. org.uk, email: nvc@LifeResources.org.uk.

Peace workers UK: Peace workers UK aim to contribute to the alleviation of suffering caused by violent conflict through the promotion and encouragement of civilian strategies for the prevention, management and resolution of conflict. They do this by developing and running training courses to prepare people for practical work in conflict areas, developing assessment standards for ensuring the quality of personnel working in this field, setting up a register of qualified personnel available in the UK, by promoting the establishment of a UK Civilian Peace Service and supporting similar international efforts in this field.

18a Victoria Park Square, London E2 9PB, UK. Tel: +44 (0)20 8880 6070, fax: +44 (0)20 8880 6089, email: info@peaceworkers. org.uk.

Responding to Conflict: They provide advice, cross-cultural training and longer-term support to people working for peace, development, rights and humanitarian assistance in societies affected or threatened by violent conflict.

1046 Bristol Road, Birmingham B29 6LJ, UK. Tel: +44 (0)121 415 5641, fax/answerphone: +44 (0)121 415 4119, email: enquiries@ respond.org.

International Alert: Aim to address the root causes of violence and contribute to the just and peaceful transformation of violent internal conflict.

1 Glyn Street, London, SE11 5HT, UK. Tel: +44 (0)20 7793 8383, fax: +44 (0)20 7793 7975, email: firstinitialfamilyname@ international-alert.org.

Conciliation Resources: CR's organizational objective is to provide practical and sustained assistance to people and groups in areas of armed conflict or potential violence who work at community or national level in order to prevent violence or transform conflict into opportunities for social, economic and political development based on more just relationships.

173 Upper Street, London N1 1RG, UK. Tel: +44 (0)20 7359 772, Fax: +44 (0)20 7359 4081, email: conres@c-r.org.

Safer world: aims to spread information across borders, create a network of all environmentally interested people and above all encourage people to stand up for a healthier environment and a safer world.

Web: www.safer-world.org, email: info@safer-world.org.

Centre for Conflict Resolution: is located within Bradford University's Peace Studies Department. From the beginning, emphasis has been placed on combining the ideas and experiences of both academics and practitioners and on the transference of research findings into practical applications.

Centre for Conflict Resolution, Department of Peace Studies, University of Bradford, West Yorkshire BD7 1DP, UK. Tel/fax: +44 (0)1274 234 197, email: l.k.reynolds@bradford.ac.uk.

INCORE: was founded in 1993 as a joint initiative between the University of Ulster and the United Nations University. INCORE aims to address the management and resolution of conflict via a combination of research, training and other activities that inform and influence national and international organizations working in the field of conflict.

Aberfoyle House, Northland Road, Londonderry BT48 7JA, Northern Ireland. Tel: +44 (0)28 7137 5500, fax +44 (0)28 7137 5510, email: incore@incore.ulst.ac.uk.

The International Crisis Group (ICG): is a private, multinational organization, with over 80 staff members on five continents, working through field-based analysis and high-level advocacy to prevent and contain conflict.

PO Box 32354, London SW17 7YP, UK. Tel: +44 (0)20 8682 9351, fax: +44 (0)20 8682 9293, email: kcronin@crisisweb.org.

CHAPTER 36

The Wise Minds experience

Teacher education in action

Morag Hunter-Carsch and Yonca Tiknaz

Introduction

Having an empathetic understanding is vital in teaching young people with SEBD. In this chapter we analyse one inspirational CPD (continuing professional development) experience in order to explore the dynamics of effective CPD. Our focus on deepening teachers' empathetic understanding. In the process of reflecting on our own experience and considering the views of others, we derive information about vital components of CPD designed to increase teachers' and students' ability to make wise choices.

Our stance

Throughout this chapter, we adopt the stance that CPD is not only desirable but essential for achieving and sustaining good practice and building on existing knowledge, professional skills and insights into ways of promoting wisdom in the community within and beyond schools.

We believe strongly that nurturing the development of empathy in our children today is one way in which we can, perhaps, assist them to recognize and find the courage to deal with the complexities of international social challenges that we all face in families, schools and in increasingly multilingual and multi-ethnic communities. Teachers have a rare and valuable opportunity to make a difference to children's experiencing of 'hope' – which is the stuff of the will to learn. It forms the basis on which to seek to live together peacefully. If our children are to learn these vital survival lessons for all of us as kindred beings, we have to be clear about what makes us more humane and what is involved in becoming wiser and making wise choices. We also recognize that many teachers like to engage in interactive CPD, not solely private study reading. Also, since attitude to learning is informed by prior experience, for teachers seeking CPD it is important that they have positive prior experiences of professional debate and discussion. For many reasons, for example pressures with increasingly demanding timetables and new curriculum content, their daily experiences in schools may not provide the quality of reflective collegial discussion that is likely to predispose them to want to engage in formal CPD in or beyond the school.

Planned or incidental research on CPD? A chance to attend 'Wise Minds'

This chapter shares our account of one memorable CPD experience – participation as delegates at the Wise Minds Conference in Cumbria in 2003. As 'action researchers' in the process of preparing for a subsequent international conference on SEBD, we were engaged in monitoring our own experience of 'Wise Minds'. Our findings persuade us that the experience of the whole of a conference is greater than any report of the sum of the parts. However, in written mode, we seek to share what we can of our CPD experience through this brief discussion.

We invite you to accompany us on a short CPD journey. The first step is to hear about the background to Wise Minds and to hear some of the voices, and the next step is to see how and why it has been helpful in pointing out some facets of the dynamics of CPD that we now consider to be vital in the tailoring of specialist teacher education in order to support young people with SEBD.

Background to Wise Minds

Wise Minds was a residential, two-day conference that took place in Windermere in a beautiful location by the lakeside. It followed two years after a highly successful conference called 'Inspiring Minds', which had brought together a group of over 100 highly committed teachers. The planners in Cumbria LA were aware that, in a sense, they were 'preaching to the converted'. Their concerns, however, were to engage with the larger question beyond initial inspiration, to discover 'How do we keep our teachers inspired and engaged with creative teaching so that young minds are being nurtured?' They were aware that, too often, substantial sums of money are invested in events or production of materials which are not then sustained by the essential ongoing professional support. They were not thinking of expensive tangible resources, but of the intangible aspects – the quality of experience that goes on providing sustenance so that teachers keep on inspiring their students.

They made a distinction between inspiration from 'outside' and the kinds of inspiration that seem to have an 'inside' source, or which become effectively internalized. They recognized that even the most inspirational teachers need not only the nurturing experiences which derive from hearing and seeing exceptionally fine professional models, but they also need to be professionally recognized and their own creativity acknowledged by themselves as well as by others (Veni, Vidi, Vici! – I came, I saw, I conquered – in the sense of seeking their own vision, overcoming their own fears and creating the 'reality' interactively, with others).

The rationale, themes and tone of the programme

On the programme notes, the conference title Wise Minds was followed by the subtitle 'Cumbria's Conference on Emotional Resilience, Social Competence and Quality Thinking'. The subtitle encompasses the ideas underpinning the four themes:

- quality thinking and reflection;
- working, playing and living together;
- promoting self-esteem and self-worth; and
- learning to make wise choices in all we do.

You will appreciate that reading about an event, as distinct from experiencing it first hand, lacks the atmospheric 'buzz' which constituted a vital part of the social experience. We can only report here, very briefly, some of the ideas that we consider reflect the design and informal nature of the planned yet creative experience which evolved.

The conference tone was set by John Nellist, Director of Education for Cumbria, who not only opened the conference and coordinated the final discussions but also participated in and supported presenters and participants throughout the two-day event in a manner described by a colleague as 'enabling and empowering'. His words in the foreword in the conference programme explained that:

the bold conference theme, 'Wise Minds', makes formal recognition of the fact that educational achievement and personal growth require more than narrow subject knowledge ... my hope is that you will leave the conference with some new insights and reflections on your own dealing with personal and professional lives.

The planning process for the conference involved taking the best ideas from Inspiring Minds and acting upon advice and suggestions made by delegates in their evaluations of that conference to produce another thought-provoking, stimulating event with world-class speakers and a wide range of engaging activities. *The planners listened to the teachers.*

The conference programme noted that:

> Over the past few years the UK has seen a proliferation of educational initiatives and movements, many of which are structured within and supported by the DfES. These initiatives promote specific ideas such as good citizenship, emotional literacy, thinking skills, creativity in education and speaking and listening. Wise Minds set out to examine many of these initiatives and to draw together in one place all the elements that are needed to enable us, as members of society, to make 'wise choices'.
>
> The importance to society of making wise choices is demonstrated on a daily basis. We only have to read reports in the press of serious lapses in judgement made by politicians, teachers, doctors and world leaders, for example, to become acutely aware of the consequences of behaving in ways that may be decisive, but not reasonable. As members of the human race, every one of us has the potential to make regular lapses in judgement, albeit in a much less public way. Through exploring pathways to wise decision-making, the conference hopes to highlight and develop the good practice that exists in our schools and in society at large.

The programme also indicated that the conference would 'seek to create a wise learning community among delegates', and asked them to 'please come prepared to think critically, creatively and reflectively, to communicate your thoughts, feelings, beliefs and vision to your fellow delegates, to speak, listen – and to enjoy growing in wisdom!' So the delegates were alerted to the expectation that they would enter into the spirit of the event and become participants, not only observers or listeners.

Key messages from the five keynote speakers

The first keynote speaker, Chris Watkins from the London Institute of Education, set the scene and engaged everyone in *deepening their understanding by learning more about the nature and process of learning* for teachers as well as for pupils. The relationship of theory to practice, research and participation in active continuing professional development was illuminated in the process of illustrating new ways of facilitating learning. This proved to be a helpful introduction and communication of recent research and provided a firm basis for relating the content to the following presentations.

As the conference 'got into gear' there was increasing engagement with the issue of what currently constitutes the school curriculum content, concerns about balance, priorities and values, how the curriculum should be experienced and the impinging awareness of the current international situation and the then seeming imminence of the Iraq war. These fundamental and challenging questions were pursued in an illuminative and inspiring presentation by Scilla Elworthy, Director of the Oxford Research Group and one of the UK's leading speakers on international security and nuclear policy. She explored the vital issue of *conflict resolution at international and classroom levels*. The focus of her attention was on ways of developing the kind of power that can confront domination and violence without causing escalation. In respect for the transcendent messages that were shared, we have obtained her permission to include a short edited account of her paper as Chapter 35.

The basis for our curriculum was explored in a differently illuminative manner by Neil Hawkes, Oxfordshire Adviser, who shared ideas about both policy and practice in 'Values education'. His message, effectively presented with humour, was to point out the need for *deeper appreciation of what constitute our values* and how we can work cooperatively to promote holistic development of children and living values.

The local as well as international concerns were further shared through Jack Mapanje's address, which explored 'Creative writing and creating thinking through creative suffering'. Jack, a Malawian poet, linguist and human rights activist, carried the audience through a series of extraordinary experiences as he shared his rebellion against dictatorial situations, not only dictators. As poet in residence at the Wordsworth Trust, Dove Cottage, he provided connections with the English curriculum poetry content and its history through local, national and international associations. His renditions of his poems, and those of his young pupils learning and working on creative writing, reflected his deep understanding of the value of *developing creative ways of dealing with conflict, oppression* and, in his own case, survival in prison without trial for his radical poetry.

He inspired the work of his young pupils, which he then recognized and honoured, sharing with the audience his own appreciation of such poems as Emma's reflections on what we can create.

What we can create
We can create paintings
To lighten up any room
We can create new fragrances
Just like perfume

We can create statues
That stand up straight and tall
We can create writing
No matter if it's big or small

We can create imagination
From fairytales to murder scenes
We can create football
By having two sides of gangs or teams

We can create feelings
Like sad, happy and stubborn,
We can create newborn life
With help from man and woman.
(Emma Hughes, 10 years old, St George's Primary School,
Barrow)

It will be appreciated that each of the keynote speakers communicated many messages and that in reporting only briefly we have sought to select a single main message from each speaker. This became particularly difficult regarding Sir John Jones's address because of its abundance of practical messages. The focus was on 'inclusion'. Some 'component messages' from his presentation emerged as important underlying themes, voiced in different ways by each of the keynote speakers and communicated in their own ways by many of the workshop leaders. They came the more sharply into our awareness in the process of reviewing the conference as a whole.

Sir John, who was honoured for his service to education, spoke with palpable humour and great energy about 'creating the inclusive school'. In so doing he modelled the feelings of creation of a relaxed, trusting and confident professional team, working with his audience, sharing his own expression of warmth and joy in collaborative support for developing children's self-esteem and *recognizing and celebrating their achievements*, especially in school subject areas different from those of the core curriculum. He shared tales about his experiences as headteacher in a series of seriously 'failing schools', repeatedly *engaging everyone in laughter*, evoking *sympathy and empathy* and sharing models for identifying the needs, interests and the underlying motivation of his colleagues as well as his students. He celebrated the fact that we were all working together in a deeply valued enterprise.

The limits of space in this chapter do not permit the inclusion of even a brief note about all the conference speakers and presenters' major messages and the vitally important content of the delegates' engagement in the events but, perhaps, some sense of the pertinence and energy felt in the exchanges can be gained from the following summary of the plenary discussion. Additionally, an illustrative flavour of the creative, poetical style and lively content the Wise Minds conference experienced can be tasted in the chapters by Ollivierre (Chapter 26) and Elworthy (Chapter 35). It should be noted that *the value of the arts, especially music and dance* constituted a strongly connecting strand throughout the conference (and is reflected also in the authorship of this book).

Creating and maintaining the shared vision
In the final discussion session with the keynote speakers John Nellist, as chairperson, invited them to respond to delegates' questions. Some points from the discussion are shared below.

Question 1: What are your priorities for ways of developing wise minds in our pupils?
Answer: (Sir John Jones) We can't do that without considering how we do this for ourselves as a profession. Crucially this involves *sharing our perspective and exploring together what we experience* when we have difficulties and conflicts and attempting to find a way to resolve the conflicts. We also need a *shared vision, developed through collaboration with others*.

Question 2: How do we sustain enthusiasm necessary both to generate and to maintain the shared vision?
Answer: (Scilla Elworthy) One way in which we can do it is to *employ lateral deep thinking* and try to log on to flashback memories and images in order to try to retrieve the strength of the ideas and feelings. It might also help to *make notes in a journal* and later on you can capture the feelings that you have at the moment and make them available to be recaptured.

(Sir John Jones) Also possibly *set up an internet chatroom* and send postcards between the conference delegates, organizers, speakers and leaders remembering a particular aspect, idea or experience and making comment on it.

Question 3: Priorities for developing effective approaches to conflict resolution in older as well as younger aspiring wise minds?

Answer: (Sir John Jones) If you are a beginner teacher, *remind yourself you are not in the classrooms to win, and practise strategies to take yourself 'out of the classroom' and the context and to consider what other ways there are for dealing with the situation,* and drama gives us one form with which we can do this.

Comment: Mike Tandy's suggestion that *drama should be a core component in the curriculum* was warmly and widely supported.

(Sir John Jones) The idea of *finding a 'quiet place'* [outside the classroom] ... can help people to find, for themselves, a way of using the quiet place – we all need to find a quiet place and to take time out in order to put time into understanding what is happening. *Teachers need training and understanding if they are to realize this.*

(Scilla Elworthy) Steven Spielberg was badly bullied in school. As a result of this being perceived and understood by him, his self-image was transformed. He recognized the value of planning for creating the image ... We might think of the Chinese saying that 'you should *try to build a golden bridge for your enemy to retreat over'.* [We all need to consider how best to let all protagonists retreat with honour.] Also, we should remember *the group has more understanding than the individual* and we should consult with the group and give them the ownership of resolution of the problem and together managing the outcomes of the situation.

(Sir John Jones) Even with the willingness to work together, and success in *removing barriers to learning and promoting a culture of achievement, sometimes we have to go with the pace of the slowest.* Also we need to celebrate successes together. We should *not be afraid to be irresistibly optimistic* and we need to remember what went into the creation of the mission statement for the school:

To go further than I thought
To run faster than I hoped
To reach higher than I dreamed
To become the person that I need to be.

Why was Wise Minds perceived to be so helpful?

It was directly useful, related to real needs, practical, provided guidance and hope as well as inspiration. The main points cited above as illustrations from the keynote speakers provide us with a set of criteria for evaluating CPD events as well as good advice for life in schools and teaching in the classroom:

- the 'director' seen to be participating (e.g. in conferences), welcoming, approachable and supportive;
- collaborative planning based on listening to teachers (and children);
- being informed and prepared before the event – knowing what to expect (structured);
- collaborative development of/shared vision;
- understanding the nature and process of learning;
- grasping the values we aspire to promote, including valuing the arts and drama;
- fostering creativity, lateral deep thinking and empathy;
- communicating with ourselves (journals) and others (chatrooms);
- finding a quiet place and building golden bridges;
- being 'irresistibly optimistic'.

It would take a much longer chapter to provide a full analysis of all of the contributing speakers' points and to delineate the range of 'workshop' experiences that contributed so much to increasing delegates' confidence as well as competence in a range of learning and teaching strategies. It is also not possible to provide here the literature search that we began on the complex matter of understanding the ideas behind the title words 'wise/wisdom' and 'minds'. For example, we found that the Concise Oxford Dictionary (1946, 3rd edn, p. 723) defines 'mind' as *'seat of consciousness, thought, volition & feeling; soul as opposed to body'*, and that Donaldson (1992) defines 'mind' as *'an active system for the interpretation of events and for the construction of meanings'* (p. 76).

In searching another source for understanding the idea of 'wisdom' we consulted Russell (1959) for historical perspectives and, from a psychological perspective, we discovered that Baltes and Kunzmann (2003) relate wisdom not primarily to cognitive factors but to personality-related factors such as openness to experience, generativity, creativity. In this way, they emphasize the fact that emotions and values also have an important role to play in the acquisition and expression of wisdom.

So, it seems that in 'developing wise minds' we are concerned not only with thinking and making meaning but also with judging, evaluating and being aware of feelings – perhaps matters that concern what is currently being described as 'emotional intelligence', 'emotional literacy' and 'spiritual intelligence' (Gardner, 1987; Goleman, 1996; Steiner and Perry, 1999; Faupel, in this book).

Emergent issues and discussion

In addition to the impetus the conference had given us in relation to studying what 'wisdom' is considered to be, there emerged four salient points that summarize our reflections of our own and other delegates' experiences about the value of the Wise Minds experience and its potential relevance for CPD planning for others. These are as follows:

1. The relevance of the conference content to the professional demands made on teachers

The links between teachers as learners and students' learning were connected. The concept of facilitating the development of wise minds, unlike teaching a curricular subject, involves engaging the individual student's attention in a manner that promotes inner reflection and exploration of it in relation to its impact on self and others. This reflection involves not only developing a heightened (or deepened) metacognitive awareness but perhaps, more vitally, becoming sensitive to progressive levels of meta-affective awareness (see Chapter 5 and Hunter-Carsch, 2001).

2. Opportunities for reflection

Discussions on collaborative professional learning communities often focus on the ways in which reflection is promoted. The 'reflective practitioner' is one of the terms that is widely used to conceptualize change in teachers' practices and beliefs. Reflection *in, on* and *for* practice appears to be a very promising way of improving teacher knowledge, understanding and skills (Knight, 2002, p. 232). Making time for reflection becomes all the more important when the trend is towards steadily increasing the demands made on already overburdened teachers, and what teachers choose to reflect on can be strongly influenced by the government's agenda. It is not surprising, for example, that teachers spend considerable amounts of time reflecting on practical and cognitive aspects of moderation, checking marking for consistency purposes rather than investing time in more affective aspects of supporting pupils' learning and development (Tiknaz, 2003). It may be important also to reverse the trend for staffrooms to become places that extend and include office work, administration and professional meetings related to policy and to try to reassociate them with collegial debate as well as essential rest and revitalization for the increasingly challenging classroom leadership demands.

The Wise Minds conference created an atmosphere in which teacher reflection was actively promoted. This was partly related to the planned programme, which facilitated social bonding throughout the conference.

During the observations of the workshops, the emotional language that the teachers used to describe their experience was noticeable. Perhaps the collegial trust enabled this type of rendering explicit of the emotional reflections where practitioners openly were able to talk about challenges they face in their work. The conference mode of learning made it easier to engage, or 'get into gear', in the group situations and there was a shared sense of the entire group actually taking the learning experience seriously, while relating to each other in an easy manner. These exchanges helped teachers to relax, enjoy relating to each other as professionals, to become constructively self-critical and ready to adopt new perspectives.

Additional evidence beyond the shared discussions was provided by the written conference evaluations. Examples of teachers' reflections that signalled the emerging shifts in their priorities, beliefs and pedagogy include the following:

> This [the conference] will make me refocus on learning rather than teaching.

> I will focus on learning rather than teaching, and the value of the preciousness and uniqueness of childhood above the curriculum.

One message that became clear was an emerging shift in teachers' thinking about the interaction between teaching and learning. The evaluations and also the informal interviews indicated a paradigm change from a 'transmission teaching' (where the teacher 'delivers' expert knowledge to the learners), to the teacher as facilitator, organizer and engineer of the learning environment to promote high-quality learning by acknowledging the complex needs of the learner.

Other responses indicate some teachers' increased confidence to take on board new approaches:

I now feel confident to establish new methodologies in order to improve behaviour and results. We will aim to do a lot more learning.

I will go away from this conference reflecting on the messages, and being enriched by them.

These accounts indicate that the conference provided teachers with the opportunity to improve practice, and to feel ready to move forward.

3. *Inspiration*

The Wise Minds conference was particularly successful in inspiring teachers to feel more confident as well as clearer about their professional identity:

Thanks to all involved – it was brilliant. I came thinking that it could not be as exciting or innovative as the Inspiring Minds conference was, but I feel it was an even greater achievement and even more inspiring. The last conference took me back into the classroom – this one may well keep me there!

Thanks for another wonderful opportunity to recharge the batteries and reaffirm my own beliefs and principles. Hopefully when I go through the gate tomorrow morning I won't wonder why!

This conference reaffirmed why I became a teacher.

I found this conference inspiring and extremely thought provoking.

I will go away from here working out ways of facilitating the same quality of inspiration and aspiration for the rest of the school community. I also aim to give myself time to think, and to notice what I am thinking about.

Exemplified by the Wise Minds event, the reminder for CPD planners is that it should promote in teachers a sense of professional pride and reassurance of the value of being a member of the teaching profession.

4. *What it means to be a learner*

How often do we, the teachers, put ourselves in our students' shoes and pause to think about what it means to be a learner in the current school context? While there is a wide range of published material on learning styles (e.g. Riding and Raynor, 1998; Smith and Call, 1999; Wenham, 2001; Reid, 2005) and what it means to be a learner as a 'cognitive being', the conceptualization of what it means to be learner as a 'social and emotional being' requires more attention. In particular, we need to be more aware of: (1) the way in which the learners organize their emotional experiences; (2) the extent to which they participate constructively in learning situations; (3) the capacity they show for insightful involvement; and (4) their capacity to connect experiences both emotionally and cognitively across a range of situations (Boxall, 2002, our numbering). Children with SEBD tend to present problems with some or all of those dimensions and they can become emotionally, socially and cognitively excluded from the schooling experience (Cooper, 2005).

We believe that to enable our children to reach their full potential, especially those who have SEBD, requires an understanding of the net of emotional and social issues which enable or disable children to engage in classroom learning (see also John's story). It was about such issues that the Wise Minds experience proved to be insightful, especially in raising participants' consciousness by inviting them to switch roles from 'the one who teaches' to 'the one who is being observed, taught and monitored' (e.g. dance, see Chapter 26).

As participants in the dance workshop, and being teachers, we were accustomed to the role of 'performer' in the classroom for an audience of children. But it was particularly interesting to participate in this group context with colleagues, since we had to engage in the performer role with an adult 'audience' and, for some, this initially posed a new challenge. But because it was being experienced in a 'team' context, the shared will to succeed seemed to carry us along in a way that promoted a quality of shared pride as well as pleasure in the accomplishment of the task.

However, the sharing of such feelings of support may not 'instantly' be accessible for all children who have SEBD if they experience difficulties that impede them from effectively cooperating with their peers. While for us it was a relatively easeful rediscovery of the relationship between self-esteem and membership of the group, we reflect that for children with SEBD this is a crucial area of need and appropriate opportunities for addressing this need deserve to be promoted in the school curriculum context.

The emergent message relating to CPD is the recognition of the fact that teachers, not only their students, are lifelong learners whose professional learning needs can be identified by themselves and in collaboration with creative, visionary CPD colleagues.

Summary of recommendations

We suggest that such conferences as Wise Minds, which *enable the renewal of energy, reaffirmation of professional identity with a sense of purpose and shared values,* can be a powerful tool for teachers' professional development. To do this individual teachers need to engage in a continually deepening understanding of the nature of 'wisdom' and they relate their findings to life in the wider community as well as to the school context. That, in turn, requires the sharing of our relevant understanding of these matters. The fact that the long-term plan in Cumbria involved not one but a series of such inspirational conferences and related CPD links between the events provides a further recommendation regarding time as well as 'distance learning' for maintaining the heightened energy and its impact on sustaining creative teaching.

We conclude that further professional development of the appropriate attitudes, knowledge and skills that form essential components of effective teaching of all young people, not only those with SEBD, can be promoted by the kind of experience which has been exemplified by the Wise Minds conference series. It involves teachers in:

- engaging in sharing professional reflection experiences of the emotions of teaching to promote the development of *teacher self-esteem* in relation to their professional identity;
- recognizing the value of investing their energies in becoming *empathetic as learners* in situations in which they are attempting to understand and find ways of overcoming their pupils' learning and behavioural difficulties;
- acquiring a *deeper shared understanding* of the dynamics of the development of wise minds in children.

In this sense, we see the relationship between teachers' professional confidence and their wisdom as dynamically involving increasing insight into their own as well as their students' emotions, behaviour and communication potential.

Acknowledgements

Thanks to John Nellist, Director of Education for Cumbria Local Education Authority, Avril Ellis and Katy Fuller, and to all of the Wise Minds conference speakers, workshop leaders and delegates, the extensive support team in the background; to Emma Hughes for permission to share her poem, and all of the creative children whose work was shared at the conference; to Iain Hunter for facilitating collegial links that also inspired us to try to disseminate Wise Minds' messages more widely.

CHAPTER 37

Towards a framework for conceptualizing SEBD and intervention practices

Morag Hunter-Carsch, Rosemary Sage,
Paul Cooper and Yonca Tiknaz,

At the heart of this book is a personal story. At the time of writing, John is a young man in his early 20s. It is clear, however, that his present and his future are deeply influenced by his experience of schooling. The reader may look at John's story and conclude that he is an articulate young man with a bright future.

Having said this, it would be a mistake to ignore the many concerns he raises about his experience of education and an even bigger mistake to argue that this fine young man was not negatively affected by these experiences. John is a rare individual who has been able to come to terms with negative life experiences through the process of articulating and examining himself in the light of those experiences. In this way, John reflects the key message of this book, which can be summarized in terms of the vital importance of the individual in education. By the individual we mean the unique identity that all human beings have. It is through the realization of this uniqueness that a person achieves self-awareness and self-esteem that in turn lead to a sense of purpose and awareness of their relationship to others. John shows this process taking place as he analyses himself in the context of his educational and broader life experiences.

A missing link in John's narrative is how he came to develop these insights and the power to express them. This is not of course a problem for John. It is, however, a question that should be foremost in the thinking of the readers of this book. It is for this reason that we have presented John's story in relation to the views of professionals and academics. What these writers and John show us is that the road to selfhood can be hindered by some of the features of our education systems. These writers show us that the school curriculum is made up of far more than subjects, attainment targets and assessment procedures. In fact, the overemphasis on these limited features of the curriculum can often be held responsible for the central failure of our schools to acknowledge and nurture the developing identities of our pupils. Taken together, these chapters show some of the many different ways in which educational provision can serve to promote the willing engagement of the pupils in the social, emotional and academic dimensions of schooling.

This educational engagement is far more than the simple inclusion of pupils in particular educational settings. Rather it refers to the individuals' active and constructive participation in the learning situation. This involves their 'organization of their experiences' that Boxall has conceptualized under the following five sub-skills:

- gives purposeful attention
- participates constructively
- connects up experiences
- shows insightful involvement
- engages cognitively with peers (Bennathan and Boxall, 2003)

Boxall indicates that children who make high scores on these items show interest in classroom activities and other people and they engage actively and positively with educational experiences and people. They are alert, empathetic, purposeful, self-motivated, able to engage in sustained thought and unafraid of new experiences. They are adaptable and flexible (Boxall, 2002).

However, being able to engage successfully with learning depends upon a climate of acceptance, trust and the promotion of feelings of security and belonging. This climate is not something that can be achieved without a great deal of hard thinking and hard work on the part of teachers and all the school staff. It depends upon the personal commitment of adults to fostering warm and empathetic relationships with their pupils. Furthermore, it requires active efforts to provide pupils with new and challenging experiences as well as structured opportunities for reflecting on and communicating about these experiences.

One of the things that makes the achievement of these goals of educational engagement so difficult is the broader social and cultural context in which education takes place. In recent years greater awareness than ever before has been raised in relation to the vulnerability of our children. This has led to the development of many taboos regarding the ways in which adults relate to children. Rightly, it is important that we be aware of the importance of social and personal boundaries and that we educate our children about these. However, there is perhaps a tendency, born out of fear, to deny the importance of emotional and personal dimensions in adult–child relationships. This is reflected, for example, in taboos relating to physical contact between adults and children in schools. These problems are further exacerbated by the way in which children's school experiences are being increasingly dominated by an academic/cognitive curriculum that reduces pupils' identities to scores on achievement tests and marks in examinations, and worse still to labels describing their degree of cooperativeness. The irony of this situation is that as the curriculum becomes increasingly mechanistic and alien to the daily lives of children, as well as ever more challenging, the emotional resources that children require in order to meet these educational challenges. In other words, there is perhaps today a greater need than ever before not only for schools to become consciously and actively nurturing organizations but also for the spirit of 'nurturing' to be better understood and more widely practised in teacher education and throughout multidisciplinary communications and community as well as national and inter- national leadership.

This is not a plea for 'domination' of any one approach. It is a plea for recognition that we need to go beyond the particular termi- nology we employ in tackling any challenging tasks, whether in the nuclear family, the committee or internationally. We need to seek the connection between our words and our intended meanings and to grasp the 'communication challenge' (see Chapter 6 and Chapter 7), read through the 'masks' and 'manners' to the motivation and minds of those with whom we live and work (see Chapter 5). This, in turn, will assist us to find both the courage and humility to discover ways of listening more keenly to each other so that we can see through each other's eyes, move through and beyond (e.g. profes- sional arguments of whether to employ descriptive terminology or 'diagnostic terminology' that seeks to connect with causal factors for 'impediments' to successful learning) and/or, for example, how best to bring together parents, teachers and young people with SEBD, to a clearer and caring dialogue. Our line of 'argument' (i.e. discourse) in this chapter seeks to be 'inclusive' in the sense that it is informed by all that precedes in this book and goes beyond the printed word to draw on diverse discussions among the CIREA team members. References at the end of this chapter serve to illustrate the authors' and others' continuing work on understanding and supporting young people with SEBD, some of whom may also have some degree of language and communication difficulties and/or specific learning difficulties such as dyslexia (Kronick, 1965; Henry, 1984; Hunter-Carsch, 2001; Cross, 2004; Sage, 2004; Cooper, 2005; Sage *et al.*, 2005; Tahmne, 2005).

Towards an innovative framework for understanding and supporting young people with SEBD

In drawing out some key points from the chapters in this book we are now looking towards the goal of creating a shared framework for understanding and supporting young people with SEBD. We consider: (1) 'dimensions', (2) the challenge of creating wise policy and practice, and (3) the implications of these for professional training and development. We look also for (4) the common thread that runs through all three.

What are some of the key implications of this book?

1. Values

It is our view that the starting point for educational policy should be the establishing of a set of shared values. The active engagement of all participants in the formulation of this set of values is a crucial foundation for the development of policy and practice. Therefore this is a deliberately 'bottom-up' as opposed to a 'top-down' framework that is illustrated in Figure 37.1.

The following list indicates some of the values that have been shared in the preceding chapters:

- individual pupil identity and their potential for both personal and social development;
- open channels of communication between children and adults and between professionals;
- understanding behaviour in relation to its emotional, social and cultural contexts and purposes;
- maintaining a developmental awareness regarding language, communication and literacy, including 'emotional literacy' and expression through the arts;
- conceptualizing 'education' holistically (social, emotional and spiritual as well as cognitive dimensions);
- active, constructive educational engagement of students;
- empowering pupils to make wise choices.

2. Professional development

In this part of the framework we summarize what we perceive to be key needs of professionals in this complex, multidisciplinary field. Practitioners need to:

- understand the ways in which social and individual factors interact and how these affect behavioural and cognitive processes;
- be skilled in empathetic listening and mediating emotions;
- build trusted and caring relationships with young people with SEBD;
- be skilled in working with individuals and groups of clients;
- facilitate the development of direction and autonomy;
- understand how to interact and facilitate a constructive working partnership with the families and communities;
- understand how to cooperate with fellow professionals, within their own professional group and with allied professions;
- engage in reflective practices, e.g. action research into own practice individually or in collaboration with other professionals.

3. Dimensions

These are interacting dimensions that help us to understand the complexity of SEBD which we have conceptualized throughout this book:

- *the personal and interpersonal* (the individual with SEBD interacting with wider social communities);
- *the social* (the individual with SEBD interacting with wider social communities);
- *the professional* (individual biography/interactions within professional group/interactions across professional groups, i.e. the professional's individual circumstances, shaped by personal experience and interpersonal and social contacts together with membership of a broader professional community and policy context);
- *the sociopolitical context* (constraints and opportunities created by dominant social and political values, e.g. social policy, education policy, dominant public opinion, the purposes and practices of education).

PROFESSIONAL DEVELOPMENT

Teachers need to:

- understand the ways in which social and individual factors interact and how these affect behavioural and cognitive processes;

- be skilled in working with individuals and groups of clients in ways that facilitate the development of direction and autonomy; and understand how to interact most effectively with the families and communities their clients come from;

- understand how to cooperate with fellow professionals and within their own professional group and from allied professions.

CREATING POLICY AND PRACTICE

How do we remain true to what we understand about the deep-seated needs for therapeutic/ personal reconstruction, of individuals whose surface behaviours may appear (to the uninformed) anti-social and volitional, and requiring punitive responses?

For the examples of good practice to be implemented and developed, there needs to be a shift in the dominant ways in which educational (and other caring) professionals are perceived.

Teachers must not be seen as mere implementers of policy; they should be seen as autonomous professionals best placed to make judgements about the specific needs of their clients.

From this vantage point they become a major source of knowledge and wisdom on which policy should be built.

THE COMPOSED DIMENSIONS OF SEBD

the personal (the individual with SEBD as a culturally grounded, biological, psychological being with an individual biography)

the interpersonal (the individual with SEBD interacting with significant others, peers, professionals, etc.)

the social (the individual with SEBD interacting with wider social communities)

the professional (individual biography/interactions within professional group/interactions across professional groups)

the sociopolitical context: constraints and opportunities created by dominant social and political values.

VALUES

The fundamental importance of:

- individual pupil identity and their potential for both personal and social development. Open channels of communication between children and adults/and between professionals
- understanding behaviour in relation to its emotional, social, cultural context and purposes
- conceptualizing 'education' holistically (social, emotional and spiritual as well as cognitive dimensions)
- active constructive educational engagement of students
- empowering pupils to make wise choices.

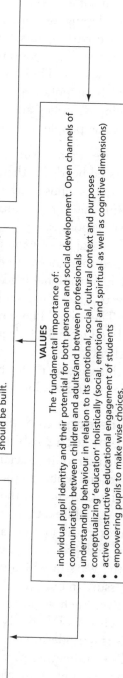

Figure 37.1 *Towards a framework for conceptualizing SEBD*

4. *Policy and practice*

Here we set out some of the challenges that need to be faced in the process of developing and bridging policies and practices. It is the role of informed participants, collectively, to make decisions about how the values and dimensions of this framework translate into policies and practices. Thus we deliberately avoid making specific prescriptions about policy and practice, but that need considerations in developing policy and practice towards understanding and supporting young people with SEBD.

- How do we remain true to what we understand about the deep-seated needs for therapeutic/personal reconstruction of individuals whose surface behaviours may appear (to the uninformed) to be anti-social, volitional and requiring punitive responses?
- For the examples of good practice to be implemented and developed there needs to be a shift in the dominant ways in which educational (and other caring) professionals are perceived. They must not be seen as mere implementers of policy. They should be seen as autonomous professionals best placed to make judgements about the specific needs of their clients.
- From this vantage point they become a major source of knowledge and wisdom on which policy should be built.

What can be done to deal with and prevent the occurrence of such problems?

Social problems require social solutions. Essentially, societies the world over get the problems they deserve. If education systems are to be taken seriously as having the goal of removing the causes of SEBD then they must address their wider causes and seek solutions at the level of values in the first instance: not only the values espoused by government and pressure groups, but the values that are demonstrated in the ways in which social problems are handled. There is massive pressure in our schools, for example, to exclude pupils who are disruptive. Such pupils are seen as an undeserving underclass whose presence in schools is regretted. The effect on schools of such pupils is to undermine the quality of life for others, to depress the school's examination performance, with the potential result of encouraging consumers to choose other schools. The assumption underpinning such punitive exclusionary action is that such pupils choose to behave in disruptive ways. As we have shown throughout this book, this view is ill-informed and counter-productive. It is highly unlikely that active and informed pupil choice plays a significant role in the development of SEBD, in any simple sense.

The educational community certainly has an important role to play in enabling social and academic engagement. Research tells us that schools which do best for children with SEBD (and all children) have a strong values structure based on a commitment to valuing all pupils as members of the school community. These values are reflected in practical measures taken to ensure that all pupils have access to the experience of success. This means broadening the way in which we view 'success', and avoiding equating educational success solely with examination results. Educational success is concerned with, on the one hand, extending one's knowledge and skills. The crucial word here is 'extending'. The most successful pupil in these terms is the one who makes the most progress, regardless of their starting point. Educational success is also concerned with personal development through engagement in the school community. In short, being a good citizen of the school community. This means that all children in a school community have to be known as individuals, and taught to see the important relationship between personal development and social community involvement. They have to be valued for their positive qualities, and efforts have to be made to develop these positive qualities. The need for control has to be balanced by care and respect for all.

We would like to give the final words to John:

I've seen these programmes like *How to Build a Human*. You can never have a child how you want it to be. 'Cos how it grows up and what it experiences changes a child.

References

Chapter 1

Bowlby, J. (1975), *Attachment and Loss*, London: Penguin.

Cooper, P. W. (1993), *Effective Schools for Disaffected Students*, London: Routledge.

Cooper. P. W., Drummond, M., Hart, S., Lovey, J. and McLaughlin, C. (2000), *Positive Alternatives to Exclusion*, London: Routledge.

DfES (2003–4), *Exclusion from Schools*, London: DfES.

Etzioni, A. (1995), *The Spirit of Community*, London: Fontana.

Frith, U. (1992), 'Cognitive development and cognitive deficit', *The Psychologist*, 5, 13–19.

Glasser, W. (1993), *Control Theory*, New York: Perennial Library.

Hargreaves, D. (1967), *Social Relations in a Secondary School*, London: Routledge.

Levy, F. and Hay, D. (eds) (2001), *Action, Genes and ADHD*, London: Psychology Press.

MacDonald, R. (1997), 'Dangerous youth and the dangerous class', in R. MacDonald (ed.), *Youth, the 'Underclass' and Social Exclusion*, London: Routledge.

Maslow, A. (1970), *Motivation and Personality*, New York: Harper & Row.

Munton, A., Silvester, J., Stratton, P. and Hank, H. (1998), *Attributions in Action*, London: Sage.

Patterson, G., Reid, J. and Dishion, T. (1992), *Anti-social Boys*, 4, Eugene, OR: Casralia.

Rutter, M. and Smith, D. (1995), *Psychosocial Disorders in Young People*, Chichester: Wiley.

Schostak, J. (1982), *Maladjusted Schooling*, Lewes: Falmer.

Shelvin, M. and Rose, R. (2003), *Encouraging Voices: Respecting the Insights of Young People Who Have Been Marginalized*, Dublin: National Disability Authority.

Chapter 3

Joyce, B. and Shower, B. (1995), *Student Achievement Through Staff Development: Fundamentals of School Power*, New York: Longman.

McNamara, S. and Moreton, G. (1993), *Understanding Differentiation: A Teachers' Guide*, London: David Fulton.

McNamara, S. and Moreton, G. (1995a), *Changing Behaviour: Teaching Children with Emotional and Behavioural Difficulties in Primary and Secondary Classrooms*, London: David Fulton.

McNamara, S. and Moreton, G. (1995b), *Teaching Special Educational Needs: Strategies and Activities for Children in the Primary Classroom*, London: David Fulton.

Chapter 4

Bullock, L. M. (1999), 'Understanding, Reaching and Teaching Today's Youth', keynote address, paper presented at Second Canadian Conference on Educating Students with Emotional and Behavioural Disorders, Quebec.

Bullock, L. M., Ellis, L. L. and Wilson, M. J. (1994), 'Knowledge/ skills needed by teachers who work with students with severe emotional/behavioural disorders: a revisitation', *Behavioural Disorders*, 19, 108–25.

Carnine, D. (1995), 'The professional context for collaboration and collaborative research', *Remedial and Special Education*, 16, 368–71.

Carnine, D. (1997), 'Bridging the research-to-practice gap', *Exceptional Children*, 63, 513–21.

Cheney, D. and Barringer, C. (1995), 'Teacher competence, student diversity, and staff training for the inclusion of middle school students with emotional and behavioural disorders', *Journal of Emotional and Behavioural Disorders*, 3, 174–82.

Cole, T., Visser, J. and Daniels, H. (1999), 'A model explaining effective practice in mainstream schools', *Emotional and Behavioural Difficulties*, 4, 12–18.

Cooper, P. (1996), 'Giving it a name: the value of descriptive categories in educational approaches to emotional and behavioural difficulties', *Support for Learning*, 11, 146–50.

Greenwood, C. R. (2001), 'Science and students with learning and behavioural problems', *Behavioural Disorders*, 27, 37–52.

Malouf, D. and Schiller, E. (1995), 'Practice and research in special education', *Exceptional Children*, 61, 414–24.

Nelson, C. M. and Rutherford, R. B. (1987), 'Behavioural interventions with behaviourally disordered students', in M. Wang, M. Reynolds and H. Walberg (eds), *Handbook of Special Education: Research and Practice*, New York: Pergamon Press, 2, 125–53.

Royer, E. (1995), 'Behaviour disorders, suspension and social skills: punishment is not education', *Therapeutic Care and Education*, 4, 32–6.

Royer, E. (2001), 'The education of students with emotional and behavioural difficulties: one size does not fit all', in J. Visser, T. Cole and H. Daniels (eds), *Emotional and Behavioural Difficulties in Mainstream Schools*, London: Elsevier Science, 1, 127–40.

Royer, E. (2003), 'What Galileo knew: school violence, research, effective practices and teacher training', in E. Royer, and E. Debarbieux, (eds), *Journal of Educational Administration*, 41 (6), 640–9.

Ruhl, K. L. and Berlinghoff, D. H. (1992), 'Research on improving behaviorally disordered students' academic performance: a review of the literature', *Behavioural Disorders*, 17, 178–90.

Schiller, E. P. (1995), 'The missing link in special education research: the practitioner', *CEC Today*, August.

Skiba, R. J. and Peterson, R. L. (2000), 'School discipline at a crossroad: from zero tolerance to early response', *Exceptional Children*, 66, 335–47.

Skiba, R. J., Peterson, R. L. and Williams, T. (1997), 'Office referrals and suspension: disciplinary intervention in middle schools', *Education and Treatment of Children*, 20, 1–21.

Strain, P. S. (2001), 'Empirically based social skill intervention: a case for quality-of-life improvement', *Behavioural Disorders*, 27, 30–6.

Sugai, G., Bullis, M. and Cumblad, C. (1997), 'Providing ongoing skill development and support', *Journal of Emotional and Behavioural Disorders*, 5, 55–64.

Tremblay, R. and Royer, E. (1992), 'Pour une perspective éducationnelle dans l'évaluation des élèves en trouble du comportement', *Sciences et comportement*, 22, 253–62.

Vaughn, S., Hughes, M. T., Schumm, J. S. and Klingner, J. K. (1998), 'A collaborative effort to enhance reading and writing instruction in inclusion classrooms', *Learning Disability Quarterly*, 21, 57–74.

Veillet, M. and Royer, E. (2001), 'Los problemas de comportamento na escola secundaria: avaliaçao de um modelo de formaçao pragmatica por acompanhamento de professores. Les problèmes de comportement à l'école secondaire: évaluation d'un modèle de formation pragmatique par accompagnement des enseignants', *Revista Portuguesa de Pedagogia*, 34, 651–72.

Visser, J. (2002), 'Eternal verities: the strongest links', *Emotional and Behavioural Difficulties*, 7, 68–84.

Walker, H. M. (2000), 'Investigating school-related behaviour disorders: lessons learned from a thirty-year research career', *Exceptional Children*, 66, 151–61.

Wehby, J. H., Symons, F. J. and Canale, J. A. (1998), 'Teaching practices in classrooms for students with emotional and behavioural disorders: discrepancies between recommendations and observations', *Behavioural Disorders*, 24, 51–6.

Chapter 5

Bettleheim, B. (1960), *The Informed Heart*, Glencoe, ILL: The Free Press.

Bois, D. (2003), *Self-awareness Through Movement: A New Approach to Psychophysical Health and Well-being*. Contact Helen Pennel, by email: helenepennel@hotmail.com noting Danis Bois method in the subject line.

BPS/DCEP (1999), *Dyslexia, Literacy and Psychological Assessment*, report by a working party of the Division of Educational and Child Psychology (DECP), Leicester: British Psychological Society.

Cooper, P. (2000), *Understanding and Supporting Children with Emotional and Behavioural Difficulties*, London: Jessica Kingsley.

Cruickshank, W., Bentzen, F. and Tannhouser, M. (1961), *A Teaching Method for Brain Injured and Hyperactive Children*, Syracuse, NY: Syracuse University Press.

Department of Education and Science, Assessment of Performance Unit (APU) (1986), *Practical Assessment of Oracy at Age 11*, London.

Donaldson, M. (1992), *Human Minds: An Exploration*, London: Penguin.

Fromm, E. (1979), *To Have or To Be?*, London: ABACUS.

Gee, (2000), 'The New Literacy Studies: from "socially situated" to the work of the social', in D. Barton, M. Hamilton and R. Ivanic (eds), *Situated Literacies*. London: Routledge, 180–96.

Green, B. and Kostogriz, A. (2002), 'Learning difficulties and the New Literacy Studies: a socially critical perspective', in J. Soler, J. Wearmouth and G. Reid (eds), *Contextualising Difficulties in Literacy Development*, London: Routledge Falmer, 102–14.

Hargreaves, A. (1998), 'The emotional practice of teaching', *Teaching and Teacher Education*, 14, 835–54.

Haring, N. G. and Phillips, E. L. (1962), *Educating Emotionally Disturbed Children*, New York: McGraw-Hill.

Holliday, A. (2005), 'Small cultures, small identities: the richness of self in a changing world', keynote address at the CELTEAL (Centre for English Language Teacher Education and Applied Linguistics) Conference: Interrogating Third Spaces in Language Teaching, Learning and Use, June, University of Leicester.

House of Commons Education and Skills Committee (2005), *Teaching Children to Read: 8th Report of Session*, London: The Stationery Office.

Hunter-Carsch, M. (2001), *Dyslexia: A Psycho-social Perspective*, London: Whurr.

Kaufmann, W. (1963), *The Faith of a Heretic*, New York: Anchor.

Kung, H. (1970), *Unfehlbar? Eine anfrage (Infallible? An inquiry)*, New York: Doubleday. (1971 transation).

Pettersson, T., 'Tina', Postholm, M. B., Flem, A. and Gudmundsdottir, S. (2004), 'The classroom as a stage and the teacher's role', *Teaching and Teacher Education*, 20, 589–605.

Reid, G. (2005), *Learning Styles and Inclusion*, London: Sage.

Soler, J. (2002), 'Policy contexts and the debates over how to teach literacy', in J. Soler, J. Wearmouth and G. Reid (eds), *Contextualising Difficulties in Literacy Development*, London: Routledge Falmer, 3–13.

Strauss, A., Werner, H. and Lehtinen, L. (1947), *The Psychopathology and Education of the Brain Injured Child*, Vols 1 and 2, New York: Grune & Stratton.

Svalberg, A. (2005), Director of the CELTEAL (Centre for English Language Teacher Education and Applied Linguistics) Conference: Interrogating Third Spaces in Language Teaching, Learning and Use, June, University of Leicester.

Vaillant, A. M. (2003), 'Presentation generale d'un travail en therapie artistique', paper on art therapy, presented at Leicester, International Conference on Communication, Emotion and Behaviour: Working with Young People with Social, Emotional and Behavioural Difficulties. With translation assistance by Jonathan Wimberley.

Vygotsky, L. S. (1978), Cole, M., John-Steiner, V., Scribner, S., and Souberman, E. (eds), *Mind in Society*, Cambridge: Cambridge University Press.

Zembylas, M. (2004), 'The emotional characteristics of teaching: an ethnographic study of one teacher', *Teaching and Teacher Education* 20, 20–04, 185–201.

Chapter 6

De Sousa, R. (1987), *The Rationality of Emotion*, Cambridge, MA: MIT Press.

Nussbaum, M. C. (2001), *Upheavals of Thought: The Intelligence of Emotions*, Cambridge: Cambridge University Press.

Spinoza, Benedict de, *Ethics*, Part IV, Proposition XIV as it appears in the James Gutman edition, following the White-Stirling translation [1883, rev. 1894, 1899]. New York: Haffner Publishing Company 1957, p. 199. (First publication of Spinoza's *Ethics* in the original Latin was in *Opera post humo*, published by his friends, Amsterdam 1677.)

Chapter 7

Barker, L., Edwards, R., Gaines, C., Gladney, K. and Holley, F. (1981), 'An investigation of proportional time spent in various communication activities by college students', *Journal of Applied Communication Research*, 8, 101–9.

Brigman, G., Lane, D. and Switzer, D. (1999), 'Teaching children school success skills', *Journal of Educational Research*, 92 (6), 323–9.

Carnegie Foundation (1992), *Ready to Learn: A Mandate for the Nation*, New York: Carnegie Corporation.

Cloven, D. H. and Roloff, M. E. (1991), 'Sense-making activities and interpersonal conflict: communicative cures for the mulling blues', *Western Journal of Speech Communication*, 55, 134–58.

Dainton, M. and Stafford, L. (1993), 'The dark side of normal family interaction', in B. H. Spitzberg and W. R. Cupach (eds), *The Dark Side of Interpersonal Communication*, Hillsdale, NJ: Lawrence Erlbaum.

Duck, S. (1990), 'Relationships as unfinished business: out of the frying pan into the 1990s', *Journal of Social and Personal Relationships*, 7, 5–28.

Lasswell, H. D. (1960), 'The structure and function of communication in society', in W. Schramm (ed.), *Mass Communication*, Urbana, ILL: University of Illinois Press.

Lees, J., Smithies, G. and Chambers, C. (2001), 'Let's talk', a community-based language promotion project for Sure Start; Proceedings of the Royal College of Speech and Language Therapy (RCSLT) National Conference, Sharing Communication, NEC Birmingham.

Plax, T. G. and Rosenfeld, L. B. (1979), 'Receiver differences and the comprehension of spoken messages', *Journal of Experimental Education*, 48, 23–8.

Pring, R. (2004), 'The skills revolution', *Oxford Review of Education*, 30 (1), 105–16.

Sage, R. (2000), *Class Talk: Successful Learning Through Effective Communication*, COGS Communication Opportunity Group Scheme, Stafford: Network Educational Press.

Sage, R. (2002), 'Data on reading habits', unpublished paper, University of Leicester School of Education.

Sage, R. (2003), *Lend Us Your Ears*, Stafford: Network Educational Press.

Sage, R. (2004), *A World of Difference*, Stafford: Network Educational Press.

Schumacher, E. F. (1978), *A Guide for the Perplexed*, London: Sphere.

Wiio, O. A. (1987), cited in *Communication* by V. Nolan, London: Sphere.

Wiio, O. A. (1991), Conversations regarding a diploma course in Human Communication, London: Central School of Speech and Drama.

Wood, D. (1998), *How Children Think and Learn*. Oxford: Blackwell.

Chapter 8

Brown, P. (2003), Report in *New Scientist*, 30–5.

Cline, T. and Baldwin, S. (2004), *Selective Mutism in Children*, Chichester: Whurr.

Goodman, R. and Scott, S. (1997), *Child Psychiatry*, London: Blackwell Science.

Graham, P. (1987, 1999), *Child Psychiatry*, Oxford: Oxford Medical Publications.

Imich, A. (1998), 'The implication of current research for practice of educational psychologists', *Educational Psychology in Practice*, 18 (1), 4.

Johnson, M. and Glassberg, A. (1999), *Breaking Down the Barriers*, Canterbury and Thanet Speech and Language Department.

Johnson, M. and Wintgens, A. (2001), *The Selective Mutism Resource Manual*, Speechmark.

Johnson, S., 'Successful treatment of a selective mute' (personal communication).

Kagan, J. and Snidman, N. (2004), *The Long Shadow of Temperament*, Cambridge, MA and London: Harvard University Press.

Kirsch, M. (2005), 'Why words fail them', *The Times*, T2, 30 May, 8–9.

Klein, R. and Tancer, K. N. (1992), 'Elective mutism', literature review prepared for the *DSM IV Sourcebook*, 4 March 1992, p. 8.

Matthews, L. (2004), 'Pupils I'll never forget', *Times Educational Supplement*, 8 October, 7.

Sage, R. (2000), *Class Talk: Successful Learning Through Effective Communication*, COGS Communication Opportunity Group Scheme, Stafford: Network Educational Press Ltd.

Sage, R. and Sluckin, A. (2004), *Silent Children: Approaches to Selective Mutism*, University of Leicester. Accompanying the book is a video pack produced by SMIRA in conjunction with the University of Leicester School of Education. For information contact SMIRA, 13 Humberstone Drive, Leicester LE5 0RE.

Sluckin, A. (1977), 'Children who do not talk at school', *Child Care, Health and Development*, 3, 69–79.

Sluckin, A. (2005), 'Staying silent', *Nursery World*, 105 (3956), 17 February.

Tabors, P. O. (1997), *One Child: Two Languages*, Baltimore, MD: Paul Brookes.

Tough, J. (1976), *Listening to Children Talking*, Schools Council Publication.

Yeganeth, R. *et. al.* (2003), 'Clinical distinction between selective mutism and social phobia: an investigation of childhood psycho-pathology', *Child and Adolescent Psychiatry*, 42 (9), 1069–75.

Chapter 9

Amos, V., Parmer, P. and Trivedi (1984), 'Many voices, one chant: black feminist perspectives', *Feminist Review*, 17 July 1984, pp. 3–19.

Axline, V. (1975), *Dibs in Search of Self*, London: Penguin.

Bell, E. and Nkomo, S. (1992), 'Revisioning women's lives', in A. Mills and P. Tancred (eds), *Gendering Organizational Analysis*, London: Sage.

Carby, H. and Parmer, P. (1982), *The Empire Strikes Back*.

Cantle, T. (2001) The Cantle Report: 'Community Cohesion: A Report of the Independent Review Team' London: The Home Office.

Davidson, M. J. (1997) *The Black and Ethnic Minority Woman Manager: Cracking the Concrete Ceiling*, London: Paul Chapman.

Eraut, M. (1994), *Developing Professional Knowledge and Competence*, London: Falmer.

Freire, P. (1970), *Pedagogy of the Oppressed*, New York: Seabury.

Ghuman, P. (1995), *Asian Teachers in British Schools: A Study of Two Generations*, Clevedon: Multilingual Matters.

hooks, b. (1981), *Ain't I a Woman?* Boston, Southend Press.

Illich, I. (1972), *Deschooling Society*, New York: Harrow Books.

Macpherson, W. Sir, of Cluny (1999), 'The Stephen Lawrence Inquiry Report', London: HMSO.

Mirza, H. S. (1997), *Black British Feminism*, London and New York: Routledge.

Osler, A. (1997), *The Education and Careers of Black Teachers*. Buckingham: Open University Press.

Parmer, P. and Mirza, N. (1981), *Growing Angry, Growing Strong*, Spare Rib, No. 111.

Race Relations (Amendment) Act 2000, New Laws for a successful multiracial Britain, London: Home Office. February 2000.

Rampton, A. (1981) The Rampton Report: 'The West Indian Children in our Schools', London: HMSO.

Richardson, R. (1990), *Daring to Be a Teacher*, Stoke: Trentham Books.

Schon, D. (1983), *The Reflective Practitioner: How Professionals Think in Action*, New York: Basic Books.

Schon, D. (1991a), *Educating the Reflective Practitioner*, Oxford: Jossey-Bass.

Schon, D. (ed.) (1991b), *The Reflective Turn: Case Studies in and on Educational Practice*, New York and London: Teachers College, Columbia University.

SGGS, 473 (Sri Guru Granth Sahib stanza 473: The Holy Scripture of the Sikh Faith).

Sivananda, A. (1982), *From Resistance to Rebellion: Asian and Afro-Caribbean Struggles in Britain*, London: Race and Class Pamphlet No. 10.

Tripp, D. (1994), 'Teachers' lives, critical incidents, and professional practice', *International Journal of Qualitative Studies in Education*, 7 (1), 65–76.

Chapter 11

Audit Commission (2002), *Special Educational Needs: A Mainstream Issue*, www.audit-commission.gov.uk.

Booth, T., Ainscow, M., Black-Hawkins, K., Vaughan, M. and Shaw, L. (2000), *Index for Inclusion*, Bristol: Centre for Studies on Inclusive Education.

DfES Circular (1999), *10/99 and 11/99 Social Inclusion: Pupil Support*, London: DfES.

DfES (2001), *Special Educational Needs Code of Practice*, London: DfES.

DfES (2001), *Special Educational Needs and Disability Act*, London: DfES.

LA (2000/1) Strategy Paper, 3.

Ofsted (2001), *Evaluating Educational Inclusion*, London: The Stationery Office. Copies also available on www.ofsted.gov.uk.

Whitney, B. (2002), *Educational Inclusion: Head Teacher's Special Report*, London: Croner.

Chapter 12

Bennathan, M. and Boxall, M. (1998), *The Boxall Profile*, East Sutton: Association of Workers for Children with Emotional and Behavioural Difficulties.

Bennathan, M. and Boxall, M. (2000), *Effective Intervention in Primary Schools: Nurture Groups* (2nd edn), London: Fulton.

Berrueta-Clement, J., Schwein, R., Hart, L., Barnett, W., Epstein, A. and Weikart, K. (1984), *Changed Lives: The Effects of the Perry Pre-school Programme on Youths Through Age 19*, Ypsilanti, MN: Monographs of the High/Scope Press.

Boorn, C. (2002), 'Locating an NG: identifying and evaluating features within a school that would make a suitable host', unpublished MSc thesis, University of Sheffield.

Bowlby, J. (1975), *Attachment Loss*, Vol. 1, London: Pimlico.

Boxall, M. (2002), *NGs in School: Principle and Practice*, London: Paul Chapman.

Bruner, J. (1987), 'The transactional self', in J. Bruner and H. Haste (eds), *Making Sense*, London: Methuen.

Bruner, J., Oliver, R. and Greenfield, P. (1966), *Studies in Cognitive Growth*, New York: Wiley.

Castle, F. and Parsons, C. (1998), 'Disruptive behaviour and exclusions from school: redefining and responding to the problem', *Emotional and Behavioural Difficulties*, 2 (3), 1–15.

Connor, M. (2001), 'Pupil stress and standard assessment tasks', *Emotional and Behavioural Difficulties*, 6 (2), 103–11.

Connor, M. (2003), 'Pupil stress and standard assessment tasks: an update', *Emotional and Behavioural Difficulties*, 8 (2), 101–7.

Cooper, P., Arnold, R. and Boyd, E. (1998), *The Nature and Distribution of NGs in England and Wales*, Cambridge: University of Cambridge School of Education.

Cooper, P. and Lovey, J. (2003), 'Early intervention in emotional and behavioural difficulties: the role of nurture groups', in M. Nind, K. Sheehy and K. Simms (eds), *Inclusive Education: Learners and Learning Contexts*, London: David Fulton.

Cooper, P. and McIntyre, D. (1993), 'Commonality in teachers' and pupils' perceptions of effective teaching and learning', *British Journal of Educational Psychology*, 63, 381–99.

Cooper, P. and McIntyre, D. (1996), *Effective Teaching and Learning: Teachers' and Students' Perspectives*, Buckingham: Open University Press.

Cooper, P. and Whitebread, D. (2003), 'The effectiveness of nurture groups: evidence from a national research study', unpublished research report, University of Leicester.

DfEE (1997), *Excellence for All Children: Meeting Special Educational Needs*, London: The Stationery Office.

Doyle, R. (2001), 'Using a readiness scale for reintegrating pupils with social, emotional and behavioural difficulties from an NG into their mainstream classroom: a pilot study', *British Journal of Special Education*, 28 (3), 126–32.

Doyle, R. (2003), 'Developing the nurturing school: spreading NG principles and practices into mainstream classrooms', *Emotional and Behavioural Difficulties*, 8 (4), 253–67.

Feuerstein, R. (1969), *The Instrumental Enrichment Method: An Outline of Theory and Technique*, Jerusalem: HWCRI.

Geddes, H. (2003), 'Attachment and the child in school. Part 1:

attachment theory and the dependent child', *Emotional and Behavioural Difficulties*, 8 (3), 231–42.

Iszatt, J. and Wasilewska, T. (1997), 'NGs: an early intervention model enabling vulnerable children with emotional and behavioural difficulties to integrate successfully into school', *Educational and Child Psychology*, 14 (3), 121–39.

Johnson, M. and Hallgarten, J. (2002), *From Victims of Change to Agents of Change: The Future of the Teaching Profession*, London: Policy Studies Institute.

Lucas, S. (1999), 'The nurturing school: the impact of NG principles and practice on the whole school', *Emotional and Behavioural Difficulties*, 4 (3), 14–19.

Maslow, A. (1970), *Motivation and Personality*, New York: Harper & Row.

Monro, J. (1999), 'Learning more about learning improves teacher effectiveness', *School Effectiveness and School Improvement*, 10 (2), 151–71.

Nind, M. (1999), 'Intensive interaction and autism: a useful approach?', *British Journal of Special Education*, 26 (2), 96–102.

Noddings, N. (1996), 'Caring pedagogy and Vygotsky', *Educational Psychologist*, 31 (3).

O'Connor, T. and Colwell, J. (2002), 'The effectiveness and rationale of the "NG" approach to helping children with emotional and behavioural difficulties remain within mainstream education', *British Journal of Special Education*, 29 (2), 96–10.

Sylva, K. (1986), 'Findings and recommendations', in C. Ball, (ed.), *Start Right: The Importance of Early Learning*, London: Royal Society of Arts.

Sylva, K. and Ilsley, J. (1992), 'The High/Scope approach to working with young children', *Early Education*, Spring.

Vygotsky, L. S. (1987), *Collected Works*, New York: Plenum.

Chapter 13

Bell, N. (1991), *Visualising and Verbalizing*, Paso Robles, CA: Academy of Reading Publications.

Brigman, G., Lane, D. and Switzer, D. (1999), 'Teaching children school success skills', *The Journal of Educational Research*, 92 (6), 323–9.

Brown, G., Anderson, A., Shillcock, R. and Yule, G. (1984), *Teaching Talk: Strategies for Production and Assessment*, Cambridge: Cambridge University Press.

Carnegie Foundation (1992), *Ready to Learn: A Mandate for the Nation*, New York: Carnegie Corporation.

Cohen, N. J. (1996), 'Unsuspected language impairments in psychiatrically disturbed children: developmental issues and associated conditions', in J. H. Beitchman, N. J. Cohen, M. M. Konstantareas and R. Tannock (eds), *Language, Learning and Behaviour Disorders: Developmental, Biological and Clinical Perspectives*, Cambridge: Cambridge University Press, 105–27.

Cross, M. (2005), *Communication and Behaviour Problems*, London, Sage.

DfEE/QCA (1997), *The National Curriculum Handbook for Primary Teachers in England*, London: DfEE/QCA (Preliminary White Paper).

Gardner, H. (1997), 'Multiple intelligences as a partner in school improvement', *Educational Leadership*, 55, 20–1.

Lees, J., Smithies, G. and Chambers, C. (2001), *Let's Talk: A Community-based Language Promotion Project for Sure Start*, Proceedings of the Royal College of Speech and Language Therapists National Conference: Sharing Communication.

Mathematics Report (2005), available at www.ma.umist.ac.uk/avb/whereform.html.

Nelson, D. and Burchell, K. (1998), *Evaluation of the Communication Opportunity Group Scheme*, South Warwickshire Combined Care NHS Trust, Department of Speech and Language Therapy, Warwick: South Warwickshire Health Authority.

Orton, K. (2005), COGS with FE students, in *COGS in the Classroom*, Stafford: Network Educational Press.

Sage, R. (1992), 'Communication in the classroom', PhD, Leicester: University of Leicester.

Sage, R. (1998), *Communication Support for Students in Senior School*, Leicester: University of Leicester.

Sage, R. (2000a), *Class Talk*, Stafford: Network Educational Press.

Sage, R. (2000b), The Communication Opportunity Group Scheme, Leicester: University of Leicester.

Sage, R. (2000c), *Successful Students: A Project to Teach Communcation Skills and Support Learning*, Leicester: University of Leicester.

Sage, R. (2003), *Lend Us Your Ears: Listen and Learn*, Stafford: Network Educational Press.

Sage, R. (2004), *Assessing Learning Competence at Entry to Secondary School*, Leicester: University of Leicester.

Sage, R. (2005), *Assessing Learning Competence at Entry to Secondary School*, Leicester: University of Leicester.

Sage, R., Rogers, J. and Cwenar, S. (2004), *The Dialogue, Innovation, Achievement and Learning Project: An East–West Collaboration to Raise Educational Achievement*, Leicester: University of Leicester.

Sage, R. and Shaw, P. (1992), *Collaborative Teaching and Learning*, London: CSSD Publications.

Sage, R. and Whittingham, J. (1997), *Using the Communication Opportunity Group Scheme in Senior Schools: A Speech and Language Therapy and Teaching Initiative*, Warwick: Warwickshire LA/AHA.

Teele, S. (2000), *Rainbows of Intelligence: Exploring How Students Learn*, California: Corwin Press, Inc. Sage Publications.

Wang, M. C., Haertel, G. D. and Walberg, H. J. (1994), 'What helps students learn?', *Educational Leadership*, 51 (4), 74–9.

Wilde, M. (2005), *Evaluating the COGS in Leicester Schools*. Leicester: University of Leicester.

CIREA (Centre for Innovation in Raising Educational Achievement), University of Leicester, School of Education, 162 Upper New Walk, Leicester LE1 7RF.

Website: www.le.ac.uk/bulletin.

*The Communication Opportunity Group Scheme is part of the activities of Human Communication International (HCI), an educational charity (Registered No.: 1081253). The COGS with instruction video is available from the University of Leicester (address above) in conjunction with a two-day accredited course.

Chapter 14

Bruner, J. S. (1973), *Beyond the Information Given*, London: Allen & Unwin.

Cockcroft, U. H. (1982), *Mathematics Counts*, Report of the Committee of Enquiry into the Teaching of Mathematics in Schools, London: HMSO.

Cwenar, S., Rogers, J. and Sage, R. (2005), *The DIAL Project (Dialogue, Innovation, Achievement & Learning): An East–West Collaboration to Raise Educational Achievement*, Leicester: University of Leicester, School of Education.

DES (1989), *Discipline in Schools*, Report of the Committee of Enquiry, chaired by Lord Elton, London: HMSO.

Hersocovics, N. and Bergeron, J. C. (1984), *A Constructivist versus Formalist Approach in the Teaching of Mathematics*, Proceedings of the Eighth International Conference on the Psychology of Mathematics Education, Sydney, Australia.

Rogers, J. (1996) *Apprentices to Number. Early Childhood Development and Care*, Vol. 125, pp. 15–25.

Rogers, J. (1997) 'Shopping Around for Answers' *The Times Educational Supplement* (2), 17 November 1997.

Rogers, J. (2004a), 'Communication? It's mathematical magic', *Communication Matters: The Journal of Human Communication International*, 6 (1).

Rogers, J. (2004b), 'Teacher autonomy and problem solving in numeracy in the early years', *Education 3–13*, 32 (3), 24–31.

Vygotsky, L. S. (1978), *Mind in Society*, Cambridge, MA: Harvard University Press.

Chapter 16

Alliger, D. (2000), in P. Haase (ed.), *Schreiben und Lesen sicher lehren lernen*, Dortmund: Borgmann, 351.

Eggert, D. and Bertrand, L., Deeken, N. and Wegner-Bleissen, N. (2002), *Raum-Zeit-Inventar der Entwicklung der räumlichen und zeitlichen Dimension bei Kindern im Vorschulalter und deren Bedeutung für den Erwerb der Kulturtechniken Lesen, Schreiben und Rechnen*, Dortmund: Borgmann.

Haase, P. (2000) (ed.) *Schreiben und Lesen sicher lehren lernen*, Dortmund: Borgmann.

Hebb, D. O. (1949), *The Organization of Behavior*, New York: Wiley.

Hunter-Carsch, C. M., Cavendish, S. and Carsch, H. (1998), An unpublished report to the Leicestershire Dyslexia Association and to the University of Leicester, School of Education based on classroom observation and contributing to ongoing collaborative research towards the development of the 'Linguae Mundi' computer project reported by Hunter-Carsch and Haase at the international conference of the British Dyslexia Association (BDA) in 2000 in Manchester and by Haase at the international conference of the Social, Emotional and Behavioural Difficulties Association (SEBDA) in Leicester in 2002.

Sczukras, R. (1903), reported at an international reading conference in Malmo, in 1993. Original source is being sent to the editor from Czechoslovakia.

Valtin, R. (1993), *Lese-achschreibe schwirichkeiten*, in Grundschulle II, 62–3, Braunshweig: Westermann.

Vygotsky, L. S. (1971, 1991), *Denken und Sprechen*, Frankfurt Main: Fischer Taschenbuch.

Chapter 18

Bennathan, M. and Boxall, M. (1996, 2000), *Effective Intervention in Primary Schools: Nurture Groups* (2nd edn), London: David Fulton.

Bettelheim, B. (1990), *Recollections and Reflections*, London: Thames & Hudson.

Bettelheim, B. and Rosenfeld, A. A. (1993), *The Art of the Obvious*, London: Thames & Hudson.

Bowlby, J. (1969), *Attachment and Loss*, London: Hogarth Press.

Brookmyre, C. (2005), 'My favourite lesson', *Guardian* Education, 24 May, 11.

Claxton, G. (1998), *Hare Brain: Tortoise Mind: Why Intelligence Increases When You Think Less*, London: Fourth Estate.

Corbett, J. (2001), *Supporting Inclusive Education: A Connective Pedagogy*, London: Routledge Falmer.

Damasio, A. R. (2003), *Looking for Spinoza: Joy, Sorrow and the Feeling Brain*, London: Heinemann.

Erikson, E. R. (1964), *Childhood and Society*, Harmondsworth: Hogarth with Pelican.

Gamman, R. (2003), 'Sharing the load: supporting the staff: collaborative management of difficult behaviour in primary schools', *Emotional and Behavioural Difficulties*, 8 (3), 217–29.

Geddes, H. (2003), 'Attachment and the child in school: Part 1: attachment theory and the "dependent" child', *Emotional and Behavioural Difficulties*, 8 (3), 231–42.

Hanko, G. (1991), 'Breaking down professional barriers. The 1990 David Wills lecture', *Maladjustment and Therapeutic Education*, 9 (1), 1–15.

Hanko, G. (1995), *Special Needs in Ordinary Schools: From Staff Support to Staff Development* (3rd edn), London: David Fulton.

Hanko, G. (1999, 2001), *Increasing Competence Through Collaborative Problem Solving: Using Insight into Social and Emotional Factors in Children's Learning*, London: David Fulton.

Hanko, G. (2002a), 'The emotional experience of teaching: a priority for professional development', in P. Gray (ed.), *Working with Emotions*, London: Routledge Falmer.

Hanko, G. (2002b), 'Making psychodynamic insights accessible to teachers as an integral part of their professional task', *Psychodynamic Practice*, 8 (3), 375–89.

Hanko, G. (2003), 'Towards an inclusive school culture: but what happened to Elton's "affective curriculum"?', *British Journal of Special Education*, 30 (3), 125–31.

Hanko, G. (2004), 'Towards inclusive education: inter-professional support strategies within and across schools and school services', *Education Review*, 17 (2), 60–5.

Mittler, P. (2000), *Working Towards Inclusive Education*, London: David Fulton.

Morris, B. (1991), *Presidential Address*, reprint, Forum for the Advancement of Educational Therapy and Therapeutic Teaching.

Mosse, J. (1994), 'The institutional roots of consulting in institutions', in A. Obholzer and Z. Roberts (eds), *The Unconscious at Work*, London: Routledge.

Norwich, B. (1996), 'Special needs education or education for all? Connective specialisation and ideological impurity', *British Journal of Special Education*, 23 (3), 100–3.

Peters, R. S. (1974), 'The education of the emotions', in R. S. Peters (ed.), *Psychology and Ethical Development*, London: Allen & Unwin.

Quinton, D. (1987), 'The consequences of care', *Maladjustment and Therapeutic Education*, 5 (2), 18–29.

Rutter, M. (1991), 'Pathways from childhood to adult life: the role of schooling', *Pastoral Care in Education*, 9 (3), 3–10.

Sennett, R. (2003), *Respect: The Formation of Character in an Age of Inequality*, London: Penguin.

Spalding, B. (2000), 'The contribution of a "quiet place" to early intervention strategies for children with emotional and behavioural difficulties in mainstream schools', *British Journal of Special Education*, 27 (3), 129–34.

Steinberg, D. (1989), *Interprofessional Consultation*, Oxford: Blackwell Scientific.

Vygotsky, L. S. (1978), *Mind in Society*, Cambridge, MA: Harvard University Press.

Waddell, M. (1998), *Inside Lives: Psychoanalysis and the Growth of Personality*, London: Tavistock.

Winnicott, D. (1965), *Maturational Processes and the Facilitating Environment*, London: Hogarth.

Woodhouse, D. and Pengelly, P. (1991), *Anxiety and the Dynamics of Collaboration*, Aberdeen: Aberdeen University Press.

Chapter 19

Adler, A. (1930), *The Education of Children*, London: George Allen & Unwin.

Aichorn, A. (1925), *Wayward Youth*, New York: Meridian Press.

Ainsworth, M. D. S. and Bowlby, J. (1991), 'An ethological approach to personality development', *American Psychologist*, 46, 333–41.

Alexander, F. and French, T. (1946), *Psycho-analytic Therapy*, New York: Ronald Press.

Armstrong, T. (2000), *Multiple Intelligences in the Classroom*, Alexandria, VA: Association for Supervision and Curriculum Development.

Bettelheim, B. (1955), *Truants from Life*, New York: Free Press/Macmillan.

Bocchino, R. (1999), *Emotional Literacy: To Be a Different Kind of Smart*, Thousand Oaks, CA: Corwin Press.

Dreikurs, R. (1968), *Psychology in the Classroom* (2nd edn), New York: Harper & Row.

Erickson, E. H. (1950), *Childhood and Society*, New York: W. W. Norton.

Freud, A. (1936), *The Ego and the Mechanisms of Defence*, New York: International Universities Press.

Freud, A. (1976), 'Dynamic psychology and education', in *Collected Papers*, 8, 307–14, New York: International Universities Press.

Gardner, H. (1993), *Multiple Intelligences: The Theory in Practice*, New York: Basic Books.

Ginott, H. (1965), *Between Parent and Child*, New York: Macmillan.

Ginott, H. (1972), *Teacher and Child*, New York: Macmillan.

Good, T. and Brophy, I. (1994), *Looking in Classrooms* (6th edn), New York: HarperCollins.

Gordon, T. (1974), *Teacher Effectiveness Training*, New York: David McKay.

Jones, E. (1953), *The Life and Work of Sigmund Freud*, Vol. 3, New York: Basic Books.

Knoblock, P. (1983), *Teaching Emotionally Disturbed Children*, Boston, MA: Houghton Mifflin.

Kounin, J. (1970), *Discipline and Group Management in Classrooms*, New York: Holt, Rinehart & Winston.

Long, N. J., Morse, W. C. and Newman, R. G. (eds) (1980), *Conflict in the Classroom* (4th edn), Belmont, CA: Wadsworth.

Ouzts, D. (1991), 'The emergence of bibliotherapy as a discipline', *Reading Horizons*, 31 (3), 199–206.

Pollock, G. (1989), 'Foreword', in K. Field, B. Cohler and G. Wool (eds), *Learning and Education: Psychoanalytic Perspectives*, Madison, CT: International Universities Press.

Redl, F. (1959), 'The life space interview', *American Journal of Psychotherapy*, 29, 1–18.

Redl, F. (1966), *When We Deal with Children: Selected Writings*, New York: Free Press.

Redl, F. and Wattenberg, W. (1959), *Mental Hygiene in Teaching*, New York: Harcourt, Brace Jovanovich.

Redl, F. and Wineman, D. (1957), *The Aggressive Child*, Glencoe, ILL: Free Press.

Rogers, C. (1957), 'The necessary and sufficient conditions of therapeutic personality change', *Journal of Consulting Psychology*, 21, 95–103.

Rogers, C. (1979), *Freedom to Learn*, New York: Charles E. Merrill.

Schon, D. (1983), *The Reflective Practitioner: How Professionals Think in Action*, New York: Basic Books.

Skinner, B. F. (1972), *Beyond Freedom and Dignity*, New York: Bantam Books.

Stronge, J. H. (2002), *Qualities of Effective Teachers*, Alexandria, VA: Association for Supervision and Curriculum Development.

Weiss, S. (2002), 'How teachers' autobiographies influence their response to children's behaviours: the psychodynamic concept of transference in the classroom, Part II', *Emotional and Behavioural Difficulties*, 7 (1), 109–27.

Chapter 20

Damasio, A. (2000), *The Feeling of What Happens: Body, Emotion and the Making of Consciousness*, London: Heinemann.

Faupel, A., Herrick, E. and Sharp, P. (1998), *Anger Management: A Practical Guide*, London: David Fulton.

Goleman, D. (1996), *Emotional Intelligence*, London: Bloomsbury.

LeDoux, J. (1998), *The Emotional Brain*, London: Phoenix.

Maslow, A. H. (1987), *Motivation and Personality*, New York: Harper & Row.

Ofsted (2001), *Southampton LEA Inspection Report*, London: Office for Standards in Education.

Rutter, M. (1991), 'Services for children with emotional disorders:

needs, accomplishments and future developments', *Young Minds* Newsletter, No. 9, London: Young Minds.

Salovey, P. and Sluyter, D. J. (eds) (1997), *Emotional Development and Emotional Intelligence: Educational Implications*, New York: Basic Books.

Sharp, P. (2001), *Nurturing Emotional Literacy: A Practical Guide for Teachers, Parents and Those in the Caring Professions*, London: David Fulton.

Weare, K. (2004), *Developing the Emotional Literate School*, London: Paul Chapman (Sage).

Chapter 21

De Saint-Exupéry, A. (1999), *Le Petit Prince* (2nd edn), Collection Folio, Gallimard.

Chapter 22

Goleman, D. (1997), *Working with Emotional Intelligence*, New York: Bantum Books.

Goleman, D. (2002), *The New Leaders*, London: Little, Brown.

Mullen. J. (2004), *IPH Evaluation Report*, London: British Council.

Stoll, L. (2002), 'Professional learning communities', paper, London: National Council for School Leadership.

West-Burnham, J. (2003), 'The emotionally intelligent school', paper, London: National Council for School Leadership.

Chapter 24

Bittman, B., Berk, L., Shannon, M., Sharaf, M., Westengard, J., Guegler, K. and Ruff, D. (2005), 'Recreational music-making modulates the human stress response: a preliminary individualized gene expression strategy', *Medical Science Monitor*, 11 (2).

DeNoon, D. (2005), 'Making music switches off stress: recreational music making turns off fired-up stress genes', *WebMD Medical News*.

Duxbury, R. (1990), 'Atma's Flight', recorded on *On Wings of Light* CD, Leicester, www.rosemaryduxbury.com.

Duxbury, R. (1992), 'Awakenings', recorded on *On Wings of Light* CD, Leicester, www.rosemaryduxbury.com.

Duxbury, R. (2000), 'Passage' for piano solo, www.rosemaryduxbury. com

Duxbury, R. (2003), *Angel Whisper*, CD, Leicester, www.rosemary duxbury.com.

Dwoskin, H. (1991), *Freedom Now: Your Key to Lasting Happiness*,

Abundance and Well Being, The Sedona Method © Basic Course,Sedona, AZ: Sedona Training Associates.

Emerson, R. W. (1844), *Experience from Essays: Second Series*, http://rwe.org/works/Essays-2nd_Series_2_Experience.htm.

HU, http://www.eckankar.org/index.html

Inayat Khan, P. V. (1979), *The Message in Our Time*, New York: Harper & Row.

Jarrett, K. (1987), *Changeless*, Keith Jarrett, Gary Peacock, Jack de Johnette, CD sleeve notes, ECM1392.

Klemp, H. (1979), www.eckankar.org.

M (2002), *MCPS PRS Members Music Magazine*, issue 3, 7.

Morris, R. (2002), 'Libretto 2002:3 p. 2', *Journal of the Associated Board of the Royal Schools of Music*.

Nieves, A. (2005), 'Playing a musical instrument reverses stress on the genomic level', American Music Conference (AMC News) press release, February.

Performing Rights Society (2001), 'The power of music report'.

Pinkett, E. (1969), *Time to Remember*, Leicester: Leicestershire County School of Music.

Raucher, F. and Shaw, G. L. (2005), *The Term 'Mozart Effect'*, USA, University of California.

Chapter 25

Alvin, J. (1968), *Music Therapy for the Autistic Child*, Oxford: Oxford University Press.

Ansdell, G. (1995), *Music for Life*, London: Jessica Kingsley.

Bunt, L. (1994), *Music Therapy: An Art Beyond Words*, London: Routledge.

De Backer, J. (1993), 'Containment in music therapy', in M. Heal and T. Wigram (eds), *Music Therapy in Health and Education*, London: Jessica Kingsley.

Heal, M. and Wigram, T. (eds) (1993), *Music Therapy in Health and Education*, London: Jessica Kingsley.

Moranto, C., Woolfolk, R. and Lehrer, P. (eds) (1993), *Principles and Practices of Stress Management*, New York: Guildford Press.

Pavlicevic, M. (1997), *Music Therapy in Context*, London: Jessica Kingsley.

Storr, A. (1993), *Music Therapy in Health and Education*, London: Jessica Kingsley.

Trevarthen, C., Aitken, K., Papouda, D. and Robarts, J. (1998), *Children with Autism: Diagnosis and Interventions to Meet Their Needs*, London: Jessica Kingsley.

Chapter 31

Cole, T., Daniels, H. and Visser, J. (2003), 'Patterns of provision for pupils with behavioural difficulties in England: a study of government statistics and behaviour support plan data', *Oxford Review of Education*, 29 (2), 188–205.

Cole, T., Sellman, E., Daniels, H. and Visser, J. (2002), *The Mental Health Needs of Children with Emotional and Behavioural Difficulties*, London: Mental Health Foundation, www.mental health.org.

Cole, T. and Visser, J. (1998), 'How should the effectiveness of schools for pupils with EBD be assessed?', *Emotional and Behavioural Difficulties*, 3 (1), 37–43.

Cole, T., Visser, J. and Upton, G. (1998), *Effective Schooling for Pupils with Emotional and Behavioural Difficulties*, London: David Fulton.

Cooper, P., Smith, C. and Upton, G. (1994), *Emotional and Behavioural Difficulties*, London: Routledge.

Daniels, H. and Cole, T. (2002), 'The development of provision for young people with emotional and behavioural difficulties: an activity theory analysis', *Oxford Review of Education*, 28 (2&3), 312–29.

Daniels, H., Cole, T., Sellman, E., Sutton, J., Visser, J. with Bedward, J. (2003), *Study of Young People Permanently Excluded from School*, London: DfES.

Daniels, H., Visser, J., Cole, T. and De Reybekill, N. (1998), *Emotional and Behavioural Difficulties in the Mainstream*, research report RR90, London: DfEE.

DfES (2003), *The Report of the Special Schools Working Group*, London: Department for Education and Skills.

Franklin, M. (1945), *The Use and Misuse of Planned Environmental Therapy*, London: Psychological and Social Services.

Greenhalgh, P. (1994), *Emotional Growth and Learning*, London: Routledge.

Kauffman, J. M. (2001), *Characteristics of Emotional and Behavioral Disorders of Children and Youth* (7th edn), New Jersey: Merrill Prentice-Hall.

Laslett, R. (1977), *Educating Maladjusted Children*, London: Granada.

Ofsted (1999), *Principles into Practice: Effective Education with Pupils with EBD*, HMI report, London: Ofsted.

Powers, S. (1996), *The Pastoral and the Academic*, London: Cassell.

Wilson, M. and Evans, M. (1980), *Education of Disturbed Pupils*, London: Methuen.

Chapter 32

Anastopoulos, A. (1999), 'AD/HD', in S. Netherton, C. Holmes and C. Walker (eds), *Child and Adolescent Psychological Disorders: A Comprehensive Textbook*, Oxford: Oxford University Press.

Angold, A., Costello, E. and Erkanli, A. (1999), 'Comorbidity', *Journal of Child Psychology and Psychiatry*, 40 (1), 57–88.

APA (1968), *Diagnostic and Statistical Manual of Mental Disorders* (2nd edn), Washington, DC: APA.

APA (1994), *Diagnostic and Statistical Manual of Mental Disorders* (4th edn), Washington, DC: APA.

Baldwin, S. and Cooper, P. (2000), 'How should ADHD be treated?' *The Psychologist*, 13 (12), 623–5.

Barkley, R. (1990), *AD/HD: A Handbook for Diagnosis and Treatment*, New York: Guilford.

Barkley, R. (1997), *AD/HD and the Nature of Self Control*, New York: Guilford.

BPS (1996), *AD/HD: A Psychological Response to an Evolving Concept*, Leicester: BPS.

BPS (2000), *AD/HD: Guidelines and Principles for Successful Multi-agency Working*, Leicester, BPS.

Cooper, P. (1997a), 'Biology, behaviour and education: AD/HD and the bio-psychosocial perspective', *Educational and Child Psychology*, 14 (1) 31–8.

Cooper, P. (1997b), 'The reality and hyperreality of AD/HD: an educational and cultural analysis', in P. Cooper and K. Ideus (eds), *Attention Deficit/Hyperactivity Disorder: Medical, Educational and Cultural Issues* (2nd rev. edn), East Sutton: The Association of Workers for Children with Emotional and Behavioural Difficulties.

Cooper, P. and Ideus, K. (1996), *ADHD: A Practical Guide for Teachers*, London: Fulton.

Cooper, P. and Shea, (1998), *Pupils' Perceptions of ADHD, Emotional and Behavioural Difficulties*, Vol. 3, No. 3, pp. 36–48.

Detweiler, R., Hicks, M. and Hicks, A. (1999), 'A multimodal approach to the assessment of ADHD', in P. Cooper and K. Bilton (eds), *ADHD: Research, Practice and Opinion*, London: Whurr.

DuPaul, G. and Stoner, G. (1994), *ADHD in the Schools*, New York: Guilford.

Ellis, A. and Young, A. (1988), *Human Cognitive Neuropsychology*, Hove: Lawrence Erlbaum Associates.

Farrington, D. (1990), 'Implications of criminal career research for the prevention of offending', *The Journal of Adolescence*, 13, 93–113.

Frith, U. (1992), 'Cognitive development and cognitive deficit', *The Psychologist*, 5, 13–19.

Greenhill, L. (1998), 'Childhood ADHD: pharmacological treatments', in X. P. Nathan and M. Gorman (eds), *A Guide to Treatments that Work*, Oxford: Oxford University Press.

Hayden, C. (1997), 'Exclusion from primary school: children in need and children with special educational need', *Emotional and Behavioural Difficulties* 2 (3), 36–44.

Hill, P. and Cameron, M. (1999), 'Recognising hyperactivity: a guide for the cautious clinician', *Child Psychology and Psychiatry Review*, 4 (2), 50–60.

Hinshaw, S. (1994), *Attention Deficits and Hyperactivity in Children*, London/New York/New Delhi: Sage.

Hinshaw, S., Klein, R. and Abikoff, H. (1998), 'Childhood ADHD: non-pharmacological and combination treatments', in X. P. Nathan and M. Gorman (eds), *A Guide to Treatments that Work*, Oxford: Oxford University Press.

Hughes, L. (1999), 'Professionals' perceptions of AD/HD', in P. Cooper (ed.), *AD/HD Research, Practice and Opinion*, London: Whurr.

Ideus, K. (1997), 'A sociological critique of an American concept', in P. Cooper and K. Ideus (eds), *Attention Deficit/Hyperactivity Disorder: Medical, Educational and Cultural Issues* (2nd rev. edn), East Sutton: The Association of Workers for Children with Emotional and Behavioural Difficulties.

Kewley, G. (1998), 'Medical aspects of assessment and treatment of children with ADHD', in P. Cooper and K. Ideus (eds), *Attention Deficit/Hyperactivity Disorder Issues*, East Sutton: The Association of Workers for Children with Emotional and Behavioural Difficulties.

Lahey, B., Waldman, I. and McBurnett, K. (1999), 'The development of antisocial behaviour: an integrative and causal model', *Journal of Child Psychology and Psychiatry*, 40 (5), 669–82.

Levy, F. and Hay, D. (eds) (2001), *Attention, Genes and ADHD*, London: Brunner-Routledge.

Munden, A. and Arcelus, J. (1999), *The AD/HD Handbook*, London: Jessica Kingsley.

Neill, A. S. (1968), *Summerhill*, Harmondsworth: Penguin.

NICE (2000), *Guidance on the Use of Methylphenidate for AD/HD*, London: National Institute of Clinical Excellence.

Nigg, J. and Hinshaw, S. (1998), 'Parent personality traits and psycho pathology associated with antisocial behaviours in childhood AD/HD', *Journal of Child Psychology and Psychiatry*, 39 (2), 145–59.

Palmer, E. and Finger, S. (2001), *The Educational Psychology Review*.

Patterson, G., Reid, R. and Dishion, T. (1992), *Antisocial Boys*, Vol. 4. Eugene.

Pellegrini, A. and Horvat, M. (1995), 'A developmental contextualist critique of AD/HD', *Educational Researcher*, 24 (1), 13–20.

Richards, I. (1995), 'ADHD and dyslexia', in P. Cooper and K. Ideus (eds), *Attention Deficit/Hyperactivity Disorder: Education, Medical and Cultural Issues*, East Sutton, The Association of Workers for Children with Emotional and Behavioural Difficulties.

Rutter, M. and Smith, D. (eds) (1995), *Psychosocial Disorders in Young People*, Chichester: Wiley.

Schostak, J. (1982), *Maladjusted Schooling*, Lewes: Falmer.

Sergeant, J. (1995), 'Hyperkinetic disorder revisited', in J. Sergeant (ed.), *Eunythydis: European Approaches to Hyperkinetic Disorder*, Amsterdam: Sergeant.

Silberman, C. (1971), *Crisis in the Classroom*, New York: Random House.

Sonuga-Barke, E., Taylor, E. and Hepenstall, E. (1992), 'Hyperactivity and delay aversion II: the effects of self versus externally imposed stimulus presentation periods on memory', *Journal of Child Psychology and Psychiatry*, 33, 399–409.

Tannock, R. (1998), 'AD/HD: advances in cognitive, neurobiological and genetic research', *Journal of Child Psychology and Psychiatry*, 39 (1), 65–99.

Thompson, R. (1993), *The Brain: A Neuroscience Primer* (2nd edn), New York: Freeman.

Van der Meere, J. (1996), 'The role of attention', in S. Sandberg (ed.), *Monographs in Child and Adolescent Psychiatry: Hyperactivity Disorders of Childhood*, Cambridge: Cambridge University Press.

Weaver, C. (ed.) (1994), *Success at Last: Helping Students with AD(H)D Achieve their Potential*, Portsmouth, NH: Heinemann.

Weiss, G. and Hechtman, L. (1993), *Hyperactive Children Grown Up* (2nd edn), New York: Guilford Press.

WHO (1990), *International Classification of Diseases* (10th edn), Geneva: WHO.

Chapter 34

Aristotle (1953), 'The ethics of Aristotle' in *The Nicomachean Ethics*, p. 56.

Rogers, B. (1998), *You Know the Fair Rule and Much More*. London: Pearson Education.

Rogers, B. (2002a), *Classroom Behaviour*, London: Paul Chapman.

Rogers, B. (2002b), *I Get By with a Little Help: Colleague Support in Schools*, Melbourne: Australian Council for Educational Research.

Rogers, B. (2004), *Behaviour Recovery: A Whole School Program for Mainstream Schools* (2nd edn), Melbourne/London: Paul Chapman.

Chapter 36

Baltes, P. B. and Kunzmann, U. (2003), 'Wisdom', *The Psychologist*, 16, 131–2.

Boxall, M. (2002), *Nurture Groups in School: Principle and Practice*, London: Paul Chapman.

Concise Oxford Dictionary (1946) (3rd edn), Oxford: OUP.

Cooper, P. (2005), 'Is inclusion just a buzz-word?', *Emotional and Behavioural Difficulties*, 9 (4), 219–22.

Cooper, P. and Tiknaz, Y. (forthcoming), 'Progress and challenge in nurture groups: evidence from three case studies', *British Journal of Special Education*.

Cumbria Local Authority Wise Minds Conference (2003) Programme, Lancaster Cumbria LA.

Donaldson, M. (1992), *Human Minds*, London: Penguin.

Gardner, H. (1985), *Frames of Mind: The Theory of Multiple Intelligences* (10th edn), Tucson, AZ: Zephyr.

Goleman, D. (1996), *Emotional Intelligence*, London: Bloomsbury.

Hargreaves, A. (2000), 'Mixed emotions: teachers' perceptions of their interactions with students', *Teaching and Teacher Education*, 16, 811–26.

Hunter-Carsch, M. (2001), *Dyslexia: A Psycho-social Perspective*, London, Whurr.

Knight, P. (2002), 'A systemic approach to professional development: learning as practice', *Teaching and Teacher Education*, 18, 229–41.

Kwakman, K. (2003), 'Factors affecting teachers' participation in professional learning activities', *Teaching and Teacher Education*, 19, 149–70.

Moyles, J., Hargreaves, L., Merry, R., Paterson, P. and Escarte-

Sarries, V. (2003) *Interactive Teaching in the Primary School*, Buckingham: Open University Press.

Nigg, J. and Hinshaw, S. (1998), 'Parent personality traits and psycho pathology associated with antisocial behaviours in childhood AD/HD', *Journal of Child Psychology and Psychiatry*, 39 (2), 145–59.

Paterson, F., and Hunter-Carsch, M. (2003), 'Teachers' voices: case studies from the SPRINT project', in M. Moyles *et al.* (2003).

Pines, A. M. (2004), 'Essay review:"The emotions of teacher stress"', in D. Caryle and P. Woods, *Teaching and Teacher Education*, 20, 537–41.

Reynolds, J. (2004), *Helping People Learn: Strategies for Moving from Training to Learning*, London: Charted Institute of Personnel and Development.

Riding, R. and Raynor, S. (1998), *Cognitive Styles and Learning Strategies: Understanding Style Differences in Learning and Behaviour*, London: David Fulton.

Russell, B. (1959), *Wisdom of the West*, Garden City, New York: Doubleday.

Sloman, M. (2003), *Training in the Age of the Learner*, London: Chartered Institute of Personnel and Development.

Sloman, M. (2005), 'Twenty years in training', *Training Magazine*, April 2005, 24–5.

Smith, A. and Call, N. (1999), *The Alps Approach: Accelerated Learning in the Primary School*, Stafford: Network Educational Press.

Steiner, C. and Perry P. (1999), *Achieving Emotional Literacy*, London: Bloomsbury.

Tiknaz, Y. (2003), 'An investigation into the theory and practice of formative assessment in Key Stage 3 Geography', unpublished EdD thesis, University of Leicester.

Wenham, M. (2001), *Understanding Science*, London: Paul Chapman (Sage).

Zembylas, M. (2004), 'The emotional characteristics of teaching: an ethnographic study of one teacher', *Teaching and Teacher Education*, 20, 185–201.

Chapter 37

Benretham, M. and Boxall, M. (2002), *Nurture Groups in Schools: Principles and Practices*, London: Paul Chapman Educational Publishing.

Cooper, P. (2005), 'Is inclusion just a buzz-word?', *Emotional and Behavioural Difficulties*, 9 (4), 219–22.

Cross, M. (2004), *Children with Emotional and Behavioural Difficulties and Communication Problems: There is Always a Reason*, London: Jessica Kingsley.

Henry, S. (1984) 'Work with parents of young people with SEBD and dyslexia', unpublished, Leicestershire Dyslexia Association (contact M. Hunter-Carsch).

Hunter-Carsch, M. (2001), *Dyslexia: A Psycho-social Perspective*, London, Whurr.

Kronick, D. (1965), *Parents of Children with Learning Disabilities*, Toronto; Association for Children with Learning Disabilities.

Sage, R. (2004), *A World of Difference*, Stafford: Network Educational Press.

Sage, R., Cwenar, S. and Rogers, J. (2005), DIAL Project (ref to be completed)

Tamhne, R. (2004), Bioecogram tm, in Blair, M., Tamhne, R. and Stiyn, M. (2004), Proceedings of the Paediatric Academic Society Annual Meeting, San Francisco, USA.

INDEX